THE SOFTWARE MARKETPLACE

THE SOFTWARE MARKETPLACE

Where to Sell What You Program

Suzan D. Prince

McGraw-Hill Book Company

New York	Hamburg	Montreal	Singapore
St. Louis	Johannesburg	New Delhi	Sydney
San Francisco	London	Panama	Tokyo
Auckland	Madrid	Paris	Toronto
Bogotá	Mexico	São Paulo	

Library of Congress Cataloging in Publication Data

Prince, Suzan D.
    The software marketplace.

    Includes indexes.
    1.Selling—Computer programs.   2.Computer programs
—Marketing.   I.Title.
HF5439.C67P75 1984   001.64'25'0688   84-4343
ISBN 0-07-050859-3

123456789   DOC/DOC   890987654

ISBN 0-07-050859-3

The editors for this book were Stephen G. Guty and William B. O'Neal,
the designer was Mark E. Safran, and the production supervisor was Sally
L. Fliess. It was set in Optima by Centennial Graphics.

Printed and bound by R. R. Donnelley & Sons Company.

To Sandy and Charles Prince, and Dora and Sam Trost
"No experience in life is ever wasted."

Contents

Preface

The premise for the book you are about to thumb through, peruse, and I hope refer to often in your software writing career was born one warm and sunny January afternoon in a Las Vegas convention hall. It was there, during the consumer electronics industry's annual trade show, where manufacturers take the wraps off hundreds and hundreds of new products, that a software publishing executive remarked to a reporter, "If we're going to continue to make it in this crazy business, we're going to have to go after those garage folk—the people who're hunched over their keyboards night after night cooking up great programs. We know they're out there, and we aim to find them—somehow."

That remark triggered a responsive chord, because ever since that particular meeting occurred, it's been echoed over and over again by dozens of marketers in similar publishing capacities. Despite the 40,000-odd software packages already on the market today and despite the fact that more than 200 new programs hit computer store shelves every month of the year, software producers have made it perfectly clear that the demand for fresh, innovative material is a constant, and that the market is wide open to anyone with a micro, a good C compiler (or fluency in BASIC or assembly language), and ample imagination (the wilder the imagination, the better). According to the people who are eager to publish your programs, there's no such thing as talent saturation; there's always room for one more *good* program and program designer.

But why would major hardware and software companies, e.g., Atari, Tandy, IBM, Sierra On-Line, Broderbund, Datasoft, and a few hundred others, along with large traditional book publishers like McGraw-Hill, Harper & Row, Simon and Schuster, Addison-Wesley, John Wiley, and similar firms now wetting their feet in the explosive growth industry, need to worry about how to find you—the individual program author? For one thing, other than by alerting the local computer clubs and canvassing the micro flea fairs, to date there has been very little in the way of a formal network or organized search procedure for discovering new software talent. And that is not expected to change, even with the recent rise of software agents, who represent only a minute fraction of available design resources. As so often happens in the traditional publishing fields of magazines, books, and newspapers, in which editors rely on a scattered community of free-lance journalists and authors to meet their article and manuscript needs, software publishers unhesitatingly place their faith in programs that come in "over the transom" via unsolicited submissions, referrals by colleagues and outside sources, word of mouth, or whatever other witchcraft that acquisitions managers perform to get their hands on new programs.

For example, given the hit-or-miss process of locating talent, during the past few years it has not been unusual for readers of various computer magazines to witness an ongoing dialogue in the letters columns that is vaguely reminiscent of the small-town swap meet: "*Dear Editor:* I just wrote this fantastic program that allows beekeepers to manage their hives from anywhere in the western hemisphere. Have any idea where I might be able to sell it?"

A few issues (i.e., months) later, the editor prints a reply from the prospective publisher: "*Dear Editor:* Regarding your reader's letter about the 64K beekeeping disk, please tell him we are anxious to review and he can reach us at his convenience at our headquarters. . . . "

Obviously, this sort of spotty correspondence can bog down the creative process considerably. So rather than risk letting even one more perfectly wonderful program idea go astray at the dead letter office, my colleagues and I decided to make the whole thing formal. Very simply, we appointed ourselves matchmakers for the industry by creating a comprehensive, "one-stop shopping" directory, both for the publisher in search of a program designer and for the individual author in search of a software publisher. Culled from a direct-mail and telephone survey of nearly 1000 software publishers, the directory listings presented in this book represent all walks of the industry—games and recreation, personal management and productivity, systems and utilities, business and professional management, and home and classroom education. The final result, the Software Marketplace Directory, which constitutes Part Two of the book, presents solid program submission requirements and guidelines from over 300 *actively soliciting* companies, plus crucial tips on the publishers' immediate, as well as long-term, interests and on the kinds of programs most in demand now.

That's right, folks—the guessing game is over. The Software Marketplace Directory presents the microcomputer software author with a thorough reference guide to:

- The primary product lines marketed by each company—arcade and action games, math drill and practice, tax preparation for the medical professional, and so on.

- Secondary product lines, or areas into which the company has expressed a desire to expand (thus arming you with double ammunition to sell your programs successfully).

- The microcomputers and operating systems supported by the publishers.

- Major distribution channels (to let you know whether your prospective program will gain national computer store exposure, or perhaps languish unattended and unpromoted in a mail-order catalog).

- Annual acquisition plans—how many programs the company purchases each year—plus the extended buying outlook.

- Explicit submission requirements, including preferred evaluation medium, documentation, and average company response time—how long you can expect to wait for an answer.

- Payment terms—royalty rates, purchasing characteristics (outright purchase or other procedure), schedule of payments.

- Distribution and marketing rights—Can you sell your program elsewhere, or in a different machine-specific format, or are you locked into a single contract with a single publisher?

There's even a section of selected computer magazines (with editorial guidelines) that purchase original programs—an excellent source for beginners.

Best of all, the directory portion of *Software Marketplace* lets you "plug in" to each market with firsthand comments from the software development and acquisitions managers you'll need to contact for project evaluation.

While Chapter 7 tells you more about how to use the directory to your best advantage, Chapters 1 through 6 contain vital marketing information for approaching this blossoming industry as a knowledgeable insider—as confident professional versus unprepared amateur.

Chapter 1, The Marketplace, presents an overview of the entire microcomputer industry, for both hardware and software. Some facts and figures on the growth forecast for computers and programs in the next several years give a sense of the size, opportunity, and excitement of the business in which you are competing, or hope to compete. Also covered are important economic, consumer, and technology trends that are likely to influence your choice of publishers, program projects, and machine compatibility.

The next section of the chapter is designed to give you the following insights into how publishers function:

- An overview of the publishers (size and structure of the industry)

- What a development team looks for in an outside submission and why certain software packages are chosen for immediate evaluation and eventual selection, while others are routinely rejected

- The general criteria used by companies in evaluating program submissions

The final section examines the role of the software agent (and whether you should consider working with one).

Chapter 2, Getting Started, briefly offers some basic information and commonsense tips for launching your software authoring career:

- Going payment rates, including what a beginner can expect to earn; factors affecting earning potential

- How to generate ideas in accordance with what publishers are looking for; the evaluation process

- How to stay organized; the importance of "good housekeeping"—setting up and keeping accurate records of your submissions, publisher correspondence, bookkeeping chores, etc.

- Ideas for the nonprogrammer and the neophyte software author

Chapter 3, Targeting the Market, takes you several crucial steps further than the general market overview in Chapter 1. Here we examine in some detail the three broad market segments of software application which are ripe for fresh ideas:

- Recreation—including games as well as leisure time and hobby-oriented programs
- Home and classroom education—including traditional drill and practice, simulations and tutorials, learning games ("edutainment"), self-improvement programs, and other innovative trends such as computer-assisted video training
- Business and professional management and personal productivity—including the market for word processors, spread sheets, and database managers; household chore management and home financial applications

Also pinpointed are many of the subset, or offbeat, markets that are often overlooked by prospective designers but for which publishers cite increasing demand. This chapter also tells you how to study your chosen marketplace, match ideas to possible publishers, and narrow down the prospective publishers in your field of interest. Finally, the chapter offers some miscellaneous income sources available to the independent program author and aimed at advancing careers, increasing beginners' opportunities, or simply providing fun and profit. These include educational grants, contests and competitions, and retail incentive programs, all of which are sponsored by publishers or other organizations on a regular basis.

Chapter 4, Submitting Programs, shows you how to begin the submission process, covering acceptable formats (no instruction manuals written in crayon, please), the query letter, the nondisclosure statement, and the covering letter (including samples); brief guidelines for testing your program and preparing the documentation; proper mailing procedures; and following up on your correspondence (patience is always the watchword).

Chapter 5, Acceptance, directs you through a "typical" publishing agreement (there's really no such thing as "typical" in this industry, but there are certain established precedents on which authors and publishers can build a relationship that ideally will be lasting and satisfactory to both parties). The chapter clarifies specific contract ingredients, such as exclusive versus nonexclusive distribution rights, and payment terms. Where to find legal assistance is also touched on, as are your legal alternatives, should you find yourself in an unsatisfactory arrangement. In the event that your submission is rejected by a publisher, the chapter offers some ways to cope, such as restructuring and resubmitting the program.

Chapter 6, Profiles, contains 10 instructive and inspiring ministories of major publishers and editors who offer vital dos and don'ts for succeeding in their particular markets, as well as encouraging advice from "those who have been there"—the independent and affiliated designers who've made it in an exciting, yet increasingly competitive, industry:

- **The publishers:** IBM, Lifeboat Associates, The Software Guild, CBS Software, Sierra On-Line
- **The publisher turned agent:** Synergistic
- **The authors:** Alan Miller (Activision), Fernando Herrera (First Star Software), Mitchell Kapor (Lotus Development Corporation), Jerry Koret (InfoSoft)

Chapter 7, How to Use the Software Marketplace Directory, as noted, explains how to get the most from the listings, and sets the stage for Part Two, which comprises the actual directory.

Following Part Two is a glossary of software publishing and marketing terms.

That's *The Software Marketplace* in a nutshell. It's written expressly for you, the independent software author, whether you're one of the "garage folk . . . hunched over their keyboards night after night," or an independent design house; whether you simply wish to share the original games that give you and your friends pleasure, or have mapped out an invaluable teaching aid or revolutionary office procedure. As you read the following pages, keep the book close by your keyboard and refer to it each time the program idea bulb lights up in your brain. Before long, you too will join the ranks of software celebrities who have gotten their best creations a place on store shelves, put their names up in pixels, and achieved micro immortality.

SUZAN D. PRINCE

Acknowledgments

Conducting and completing a survey of this size and nature constitute a massive undertaking. The marketing and editorial expertise of two tireless professionals—Mark G. Trost and Greg L. Prince—virtually assured the study's comprehensive and valuable results. Both are responsible for the survey's conception, design, and follow-up, and for the structure and compilation of the company listings. Without them, deadlines simply could not have been met, and met well. I am grateful to them.

Also, deepest appreciation to the hundreds of company representatives who responded so thoroughly and enthusiastically to the survey upon which this book is based.

THE SOFTWARE MARKETPLACE

PART ONE
Getting to Know the Marketplace

CHAPTER ONE

The Marketplace

Chapter 1 offers the independent program author a broad overview of the microcomputer hardware and software marketplace, calling special attention to recent developments in technology, consumer demand, distribution, and industry pricing that will probably influence creative direction. A discussion of long- and short-term sales growth patterns for hardware and software gives a handle on the total size of the market and potential demand for new programs. The software publisher's function is examined, as is the role of the software agent.

HARDWARE AND SOFTWARE AT A GLANCE: AN OVERVIEW

Ever since Steve Jobs and his partner, Steve Wozniak, placed their first Apple computer on store shelves (followed quickly by Tandy's TRS-80 and Commodore's PET), microcomputers in dozens of brands, sizes, and prices have become standard fixtures in several million households, classrooms, and offices. By far, however, the business segment of the market has evolved as the largest and fastest-growing installed base. Corporations, small businesses, professionals, and entrepreneurs were the first mass market users to capitalize on the micro's nearly limitless potential to accomplish efficiently and inexpensively tasks such as bookkeeping, report writing, and data processing formerly performed by hand or by huge, costly mainframe computers. The business market has also put the desktop micro to work on a variety of highly specialized tasks in such vertical markets as dentistry, medical labs, law offices, real estate, and insurance.

According to industry analysts, sales of desktop computers used in business applications are growing at an annual rate of over 40 percent and are expected to account for more than $20 billion in U.S. sales annually near the end of the decade. There are now over 3.5 million units in offices, factories, and other business locations.

However, the household market for low-priced microcomputers is somewhat puzzling to those who follow the segment closely. Although there are currently more than 10 million home computers in place, the long-predicted "mass" market, in which a majority of the United States's more than 83 million households are supposed to own not just one, but two, or even three, home computers, has yet to materialize. Reasons for the steady but slow growth are discussed below; however, analysts believe that the sales outlook for the $2 billion-a-year industry remains bright. By the middle of the decade, many predict, well over 25 million units will hum away on kitchen tables, in dens, and in family playrooms (see Figure 1-1).

Micros in the schools also continue multiplying but at a slower than anticipated rate for reasons discussed later; approximately 300,000 current units will expand to nearly 2 million in 1986, according to recent estimates. Overall growth of microcomputer sales to public and private schools, colleges, universities, and continuing education and vocational training centers is expected to keep pace at an annual rate of over 30 percent.

Microcomputer software, once a business largely overlooked by manufacturers as "unprofitable," accounts for over $2 billion in annual sales. Until recently, games captured over half the entire consumer marketplace, but that is changing as people ask themselves— and their computer store dealers—if there's life after *PAC-MAN!* Although games and recreation programs involving hobby interests, self-improvement, home learning, and other leisure pursuits will still lead the industry in the coming years, personal productivity programs that allow people to conquer mundane household chores (a grocery list program is enjoying some popularity, according to one publisher) or perform sophisticated home financial management will play an increasingly important role in the family-oriented segment. Sales growth of classroom education and business and professional programs is also expected to show continued strength. As the 1980s draw to a close, look for recreation to stabilize at

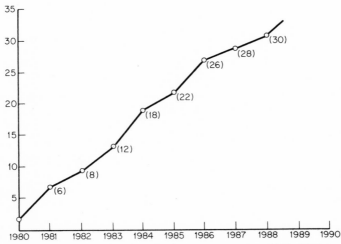

Figure 1-1   Past and projected microcomputer sales, 1980–1988 (in millions).

about 40 percent of the market, the school segment to account for nearly 25 percent, and business and professional use to maintain about 35 percent. Overall, by 1990, microcomputer software is expected to reach $12 billion in annual sales.

The short-term program acquisition plans of buyers of recreation, education, and business software listed in the Software Marketplace Directory (SMD) clearly reflect analysts' prognoses (see Figure 1-2). For example, of the 272 total publishers, the majority—107 companies, or nearly 40 percent—actively acquire recreation programs, including games, hobby aids, music, art, self-instruction and learning, self-improvement, and novelty software. Those purchasing personal management and personal productivity software, covering such areas as personal finance, budgeting, spreadsheets, household chores, word processing, mail lists, recipes, mortgages, and auto management, number 29 companies, nearly 11 percent of the total. However, 44 percent (107 companies) indicate that they are expanding acquisitions in this important segment.

Forty-eight companies (17.6 percent) purchase classroom software, including software for drill and practice, learning games, tutorials, simulations, and teacher management for kindergarten through twelfth grade (K–12), college level, adult or continuing education, and vocational or corporate training; more than 46 percent (103 companies) noted a stepped-up demand in this area. Meanwhile, business and professional management buyers of office-oriented word processing, scheduling, accounting, spreadsheets, records management, graphics, and software serving vertical markets total 59 companies, or almost 22 percent of the publishers, and another 88 respondents, or 41.3 percent, cited expansion of program needs in this area.

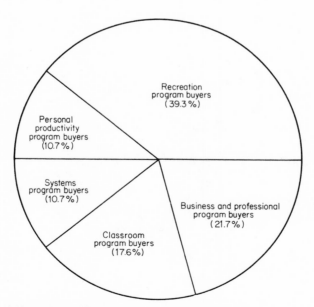

Figure 1-2 Publishers' program acquisition plans. Total companies surveyed: 272.

Operating software and programming tools, including the various utilities, database managers, debuggers, and machine languages, account for a modest portion—less than 15 percent—of the overall software publishing industry, although the segment is expected to grow moderately in the next several years. This projection, too, is accurately reflected by the buying habits of the directory's respondents—only 29 companies, or 10.7 percent, indicated an immediate need in this area. However, about 28 percent of the group (69 publishers) expressed cautious optimism that the need for such programs will increase as consumers acquire more sophisticated programming skills.

TECHNOLOGICAL TRENDS IN HARDWARE AND SOFTWARE

Remember when 4K was a big deal? Thanks to improved technology decreasing manufacturing costs, the standard amount of random-access memory (RAM) that may be included in the purchase of a home or personal computer has grown enormously. In the home segment, 64K RAM has become an acceptable new standard (e.g., Commodore 64, Atari 800 XL, Spectravideo SV-328), and desktop computers usually sport a minimum of 128K bytes of main memory (IBM PC, Apple III, Eagle PC, etc.). Expandability standards for internal memory have also broadened, and lower-cost computers commonly stretch to 128K or perhaps even 256K RAM and business-oriented machines to a comfortable 512K bytes or more.

In the area of external memory, new developments in magnetic recording methods

64K RAM is the standard in late-generation home computers. *(Spectravideo.)*

should result in the availability of inexpensive, vast storage capacity for the mass market. Eastman Kodak (along with a number of Japanese and U.S. companies), for instance, says it has perfected an ultrahigh-density magnetic recording technique that can contain millions of characters of information. Whereas the average floppy disk can currently absorb a maximum of half a megabyte, or 500,000 pieces of information, the new technology makes it possible to jam as much as 10 megabytes, or 10 million pieces of information, onto a 5¼-inch diskette. In the nearer term, many companies also forecast the arrival of low-cost rigid (Winchester) disk storage on the home scene (it is already a reality for the IBM XT), which would drastically increase the consumer's available amount of offline storage and allow users to handle substantially larger files. Yet another storage technology in development is the laser-based recordable-erasable video disk. When perfected, this medium will be able to capture and store data approaching encyclopedias in quantity.

This may be good news for the independent author who needs lots of room for creativity, but with such design freedom comes responsibility. Cost-conscious publishers continually stress the importance of design efficiency rather than elegance. Like any good writer, the successful software author strives for the fewest words with the greatest meaning.

Currently, in the home software area, important technological trends and standard media formats have emerged because lower-priced hardware and memory have made the previously unaffordable computer purchase a reality for millions of people. Games contained on read-only memory (ROM) chips, for example, are packed with more play features than ever—elaborate sound effects, music, arcadelike graphics, etc. Although more expensive to produce than diskettes, ROM chips remain the preferred medium of many developers of games and other programs requiring no user access and limited memory for another reason—they're quite difficult (but not impossible) to pirate. However, for programs that do require substantial RAM and large amounts of file storage, disks remain the overwhelmingly preferred choice of publishers. In general, despite recent improvements in the speed and reliability of data cassette tape and tape drive technology, disks are expected to account for the vast majority of all storage media in the next several years. Other broad trends in the home segment include video game companies moving to computer games and consumers increasingly shifting toward multifaceted home computers and away from game machines such as the Atari VCS.

Developers of business software increasingly depend on the use of simplified graphics to help inexperienced managers adjust quickly to computerized office functions. The trend can be traced to the introduction of Apple's LISA business computer. Apple believed that executives with little or no hands-on computer background (or typing expertise, for that matter) could relate much more easily to a pointing device called a "mouse," rather than a keyboard, which is combined with a program that illustrates a particular job with tiny pictures, or icons. For instance, when a LISA user points to a representation of a wastebasket, the program deletes (throws away) whatever file the user has designated. Since the advent of LISA, other companies are writing applications which rely on operating software and improved input devices such as mice, touch screens, and touch pads to turn the monitor into a replica of a manager's desk, using such icons as memo pads, calendars, and file cabinets, thus paving the way for a whole new wave of so-called convenience programs.

Integrated software, another important development, was brought to the forefront by

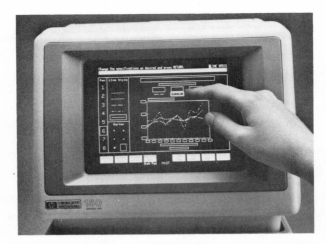

Development of pointing devices, such as touch screens *(top)* and the mouse *(middle)*, and the use of software icons *(bottom)* are changing the way people communicate with their machines, both at the office and at home. *(Hewlett-Packard; Apple; and Sierra On-Line.)*

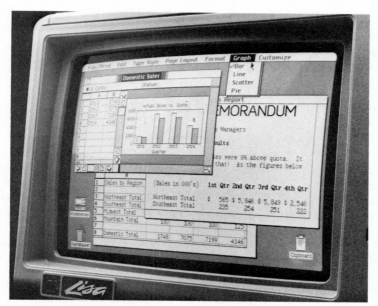

Integrated applications let users choose from among several tasks without changing disks. *(Apple.)*

Lotus Development Corporation's 1-2-3, a single program in which the user can easily switch back and forth between several functions (i.e., spreadsheet to graphing to database management). Such multitask software has rapidly gained popularity with managers because it eliminates the need to power down and reboot different disks containing complementary applications.

Classroom programming trends, from the earliest levels through high school, point less to the straight drill and practice programs of the mid to late 1970s and more to eye-catching interactive learning games that make great use of imagination, color, music, and sound as well as tutorial programs that require students to think through their answers rather than to respond to the computer like automatons. Straight drill programs may supplement a syllabus under certain conditions, but schools generally advocate that the micro isn't an electronic textbook and therefore the computer should add value to a lesson rather than imitate what is more easily accomplished with ink and paper.

At the college level, simulation programs that can give students a real-time "slice" of the subject are stressed. Simulations and interactive tutorials are also finding increased favor with corporate trainers, continuing and adult basic education instructors, and vocational training institutions. More and more programs for these users will be produced on computer-controlled, interactive video tape and disc. Video has long been an educational tool; interactive video offers instructors increased flexibility: curricula can be customized to meet individual skill levels so that students can be encouraged to accomplish goals at their own pace.

As will be discussed, major textbook publishers, as well as independent developers, have successfully adapted the principles of computer-assisted instruction (CAI) for the home environment. In fact, home-oriented learning programs covering every conceivable category and age level account for well over half of all education software sold.

CONSUMER TRENDS IN HARDWARE AND SOFTWARE

The microcomputer industry is volatile. Companies come and go, and technology hailed as ground-breaking one day is ancient history the next. However, the field has achieved several crucial standards brought forth by a few die-hard, quality-driven pioneers and aggressively supported by manufacturers, retailers, and—most important—the end user. If they haven't already, these standards should strongly influence your choice of computers, publishers, and creative subjects. Although one engineer recently noted that we can barely envision how computers at the turn of the century will look and function (so radically will they differ from today's breed), industry observers believe that the following elements will remain the status quo, at least for the foreseeable future.

CPUs: Computers (and their compatible clones) built around microprocessors from Motorola (Apple, Atari—6502), Intel (IBM PC—8088), Zilog (Radio Shack TRS-80, Timex Sinclair—Z80), and proprietary circuits (Commodore, Texas Instruments)

Operating systems: Digital Research's CP/M, CP/M-86, Concurrent CP/M; Microsoft's MS-DOS; PC-DOS; Apple's Apple DOS

Programming languages: Machine level (assembly, FORTH, Pascal); high level (BASIC, C-BASIC, MBASIC)

Our directory respondents consistently correlated these thus far widely accepted standards. In the area of industry standard operating systems, for example, Apple-DOS- and CP/M-based software, widely available since the late 1970s, overwhelmingly won out over other choices, nearly all software market respondents producing software for CP/M-equipped computers. However, the newer MS-DOS (IBM) is catching up quickly; nearly three-quarters of the SMD publishers currently make or intend to make packages using that system.

In addition, Microsoft Corporation, creator of the MS-DOS system, has developed a microprocessor and operating system for Japanese manufacturers, the MSX and MSX-DOS, which allow, for the first time, computers of different brands to run the same application programs. Resembling both MS-DOS and CP/M, MSX-DOS software could, for example, read information written on disks by IBM's PC and write information that the IBM computer can read. If the MSX standard is adopted by major hardware suppliers throughout Japan, the new computer could open up an important new export market for U.S. software publishers who would be able to create new applications for that audience as well as quickly adapt thousands of existing programs.

Besides technical standards, consumers' choice of computer (and therefore your choice) is also influenced by such important factors as manufacturers' warranty and service support,

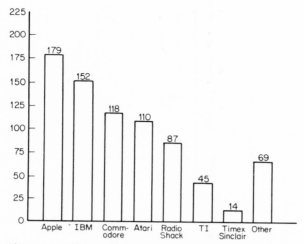

Figure 1-3 Of the publishers surveyed, the number supporting various microcomputers. Total companies surveyed: 272.

attractiveness and effectiveness of advertising and outside packaging, and ease of use. In the home computer brand wars, Commodore's model 64, with over 2 million units installed in U.S. households, appears to be winning a lucrative fight. Following behind Commodore in the home segment are Atari, Tandy, Texas Instruments (TI), and Timex Sinclair, in that order. Two new hardware additions at this writing, IBM's PCjr and Coleco's ADAM computer, may also strongly influence consumer (and author) choices in the future, as presumably will TI's decision to withdraw from the home computer market. At present, software producers say strong demand for TI education programs persists because of a heavy school-installed base.

In the higher-priced segment, IBM and Apple have been going head to head since the giant manufacturer entered the fray in 1981. Lately, IBM has grabbed nearly one-third of business users, and Apple has maintained or slightly lost share, with about one-quarter of the market. In addition, IBM may seek a larger portion of the education sector with the PCjr. The above trends are strongly indicated by our directory participants (see Figure 1-3).

Of publishers serving the home computer market, 43.3 percent said they produce for the Commodore 64; 40.4 percent produce for Atari; and 31.9 percent said they sell into the TRS-80 market. Although Apple supporters rank highly—more than 65 percent—a whopping 55.8 percent told us they now support (or intend to support in the next 12 months) IBM's PC micro and compatibles. This is especially significant to the program author. According to one recent estimate, by 1985 over one-third of all software programs sold will support "Big Blue" (IBM) and its compatibles. If you must put all your creative eggs in one basket, the IBM segment is an excellent place to start.

The final and, of course, most vital elements that determine which computers capture the public's attention and purse strings are the amount, quality, and ease of use of software for a system. As pointed out, with some 40,000 individual software products already on the market (including versions of the same title adapted for different machines), there's certainly no shortage of programs, especially those supporting the most popular computers. Commodore's software base, for example, runs to over 2000 pieces on cassette, ROM, and disk from the manufacturer itself as well as from third-party suppliers. Texas Instruments, with over 3000 games, personal management, and learning programs, boasts more than 300 educational titles from outside and in-house sources alone. Atari is quite well supported, and Apple is believed to have the world's largest program base (some 20,000 and growing). The IBM PC has purportedly spurred development of more than 5000 applications in its brief history, with more materializing daily.

Rather than quantity, quality and user friendliness spell success or disaster for a computer vendor and its suppliers. User friendliness, ease of use—these by-now-clichéd phrases are repeated over and over in the directory, but this is not mere rhetoric for today's software developers. Many a potentially great electronic brain has died a horrible death in the marketplace simply because the only programs available for it were sloppily structured, overly technical, error-plagued affairs—disks and tapes that might as well have come from Mars for all the sense they made to those unfamiliar with computers.

This dilemma was nonexistent (along with the majority of software producers) back when hobbyists and hackers ruled the micro world. Manufacturers then sold machines in kit form, and prepackaged programs were few and far between. Target audiences for computers at that time were mostly dedicated engineers and other electronics technicians and professionals who wrote their own software to their exact specifications. Only as micros have slowly circulated among the masses and the computer changed from a hobby to an everyday convenience item have manufacturers found it necessary not only to sell prefabricated units requiring first-time users to connect nothing more complex than a plug to a wall but also to supplement their "black boxes" with ready-to-run application programs. This has been more easily said than done.

It's difficult for a professional program author to comprehend, but when most first-time users sit down at the keyboard, a strange, catatonic-like spell overcomes them. The person usually can't rationally explain the feeling of terror inspired by a tiny silicon chip, but a business executive quoted in the *Wall Street Journal* put it succinctly when she said, "I just know that if I push the wrong button, I'm going to blow up Pittsburgh."

This sort of consumer fear, as irrational as it seems, is exactly the barrier that has kept microcomputers from becoming true mass market items. Today's publishers seek to correct problems in two major areas to "de-intimidate" a greater portion of potential users.

The first problem area involves three elements of program structure. The first is command inconsistencies, which are a major problem, especially in complex business packages. For example, accessing the spelling checker or word search portion of a word processing program may require the user to memorize an entirely different set of commands from those needed to use the editing functions.

Screen menus are the second element. Poorly structured menus spell nothing but trouble and discouragement to new users. For example, placing the "press any key to continue" message on different parts of the screen during different operations instead of in one designated area throughout creates needless disorientation. Menus that confuse consumers by allowing them to wander aimlessly in a routine, rather than consistently offering a main menu option, are also turnoffs.

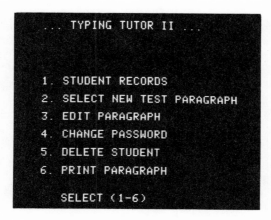

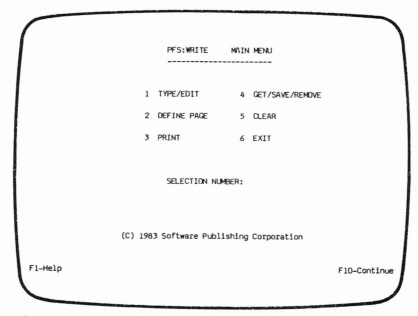

Software publishers strive for screen menus that are simple, consistent, and direct. *(Kriya Systems; Software Publishing Corporation.)*

Poor choice of screen vocabulary is the third problem. Such jargon-loaded phrases as "syntax error" or "use default drive" instead of "wrong word order" or "use Drive A" play havoc with a user's sensibilities. "Say what you mean in the simplest way" is becoming the credo of program developers. Publishers are recognizing that, for the novice, adjusting to a computer language is as complex a task as learning any foreign tongue. Since the producer obviously can't hold each user's hand, publishers firmly believe that the dialogue between user and computer must be a friendly, interactive one and that consumers must start with the simple to build confidence to go on to master increasingly complex material.

The second area receiving corrective attention from publishers today is documentation. "User documentation" is simply an expensive phrase for "instruction booklet." Unfortunately, it's also practically synonymous with many of the same problems associated with fuzzy screen instructions.

By far the most dramatic problem, with the costliest impact, is poor writing. Unclear, inconcise prose may make buyers wish they'd canceled their checks while they had the chance. Certainly, blurry instructions don't speak well for the publisher's reputation for future products. Most program manuals go unread today because neither author nor publisher has bothered to check for consistency of meanings throughout the text or to offer highly simplified, step-by-step explanations that are also well-illustrated or present specific examples with encouraging feedback for the user to try. Some don't even bother to check that what appears in the manual is actually what happens on screen! As Ken Coach, former vice president of Softsync, a New York publisher of home productivity programs, pointed out, "Too often, documentation is overlooked until two weeks after a program is ready to ship to the stores, and then it's written and edited in a rush, maybe even without going back over the program." Quality-oriented publishers today are striving to develop manuals as carefully as they engineer the software, with work progressing along with the programming so that critical changes can be inserted in both the manual and the software concurrently.

Also on the brighter side, major producers are establishing certain criteria that should set an example for the rest of the industry and bring about positive changes in consumers' attitudes and purchase decisions. For example, there is a trend toward including "quick start" flash cards or flip cards with program manuals to allow a user to move quickly and accurately into a program, leaving lengthy details for when the consumer is more familiar with the basic operations. A number of designers are also including more on-screen help, although, as others point out, too many screen aids mean less room for the actual application software. Experienced book manuscript editors in major textbook firms and elsewhere are increasingly being called on to work with program authors to create clear, concise instruction manuals.

SOFTWARE PRICING TRENDS

A publisher compensates program authors in two ways. One way is to offer a flat fee, in which all rights to the program (present and future) become the publisher's property. If a publisher doesn't buy the rights to your program outright, however, you agree to license all or certain marketing rights to the producer in exchange for a periodic royalty (percentage) based on sales. Although payment specifics are discussed in Chapter 5, this section examines general industry pricing trends, as well as a few specific pricing tendencies for the various market segments, that will ultimately affect the deal you strike with a publisher.

Overall, software produced for the home marketplace, i.e., games, home learning programs, and other applications for low-cost computers, are feeling the pinch of downward

```
        Cursor Movement                        Editing Options

                 up
                  ↑
       left ←─────┼─────→ right    Adjust a line            F8
                  ↓                Boldface a character     Shift F8
                down               Duplicate a text block   F6
   Next word          F4           Exit to Main Menu        Esc
   Previous word      F3           Insert characters        Ins
   Beginning of line  Shift F3     Join file from disk      F9
   End of line        Shift F4     Label a block of text    F5
                                   Remove
   Next tab stop      Tab            a character            Del
   Previous tab stop  Shift Tab      a word                 Shift F5
                                     a line                 Shift F6
   Next screen        PgDn         Search/search & replace  F7
   Previous screen    PgUp         Set tabs                 F2
                                   Underline a character    Shift F7
   Beginning of document  Home
   End of document        End

         ----Press F10 to return to your document---
```

Clearly written manuals, help screens, and flip charts get the user started quickly. *(Edu-Ware; Software Publishing Corporation; Bruce & James.)*

15

pricing pressure caused by intense competition in the recreation segment. The result of hundreds of new products chasing a stable but slow-growing customer base first is lower suggested retail prices and then sometimes extensive discounting as a package's life cycle progresses. Arcade games, for example, are notorious for yielding slim profit margins in very short life spans. Few of these packages are priced higher than about $30 to start, and it is estimated that 75 percent of such games' sales occur in the first 6 weeks of shelf life. Unless the disk or cartridge proves to be a "classic" with good backlist possibilities (i.e., retailers want to order it every Christmas), sales can be expected to drop off sharply after the initial distribution period, and the game is likely to be severely discounted or even dumped at cost by stores before it is finally discontinued by a publisher.

In the business market, however, prices historically have been maintained at a much higher level (the average office-oriented financial modeling package carries a suggested retail of over $200) than home software for several reasons. The demand for reliable, easy-to-operate programs in certain categories (accounting, database management, etc.) has so far outrun the supply. In addition, software for the office tends to be complex, and development time is significantly longer than for recreation software. Customers are also willing to pay a higher price if the business producer includes warranties, guarantees of updated versions, user hot lines for troubleshooting, and other buyer incentives. A trend emerging in the small-business and personal productivity segment is the marketing of a major application at a moderate suggested retail price and providing users with the option to upgrade their software with a series of products that supplement the main task. For instance, a word processor retailing for under $50 may be surrounded by a spelling checker, a mail list option, and a "super" filing system, each listing for $29.95. This strategy not only gives the user flexibility in choosing applications according to need, experience level, and budget but also affords excellent opportunities for authors who can supply a continuing series of such "companion," or "add-on," programs.

SOFTWARE DISTRIBUTION TRENDS

Where and how a program reaches its target audience greatly influences its chances for success in the marketplace. A few short years ago, the primary method for getting software into the hands of users was direct mail. But the days when a manufacturer or software publisher could place a little classified ad in the back of a computer magazine and then await an avalanche of orders has long since passed. Even experienced users of the day found buying products sight unseen—especially hardware—a risky undertaking. Not only might merchandise be of questionable quality, but often it was not guaranteed or supported by suppliers; indeed, a mail-order house could disappear from the face of the earth, leaving customers no retribution whatsoever.

In 1975, the first computer specialty shops opened their doors to the highly technical hobbyists and engineers who discovered the convenience of supporting their product habits at a central, reliable location that was increasingly accessible from homes and workplaces. Further, computer stores took on a "clubby" atmosphere where technical enthusiasts could meet to discuss the latest industry developments and exchange equipment experiences and advice with one another as well as with sales staff—usually "tekkies" themselves.

✛ Computer stores remain the dominant distribution outlet today, particularly for the business markets, with more than 15,000 independently owned and franchised chains in operation. But for obvious reasons there are now at least a half-dozen or more different and rapidly growing channels aggressively competing with computer stores, including software specialty shops; mass merchandisers such as Sears, K-Mart, and J. C. Penney; department stores; toy and video stores; record and tape outlets; audio and consumer electronics stores; bookstores; and even supermarkets.

Distribution channels have broadened drastically in a relatively short time to meet the challenges of changing customer demographics (population characteristics) such as age, education, occupation, and income level. Today's prime computer user, as we know, is no longer a professional or technical scientist, engineer, or hobbyist who enjoys tinkering with single-board micros and whose idea of a good time is a Saturday night spent debugging in COBOL. Rather, on the business side, the mainstream personal computer customer is an upwardly mobile middle manager who has already experienced the technology through a large corporate employer. Or perhaps the customer is a small business owner ready to change over from manual operations. On the home front, the customer could be an executive who brings a desktop computer home at night so Johnny can do his homework and maybe get in a few rounds of *Donkey Kong* before bedtime or the parents of a student who works on an Apple II at school who want to encourage computer education at home.

For these nouveau buyers, deciding where to buy a computer and accompanying software is as critical as choosing the right model. Many computer illiterates are intimidated by computer specialty stores, where the language spoken continues to lean more toward advanced BASIC than English. But even if they hesitate to shop at a full-service specialty store, they still need an outlet that will spend time explaining the products, be there for repairs and additional questions, and unbegrudgingly do a little hand holding. Increasingly, publishers as well as manufacturers aiming for the mass market—the "great computer unwashed"—attempt to reach these customers through familiar retail settings such as department stores or the neighborhood record store or toy shops, which might also provide the critical service and support needed to capture repeat sales. Unfortunately, not all these outlets are well-prepared to explain your particular program to the uninitiated. That's why the SMD pays close attention to publishers' distribution channels, and so should you. For example, complex business packages plainly must be entrusted to experienced merchandising specialists—the computer and software-only stores—rather than to mass merchandisers suffering from chronic staff turnover and insufficient time or training to explain the workings of an intricate application to a confused customer. However, games and programs that are largely self-starting should be broadly distributed for maximum profit potential.

In the discussion of publisher-author contract negotiations in Chapter 5, you'll learn the importance of ensuring that your programs receive not only adequate distribution but also the appropriate channel of distribution. That is, the publisher who wants exclusive distribution rights to your creations should be able to offer you either the broadest possible coverage or specific outlets, depending on the application. In general, however, our respondents show an increasing trend toward well-balanced distribution in their various target segments.

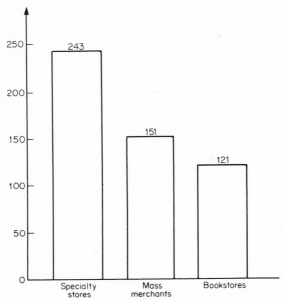

Figure 1-4   Of the publishers surveyed, the number using various distribution channels. Total companies surveyed: 272.

Over half of the program publishers indicated that they sell their recreation, education, and personal productivity products through mass market channels: department stores, mass merchandisers, consumer electronics stores, catalog showrooms and merchandisers, etc. (see Figure 1-4). Of course, most recreation producers also sell into computer stores and software-only shops, as do the majority of business and utility producers—almost 90 percent. Only a handful of recreation and business suppliers move their products only through direct mail backed by catalog ordering—these tend to be very small firms with limited human and financial resources. Business firms serving vertical markets, e.g., insurance or health industries, tend to rely heavily on direct sales forces and value-added resellers (sales organizations that specialize in packaging complete hardware and software systems for corporate customers). Major textbook publishers tend to use established direct-to-school sales forces or school supply firms to gain inroads into the classroom computer market.

In the short term, there will be much experimentation with distribution channels as publishers seek the most efficient methods for moving merchandise. Supermarkets and other heretofore unlikely outlets (one respondent told us Army PXs stock his products) increasingly are cited as either current or proposed sales channels. Significantly, 44.8 percent of SMD survey respondents note that they included bookstores as an important distribution outlet, thus confirming a parallel relationship between software and book publishing. "Software is a natural extension of the book business," says Frank Schwartz, president of Simon and Schuster's electronic publishing division. Accordingly, recent surveys have found that the average computer shopper buys from eight to ten books on the subject before, during, and after the major hardware purchase. It would seem only natural to browse and buy software in a bookshop as well. Marketers note that the big bookstore chains such as B. Dalton and Waldenbooks are already stocking home education and productivity software on a trial basis. If sales prove viable, the 10,000 bookstores nationwide could follow suit by making software part of the standard backlist.

Publishers' sales promotion departments are also working on improving software packaging and putting new emphasis on giveaway or in-store demonstration disks containing sample portions of programs and instructions so that software can help "sell itself" to consumers. (That's yet another vote for program authors to provide instructions—both on screen and in the manual—that are clear-cut, concise, and free of fancy language or technical buzzwords.)

In the longer term, as consumers become more sophisticated and computer literate, rapid growth of franchised software-only specialty stores (from less than 100 stores at the close of 1982 to a projected 2000 or more outlets by the end of the decade) could earn these sources the label of "fast food" chains for the medium.

Other distribution alternatives will enter the picture in the next few years. Commercial online database networks such as The Source, CompuServe, and Dow Jones News and Information Retrieval Service are expected to provide large-scale program distribution as their subscriber base grows. Currently, the full profit potential of electronic downloading to the software-consuming public via these remote networks cannot yet be realized because most computing households have not purchased the necessary telecommunications connection equipment (modem and software). Fewer than 10 percent of the nation's computer-owning households currently own modems, although many have expressed a desire to participate in such long-distance services as home banking and shopping as well as receiving software. Also, until now, sign-on procedures and downloading all but the shortest programs were an excruciatingly slow, complicated, and usually unreliable process. Yet another limiting factor has been the high cost of per hour telephone connect time for the average family. However, as technology improves and prices drop, analysts say electronic software distribution could well account for more than 10 percent of all software sales by 1990.

THE PUBLISHERS

At this writing more than 6000 individuals and organizations label themselves "software publishers." More than half that number, however, are single authors (maybe you're among them) or design teams who write and distribute programs on a shoestring budget—a classified ad here, a catalog or flyer there. In the "old days," it was entirely possible to earn a decent piece of change via such scattershot marketing. A diskette wrapped in a plastic bag and stapled with a business card pretty well ensured an independent a place in the industry.

The cottage era of software publishing, however, is all but finished. Such industry leaders as VisiCorp, MicroPRO International, and Digital Research may have gotten their start in a garage—literally—but as start-ups today they would no doubt be overpowered by the industry heavyweights: cash-rich textbook and commercial book publishers; media conglomerates such as Warner, Inc., CBS, and Time-Life, Inc.; and the mightiest of manu-

LOTUS 1-2-3: It took more than $1 million to launch the program in 1983. *VisiCalc:* It all started in a garage on a shoestring budget in 1978. *(Lotus Development Corporation; VisiCorp.)*

facturers—led by IBM—all muscling in with huge production, advertising, and marketing budgets and strong, long-established distribution channels. They're in the game to stay, and they're playing hardball.

To give you an idea of the potential impact of these newer entrants on current leaders, consider that, although VisiCorp, made famous by its *VisiCalc* package and subsequent *VisiSeries* of software, is the largest independent producer in terms of revenues, it earns under $100 million annually. (Indeed, fewer than 100 third-party software companies employ more than 25 employees.) Compare this figure with the multibillion-dollar-a-year revenues of a McGraw-Hill, a Gulf & Western (which owns Simon and Schuster), or a Warner Communication. Analysts expect a significant transition in the structure of software publishing in the next several years, from an entrepreneur-driven business with relatively low entry costs to a business that strongly parallels today's competitive book publishing or record industry. Late but powerful entrants signal clear changes—some of them negative, others positive—in the very character of program publishing as well as future opportunities for independents.

Although the death knell for independent start-ups hasn't entirely sounded, the major producers have already forced many "one-man bands" with inadequate financial and marketing resources to give up the ghost. Merger and acquisition activity, too, have claimed many a promising small publisher. Some observers think that the giants may foster an unhealthy consolidation and perhaps even stifle new talent. In other words, many programs will pass through the hands of a few large companies which will make the major marketing and production decisions, determine the overall trends, and fill the pipelines with packages they perceive as meeting the needs of consumers.

On the plus side of the debate, software quality and customer service and support are likely to improve greatly as formal production standards and efficient design criteria become firmly established. The obvious parallels drawn between software publishing and the record or book publishing business should also benefit the author in the long run. Just as most book authors and recording artists neither are prepared to be nor desire to be their own publishers, marketers, and distributors, the entry of well-heeled organizations lifts the financial burden off the shoulders of the struggling independents, leaving them to pursue the truly creative task of discovering and refining innovative concepts and new program ideas. With the entry of the major players, the software industry may at last shed its chaotic beginnings for an orderly mature existence.

Other notable changes that will occur with the aggressive stance of the large corporations will be the tendency for publishers to broaden their single-product lines. Until recently, even the most profitable producers made their market on a single, specialized concept: VisiCorp had *VisiCalc*, MicroPRO had *Wordstar*, Ashton-Tate had *dBase II*, and Lotus Development had *1-2-3*. Now, broad-minded traditional publishers with adequate resources will deepen and widen software lines to achieve a more balanced selection, whether they're aiming for the home, school, or office. The SMD already reflects the trend; note that many of the larger companies request programs that supplement a mainstream idea (e.g., adding an electronic dictionary to a word processing package).

Since not every program that goes to market is a best-seller, broadening the lines virtually assures publishers of large, profitable backlists—titles that sell in small quantities but are steady box office draws (witness the remarkable profitability of romance novels). The opportunity to participate in building reliable backlists in turn assures talented authors of at least a steady income, if not software stardom.

As in books and records, then, large software publishers will offer ample opportunity for the creative professional. More good news: small- and medium-sized companies that assume the intermediary role of developer-packager for the larger organizations will gain an increasing piece of the action. These smaller companies, already expert in packaging computer books which are distributed and marketed by large commercial publishers, view software as a natural extension. Some of the better-known packagers of computer books and, more recently, software, which are constantly on the lookout for talented designers are TAB Books, Wayne Green Press, Dilithium Press, and Howard W. Samms. As noted in the directory, opportunities to contribute to intermediaries abound, and it's a good way to gain a niche in the business.

Another type of intermediary is the software licenser-packager, which accepts original program designs, converts the titles into several different machine formats, prepares a cohesive advertising and promotional campaign for each (including the package artwork), and then licenses marketing and distribution rights of the finished products to major publishers. The largest worldwide licensing agency is International Computer Group, which holds the rights to over 3000 titles and was instrumental in the wildly successful across-the-board marketing of Bill Hogue's *Miner 2049er* maze game.

Major hardware manufacturers are also expected to play a vital role in large-scale software development, with IBM leading the pack. It is advisable, in fact, to follow IBM's actions closely, since it is the bellwether of industry change. Other major hardware players include Texas Instruments (professional systems) and Tandy Corporation. Apple has scaled back software development, noting that there are plenty of third parties supporting its systems worldwide.

Perhaps the ultimate overlap between the software and the book business is the recent trend of selling computer books and software in a single package. Software designers who are also good writers will profit nicely in the coming software revolution.

THE SOFTWARE AGENT

The near collision of books and software has led, not surprisingly, to the entrance of yet two more familiar characters in the industry drama, the literary agent—software author's representative and the software marketing organization.

Functioning much like any book author's agent, software agents seek the best production and distribution agreement for their clients in exchange for a percentage of the authors' profits, usually ranging from 10 to 15 percent. Nearly all the big names in literary circles are now involved with software, but the agency with the largest stake so far is John Brockman Associates in New York. That firm put together a multimillion dollar deal for its client, Bruce & James Program Publishers, Inc., producers of *Wordvision*, a word processing package. Simon and Schuster agreed to distribute and market the package through the nation's bookstores. Other big names in the business include Scott Meredith Agency, William Morris, Sterling Lord, and The Software Agency, the result of a merger between the Sanford Greenburger and Moulton agencies (see the last page of the SMD for complete addresses and telephone numbers).

The software-only representative is an offshoot of the literary agent. Such intermediaries usually limit their expertise to software authors and computer book authors and many also act as their client's attorney in negotiating the publishing agreement. Software marketing organizations may best be described as the vanity presses of the computer world. For a fee, they will help you package your program and prepare documentation so that you can market it or self-publish and distribute it. Unlike agents, marketing representatives generally don't negotiate with publishers on the author's behalf.

Should you acquire an agent's services? It depends. First, the big names in the business won't look at you or your diskettes until you have already successfully sold programs. Even then, getting through to the handful of top people is a fiercely competitive process. Instead, you might approach a lesser-known firm that is hungry for fresh talent; such representatives may alert you to team projects and other opportunities you may not otherwise discover. Certainly, an agent is not a prerequisite to going ahead with a program submission, although a few of the larger traditional book publishers say they "prefer" program proposals from agents (who also perform a vital screening function for inundated editors). On the whole, however, directory respondents don't place heavy emphasis on the agent's participation.

Indeed, sometimes a well-meaning representative may hinder your chances for a program sale or irrevocably upset a potentially beneficial author-publisher relationship. A word of caution from a Harper & Row electronic publishing editor: Make certain that the agent you choose is both educated and experienced in the field. "I find myself irritated beyond words when an agent calls and says, 'I have this thing. I don't understand it. But why don't you give it a look.' " Having the agent as the "pocket of ignorance" between programmer and publisher, she adds, is "harmful and crazy."

THE MARKETPLACE—CONCLUSION

Events in this lightning-fast business change almost daily. This book can lay the foundation for your marketing approach and alert you to significant developments that will most likely affect your publishing success; it's up to you to regularly follow your field of interest by reading any of scores of general and machine-specific computer magazines as well as important trade periodicals. Among valuable general publications are *Popular Computing* and *Creative Computing* for the nontechnical consumer and *BYTE* for highly technically oriented readers. In the trade, for a valuable "moving picture" of the consumer marketplace, a (cheap) subscription to *Infoworld*, the newsweekly of the micro industry, is recommended. For those interested in more technical developments, *Electronic News* is a weekly newspaper published by New York–based Fairchild, Inc., covering everything from semiconductors to minicomputers and mainframes.

Once upon a time writing a software program was akin to creating the great American novel. But today's software author can no longer afford to write in complete isolation. As you'll discover from the directory respondents, competition demands penetrating knowledge of both the marketplace and one's "technospecialty." The industry-savvy designer stays a step ahead of the pack.

CHAPTER TWO

Getting Started

Capturing the attention of those who count in a business that has often been described as thriving on chaos requires logical and orderly planning. This chapter shows you how to start moving all those ingenious ideas out of your micro and into the hands of the people who want to pay for them. First, we'll consider the good stuff—going payment rates, what a beginner can expect to earn on a program sale, and which program categories offer the best long-term prospects. Then we'll look at the business of generating program ideas that accord with what publishers seek in a new submission and list the steps involved in program evaluation. The importance of good housekeeping (file keeping) follows. Finally, we'll consider opportunities and ideas for beginners and nonprogrammers.

MONEY, MONEY, MONEY

Despite the wave of publicity that accompanies them, overnight millionaires in the software industry are pretty rare birds. Although it's entirely possible to earn a six-figure or better income over the life of a single program, most authors find that royalty dollars accrue at a slow, but steady, annual pace, usually from sales of several products over time.

Royalties may be based (1) on a percentage or fixed dollar amount of the per copy suggested retail price (i.e., 10 percent of each copy sold at $19.95) or (2) on a percentage of the product's total annual wholesale revenues (i.e., 20 percent of the $150,000). Small publishers as well as magazines which accept programs for publication may offer flat fees. The rates you can expect to receive vary, depending on your experience, skills, and flexibility. For example, beginners with little or no background usually get the lower end of the royalty scale or a flat fee; pros with prior successful products find their terms constantly improving. Those who can offer publishers specialized or highly valued talents—expertise in several popular programming languages and machine formats plus a flair for art, for instance—may find their services exceptionally well compensated. In addition, separate royalties are often assigned for documentation and other user materials. The only fixed rule in this business, really, is that everything is negotiable. (For additional payment information, see Chapters 5 and 6.)

If payment is calculated according to the shelf life of the various program categories, business programs, primarily horizontal applications, are considered the most lucrative long-term prospects (i.e., word processors, database managers, and financial applications—software that is useful to a broad range of office personnel, managers, and executives as well as small-business owners, home entrepreneurs, and professionals). Into the second-most-promising category fall vertical packages—applications aimed at doctors, lawyers, architects, or other narrow user groups or institutions. The majority of games live very brief selling cycles—perhaps as short as a few months.

Directory survey data throw some overall light on publishers' average royalty payments. Of the companies citing a specific royalty figure, over half said that they offer rates starting at between 10 and 15 percent of program sales and ranging up to 20 percent or better. In general, education and utilities publishers tend to offer lower rates, usually averaging 10 percent or under.

FACTORS AFFECTING EARNINGS POTENTIAL

In Chapter 1 we covered general hardware and software trends that are likely to affect your target computer, publisher, and program projects and emphasized the need to follow day-to-day market developments in your area of interest. Why you should be well-versed in your chosen market segment becomes clear when you attempt to figure a rough but realistic yearly earnings estimate for your labors.

In determining your earning power, first consider how much your time is worth on the open market. For example, given such market conditions as demand for your program, probable price, and range of distribution, do potential royalties earned in a year equal or exceed what you'd earn if you were employed full-time in a comparable programming position at a certain annual salary plus medical and other benefits? Obviously, spending 6 months creating a low-priced game for a narrow group of players is a poor investment of human resources and disastrous entrepreneurial planning. Other factors that should help determine your chances of making a satisfying living, full or part time, follow. Consider them in terms of impact on your earnings potential as well as how they might affect work opportunities.

Machine-installed base: If you author for a single system, make sure that there are enough users and potential users for your programs. Author for well-established products, veering away from off-brand or new products that haven't yet built a following in the marketplace. Authors who can prepare programs for several different systems are at a definite advantage.

Collateral effort required: Don't "byte" off more than you can chew. Ed Curry, president of Lifeboat Associates, the world's largest marketer of business software, says earning program royalties is like "making money while you sleep." And, of course, the faster you can bring a concept to market the sooner you can start collecting those royalties. But it takes many worker-hours to complete a software project to the satisfaction of all parties. First drafts of programs alone do not a sale make. The documentation must be meticulously prepared and the program reworked and repolished until it shines error-free and perfectly understandable to the potential customer.

Remember also that the authors' responsibility for their creations may not end when they complete assignments. In the business segment particularly, authors should be prepared to offer telephone support to novice users (most program producers have toll-free customer "hot lines," and the people who use them expect fast and helpful answers). Authors are also expected to update, revise, debug, and otherwise periodically adjust their works for new or upwardly compatible operating systems (e.g., converting to 16-bit from 8-bit machines).

Very few full-time authors can exist on the strength of a single program. Beyond the initial project, good authors are asked to create companion programs that support the original concept, particularly in the business and education areas. In recreation, there is great time pressure to come up with fresh, exciting ideas before the competition does.

Publisher's breadth and depth of distribution: As was suggested in the last chapter, how widely your program is distributed determines the number of potential buyers who will be exposed to it. Programs for a broad-based audience (games, for example) should sell through publishers with the widest possible distribution—mass merchandisers; department stores; consumer electronics, computer, and other specialty outlets; catalog showrooms; etc. (Small producers relying primarily on direct-mail catalogs are a good route to breaking in, but, once you're well-established, try for producers with a larger potential customer base.)

However, highly specialized programs should be sold with the expert retailer in mind—computer store, software store, or even direct sales force in the case of vertical applications designed for specific companies and industries.

How do you determine a publisher's distribution routes? Ask! Or see for yourself. Visit a local shopping center and count how many stores (and types of stores) carry the producer's products. How visible are the products (shelved up front or hidden under miscellaneous merchandise)? Does each store carry all the company's lines or just a few select "hot" products? This tells you not only the customer base a producer solicits but also how aggressively it merchandises its backlist products as well as its "stars."

GENERATING IDEAS

Intimate knowledge of the marketplace, coupled with personal or occupational expertise, leads naturally to generating salable program ideas. Learn to keep an open eye and ear on your environment. Attune yourself to program possibilities at every turn. Jot down ideas as they occur so you don't forget them (professional journalists and authors keep a pad and pen at bedside for those wee-hours inspirations).

Whatever your experience, you're brimming with program proposals you don't even realize you have. Educators and students, for example, are ideally situated to discover computer-assisted instruction packages not already available. Office managers may have their own unique filing system that would benefit complementary (not necessarily competitive) industries. Store managers may have devised a twist on a general inventory package that truly customizes that software for specialized store applications. There isn't room to list the hundreds of possibilities that will emerge with a bit of soul-searching. However, Chapter 3, Targeting the Market, pinpoints some offbeat program audiences that should spur your imagination.

If you really suffer from writer's block, a good place to start churning out ideas is the SMD. Peruse the "Plugging In" section of each company listing which divulges the publisher's immediate program interests. In a more general vein, consider the following prime areas in which publishers cite increasing interest.

- **Program conversions:**   Any practical application now on the market that hasn't yet been written for the IBM PC, PCjr, and compatible machines is fair game.
- **Upward conversions:**   The movement from 8-bit to 16-bit machines has left the newer generation behind in terms of usable software. Publishers need people who can turn 8-bit-based programs into smoothly running applications for 16-bit micros.
- **Improvement of older programs:**   Teach an old dog new tricks using the improved technology and greater memory capacity of late-generation computers.

Some companies make specific "needs" lists—lists of long- and short-term program projects—available on request. Also, remember that plans change constantly. It's a good idea to communicate frequently with companies that produce programs in your specialty.

THE EVALUATION PROCESS

Why do some authors' proposals undergo serious consideration by publishers, whereas others are read and rejected almost immediately? Knowing your marketplace is the number-one prerequisite to getting your foot—and your package—inside the publishing door. Given the cost of developing a software program, bringing it to market, and supporting it (in some cases forever) and given the number of products already fighting for market share, publishers necessarily must place themselves in a near-adversarial position—you are considered unpublishable until you've proved otherwise. Before even looking at the details of the actual program, publishers need to know if you know the bottom line. Therefore, they will seek out the following profit-minded elements upon receiving your software proposal.

- **Program purpose:**   What does the software attempt to do? What are its main features and objectives (what does it hope to accomplish for users, i.e., will it inform, entertain, educate, make people more productive)? Why does the world need this program?

- **Target audience:** Who will use this program primarily? Who are the secondary users, if any (e.g., teachers primarily, and also administrators)? What are the users' characteristics (e.g., age, sex, occupation, education level, computer and software experience level)? How large is the audience (i.e., its market size—U.S. elementary and secondary schools, over 2000 ad agencies, the nation's dairy farmers)? What percentage of the total market do you realistically expect to penetrate with your program?

- **The competition:** Who are the companies and authors who have already produced similar programs? What are the features and main advantages and disadvantages of competing programs? How does your idea stack up against what's already out there? How should the package be priced (approximately), given the competition?

- **Menu contents and overall design features:** What are your main menu items and how do they suit the user's needs? How does your program interact with the user (i.e., are error messages and other feedback proposed to increase user friendliness)? What innovative use of color, graphics, and sound do you include? Are there any major design problems that will need to be solved to ensure user friendliness?

- **System requirements:** What programming language are you using to write the program? What machine, model, and operating system is your software written for? How many bytes of memory are required to operate the program? What special peripherals or other add-ons are required to operate the program?

- **Transportability:** How easily will your program transfer to another personal computer? What machines would be recommended? Will there be any special conversion problems?

- **Packaging and marketing:** It is extremely important to visualize for the publisher how the finished package—box and all—will appear. What is the total number of diskettes on completion? Size and length of documentation (e.g., 8-page pamphlet or 50-page spiral instruction manual heavily illustrated)? Package art (include a sketch)? Distribution—where should the program be sold? How would you position it in the marketplace to advertise it effectively (e.g., a cooking program as the housewife's helper)? Would humor help sell a program to its audience? Where should the package be advertised (computer magazines, general interest magazines, billboards, etc.)?

- **Maintenance and updates:** What and how much support will users of your program need (e.g., most users will need at least a week of training to become adept)? How should support be accomplished (in store, via telephone hot line, with additional documentation, etc.)? How might your program need to be periodically revised or updated? Why? How often? If not, why not?

- **Delivery of finished product:** How soon can you deliver a prototype or program sample? Within how many weeks or months do you anticipate program and documentation completion?

- **Author's credentials:** Why are you qualified to supply the proposed program? What is your prior experience in the field?

Your ability to answer these vital preliminary questions is inextricably linked with how well you've studied the market of your choice. If satisfied, the scrupulous publisher goes on to extensively preview and pretest your proposal and sample diskette for quality and content. Finally, the package is deemed salable or unsalable. If the answer is positive, contract negotiations begin (see Chapter 5, Acceptance). If the answer is negative, all materials are returned to you. (See Chapter 4, Submitting Programs, for information regarding the nondisclosure agreement, which helps protect original ideas and source code, and additional evaluation guidelines.)

Despite the near mountain of material that must first pass through dozens of hands, the initial waiting game is relatively brief. Despite unavoidable bottlenecks, most directory respondents believe proposal reviews should take no longer than 8 weeks; some say they respond in less than 1 to 2 weeks. Once the proposal is accepted, however, project length can stretch from a few months to over a year, depending on the nature of the program and the amount of necessary editing and revision.

THE IMPORTANCE OF GOOD HOUSEKEEPING

As mentioned previously, an organized author is well-prepared to tackle the often confusing submissions process. Before you get buried under the inevitable mounds of correspondence and reams of paper that are the occupational hazards of independents, take a day or two to create the following files (on computer or with good old-fashioned manila folders—whichever is easier to maintain and update daily).

- **The idea file:**   Divide this file by market segment (e.g., recreation, education, business, utility), customer group, or other convenient subset. Into this file will go all notes, product literature, jottings, article clippings, and other "instant inspirations" that could form the basis for a brilliant program idea. Building an idea file also provides you with a backup during those "dry" brainstorming periods.

- **Publishers' correspondence file:**   Divide this file according to companies you communicate with. Each time you contact a new publishing source, be it hardware manufacturer, third-party distributor, or computer magazine, start a new folder.

- **Publishers' names, addresses, phone numbers, and personal contacts list:**   Keep this on a rotating card file, mail-merge file, or whatever form that lets you know who and where to call or write quickly and without procrastinating. People and companies move around often, so be sure to update the list regularly.

- **Accounts receivable:**   You're going to have to pay taxes on what you earn, so if you don't have a bookkeeper or accountant, keep a careful payment record. Most independents figure their income on a calendar basis—from January 1 to December 31. Thus, this file should accommodate 12 months and be set up according to publisher, statement date, amount of royalty, and which program or programs the money represents (e.g., if the program is selling through two different publishers in two different machine formats, list each as a separate entry). If you are paid separately for documentation or for providing special user support, list those amounts too. Keep a running total.

- **Accounts payable:** As a self-employed, full-time independent, you are entitled to deduct certain expenses from your gross income before taxes are figured. Keep a record of daily expenditures that are directly linked to program production, (e.g., blank diskettes, printer paper, other stationery supplies, cost of traveling to and from a publisher for editorial meetings, technical publications, and dues from club or organization memberships that assist you in your work). You may even deduct a portion of your rent or mortgage payment if you use your home as a primary workplace—check with an accountant or tax preparer or with the nearest IRS office for specific details. Even if you write programs only part time, while holding a full-time job (as many authors do), you may still be eligible to deduct certain expenses from your income. Consult a qualified professional for details.

IDEAS FOR BEGINNERS AND NONPROGRAMMERS

So what if you've only just started programming, or if you've never written a single line of code? If you have an inspiration and have sufficiently checked out the market, there are more than a few ways to "go for it."

- Consider teaming up with a technically skilled partner—with you as idea and marketing person—at least until your design skills improve enough to allow you to strike out on your own. (Even if you're a solid single designer, team planning that exploits different individuals' strengths may increase your chances of program sales.)
- Approach any of the dozens of popular computer magazines that accept short, easy-to-use programs written expressly for beginners. (For specific submission guidelines, see the SMD, Section Six, Magazines.)
- Circulate your amateur (public domain) programs around the computer clubs—if your peers find them useful and easy to use, then you've conquered a minimarket and can communicate this as evidence of your talent to potential publishers.
- Enter contests and competitions regularly run by magazines and some software companies. For a rundown on annual contests and miscellaneous selling opportunities for beginners and professionals, see Chapter 3, Targeting the Market.

CHAPTER THREE

Targeting the Market

If you're a specialist in your field—an instructor for the handicapped, for example, or a PASCAL expert, you probably have a solid notion of your potential user audience. Whether specialists or generalists, authors must pin down the appropriate market segment for their programs and then focus all design efforts on meeting that group's software needs to survive publishers' tough evaluation processes. This chapter pinpoints specific creative trends and the acquisition outlook for the three major subject areas: recreation, education (home and classroom), and business and professional management and personal productivity. The markets are considered strictly from a salability standpoint: What are some best-seller examples in each category? What are the creative and technical elements that made them best-sellers? What makes a steady seller? Then we'll explore the hidden program market— some widely overlooked audience subsets that open up many additional selling opportunities. Tips on staying alert to new targets follow, along with how to narrow your choice of publishers. Finally, some miscellaneous income opportunities for beginners and professionals are listed that perhaps are not readily apparent but are nonetheless promising.

WHERE THE ACTION IS: RECREATION

Directory respondents divide the recreation market into two broad categories: entertainment, including all kinds of games and hobby and leisure time pursuits, and home education, which includes learning games and tutorials aimed at self-improvement and self-instruction. Home learning is discussed in the next section, along with programs targeted to the classroom. Here, let's consider the market for entertainment software from the author's vantage point.

If you've always dreamed of writing the Great American Game, welcome to the club. The five major game categories—arcade, action, adventure, strategy, and simulation—

currently make up about 40 percent of all home-oriented applications purchased. That figure is expected to stabilize or decline only slightly in years to come, because, no matter how useful the computer proves, people are game players at heart. There's always room for one more good game program (emphasis on *good*), especially those offering unique twists on ordinary concepts or posing exciting new home challenges to otherwise jaded "coin-op" devotees.

No matter what the creative bent, publishers today are unanimous in their desire to acquire "classics"—programs that catch consumers' fancy and "keep 'em coming back" to the keyboard again and again. In fact, it's not the momentary best-seller riding high on a quickie fad that program buyers constantly seek but rather the steady grosser. What makes a good, i.e., perennially salable, game program in the eyes of the publisher and, ultimately, the end user? Let's examine the creative elements of each game category and then summarize the long- and short-term authoring prospects for each.

Arcade Games

According to Nolan Bushnell, the man who founded Atari and invented *PONG*, a "good game is one that keeps the player right on the edge between ecstasy and frustration." That's a very apt description of the criteria needed to distinguish your game program from the hundreds, even thousands, now on the market or in software companies' evaluation files. Examples that follow Bushnell's philosophy are the dynamic video arcade games licensed for the home, such as *Centipede, Donkey Kong, Q-Bert, Pole Position*, and other graphically mesmerizing packages that are tough enough to frustrate *and* satisfy even the most expert of experts. Although the above-mentioned examples are drawn from the coin-operated design world, many original home arcade hits abound. There are *Sneakers* (Sirius), *Crush Crumble and Chomp* (Epyx), *Apple Panic* and *Choplifter* (Broderbund), *Miner 2049er* (MicroLab), among others.

You know the feeling of playing an arcade classic. It's like plugging in an old friend; no matter how often you go at it, the thrill never ends. That's exactly the feeling publishers try to capture in new arcade programs and what you should strive for in your own work.

Maze games, although an intrinsic part of the arcade scene, deserve a separate mention because of their overwhelming popularity. Namco's *PAC-MAN* for the arcades (closely trailed by *MS. PAC-MAN*) is by far the most beloved of the genre for all ages, despite its graphic limitations on some home systems. Successful variations include Coleco's *Ladybug* and *Mousetrap*, Sierra On-Line's *Jawbreaker*, and Mattel's *Lock 'n' Chase*. Why are maze games met with such universal enthusiasm? "Universal" is the key operating word. Dan Gutman, editor of *Computer Games Player* magazine, writing in *Psychology Today*, notes that "cute, cuddly characters in nonviolent games" are instantly attractive to children, teens, and adults of both sexes, but that the real secret of *PAC-MAN's* success (and the success of his animated descendants) is his appeal to women. "He brought them into arcades in large numbers for the first time," the editor observes. The psychology of power also has something to do with it, experts believe. Overcoming a challenging maze by memorizing certain surefire patterns instills a sense of power and control in a player. Such feelings are hard to come by in everyday life at school and work.

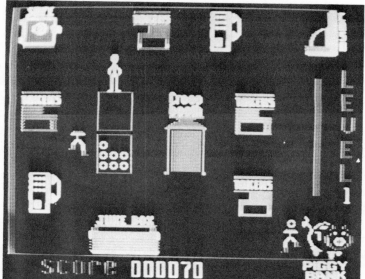

Arcade adaptions such as those pictured here are popular picks by publishers, but game companies are always on the lookout for an original "classic." *Data-soft; Broderbund Software.*)

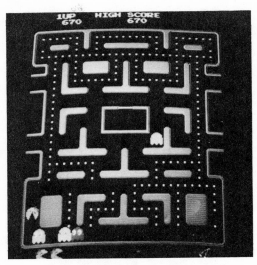

PAC-MAN won the women's hearts and paved the way
for the maze game, including MS. PAC-MAN. (Atari.)

Market outlook for arcade games: Overall demand for independently authored products is steady, hindered only by major companies' desire for "proven," audience-tested arcade hits, which has led many to license titles directly from arcade game makers such as Bally/Midway and Sega and then develop them for the home market in house. However, SMD publishers agreed that if a program posesses a unique angle or presents an original concept, the chances of acceptance are better than average.

Eye-catching graphics and meaningful use of color, sound, and, increasingly, music are additional desirable elements cited by buyers. To be avoided at all costs are simplistic "twitch" games offering little or no challenge, color and sound unrelated to the action, and video arcade knockoffs without the hint of an original theme.

Action Games

Into this group fall sports, space, military, and other pure movement games that transform the player into an active participant, either in a team situation or one-on-one against a human opponent or the computer. Best-selling *Enduro* (Activision), *Astro Chase* (First Star Software), *Superman* (Atari), and *Sea Dragon* (Adventure International) are styles that merit emulation. Here the key to successful program design, says Tom Lopez, Activision's editorial director, is using the machine's capabilities to the fullest in dreaming up a hero fantasy situation that players can relate to, possibly a scenario you have always wanted to enact. "Start with a scene—you're a race car driver in your first grand prix, or a mountain climber in the Alps—and then build the game objectives around it," he suggests. The idea, producers stress, is to totally immerse your audience in the crisis and challenge at hand.

Interestingly, although the vast majority of action games tend to place the player in a fantasy hero role, there appears to be some appetite for programs in which the major character is an "average Joe," or a "Mr. or Ms. Every American." Gary Carlston, vice president and director of product development at Broderbund, reports that his company has received several author proposals in which the hero is "everything from a waitress to a gas station attendant to a fast food preparer." Mattel's popular *Burgertime* reflects such ordinary play themes. But Broderbund has yet to accept such pedestrian proposals. "Unless future consumer market research proves otherwise, we tend to believe that most people want a chance to live out their wildest, rather than their most mundane, fantasies through the computer," he comments. Just the same, you never know. If you have a John Q. Public action game waiting in the wings, keep it handy as you peruse the directory.

Market outlook for action games: The prospect for long-term demand for independently authored products is good, with over half of SMD survey respondents in the recreation segment reporting immediate demand for the category. In general, buyers advise avoiding repetitive or clichéd situations and aiming for a balance between skill and reflex factors.

Adventure Games

An increasingly popular genre covering many of the same subject areas as action games (fantasy, the military, space, science fiction, etc.), adventures are much more complex than pure action stories and cover a lot more ground than even multiple-screen arcade and action games. Resembling novels more closely than games, in fact, the best way to contrast adventure with pure action games is to consider the difference between a television mini-series and a half-hour police show. Adventures not only involve role-playing but also require a solid plot, characters, descriptive scenery, and all the other elements that create an exciting quest, treasure hunt, revolutionary war, etc. In addition, many authors create a real-time mode for extra realism.

Among the recent best-sellers in this group are *The Dark Crystal* (Sierra On-Line, based on the movie by Jim Henson), *Time Zone* and *Deadline* (Infocom), and everyone's favorite, *Dungeons & Dragons*, originally conceived by TSR Hobbies, Inc. Several key elements resulted in these programs' success, among them, elaborate branching and mapping routines that lead players in any of several intriguing directions, user friendliness and easy-to-answer prompts, and, in appropriate circumstances, humor.

"Humor is very important in maintaining an ongoing friendly relationship between user and computer, especially in the adventure program, where game play can take several hours or even several days or weeks," advises Christopher Cerf, scriptwriter for *The Dark Crystal*. However, he adds, "You have to use discretion and not overdo it." Cerf also points out that humorous elements should have universal recognition. An example of properly implemented and well-timed humor in *The Dark Crystal* is an answer parodying a well-known television commercial. Prompted by the user command to "cut vine," the program slyly responds, "We shall cut no vine before its time."

Market outlook for adventure games: Long-term demand for adventure games is very good, as evidenced by the SMD recreation buyers, 55 percent of whom said that they actively seek quality programs in this genre.

Since a great story idea can quickly become overwhelming in the computer conversion

The adventure game as literary medium and art form. *(Sierra On-Line.)*

process, publishers suggest these basic steps in preparing an adventure program: Outline the plot, purpose, complete cast of characters, necessary scenery, objects to be retrieved or to be used as clues, and any other items and facts needed to achieve the story's goal. Then fill in the outline in a rough draft. Later, as you compose the finished game, physically map out the various directional possibilities and try to anticipate how users might respond to system prompts (e.g., north, south, forward, backward, take lamp, cut rope). Such a step-by-step process will also simplify writing the documentation and supplementary instructions.

Experts believe that new technology and the acceptance of micro software as art form and literary medium will launch the adventure genre as a primary form of expression in years to come. For example, computer-controlled video disks containing full-scale production values for a mystery adventure series called *Murder, Anyone?* was recently released by Vidimax. The first disk was partially staged with live actors at an estate and mansion in a Long Island suburb of New York and then combined with branching instructions to lead teams of players through a whodunnit scenario. Improvements in microcomputer graphics and animation also are changing the face of adventures from text-only to beautifully configured, full-color backgrounds and intricately drawn characters. The Apple II version of *The Dark Crystal*, for instance, boasts more than 200 individual color pictures.

For the talented writer, novelist, or artist who is also computer-savvy (or who can team up with programmer partners), the adventure category becomes a lucrative outlet for as many applications as the imagination can conjure.

Strategy Games

Other than straight "shoot-'em-ups" or the simplest hand-eye coordination programs, all games contain some element of strategy, from simple obstacle avoidance to elaborate plotting and decision making, and the player must carefully weigh the consequences of

Good strategy games keep players on their toes. *(Epyx.)*

each and every move. Strategy games maintain their popularity because they require thought, not just mechanical reactions.

"We think games should make a person use his noodle and not just his joystick," says Michael Katz, president of Epyx, a specialty publisher of strategy games. Similarly, "using your noodle" to design for this genre paves the path to a program sale, he believes. "A good strategy program keeps the player on his toes, keeps the game moving in an orderly, yet exciting fashion, and provides lots of room for alternative decision-making on the way to the ultimate reward," Katz explains.

You may be familiar with such strategy classics as *Temple of Apshai* (Epyx), *Artillery Duel* (Action Graphics), *Pitfall!* (Activision), and *Necromancer*, (Synapse). These hits artfully combine the adventure story or action element with thought-provoking and, in many instances, real-time tests of wit. Other forms of strategy games include traditional board game conversions such as chess, backgammon, and Reversi.

Market outlook for strategy games: Excellent; SMD recreation respondents report an increased buying outlook for the category in the short term.

Simulation Games

Consider simulation games as a subset of strategy and adventure games, but with a twist: the games are written entirely in "first person," that is, the player is (literally) in the driver's seat, in the pilot's seat, at a nuclear reactor site, on the moon, or wherever. Simulations place players right in the middle of a specific setting or situation and force them to respond as closely as possible to the real-life version. The most popular type is the flight simulator, and many successful authors, have drawn on actual aircraft takeoff and landing patterns and airport layouts. Although dozens of these packages exist, publishers don't appear to be saturated; many encourage submissions that extend the flight simulation concept to unique settings (other solar systems, for example) or offer complex and challenging "control panels." Simulations may also include just about any "real" geographic area imaginable, from Monte Carlo to Moscow or Cape Canaveral—go right ahead and transport your audience wherever your wildest desires take them.

Excellent simulation examples on the market include *Flight Simulator*, by SubLogic, Inc., for Microsoft; *Air Traffic Controller* (Avant-Garde); *Chennault's Flying Tigers* (Discovery Games); *Star Master* (Activision); and *Micro Surgeon* (Imagic). Crafting these well-received games in many cases required painstaking research of facts, maps, and other data. *Micro Surgeon*, for example, a medical mystery that takes players deep into the human body, incorporates actual principles of biology, according to William Grubb, chair of Imagic.

Another important technique that makes simulations sell is how graphics are employed. "Realism is quite important," revealed Tom Lopez, Activision's editorial director. "You've got to go that extra mile to get the most out of your system, because players expect no less than the 'real' thing from today's simulations."

Market outlook for simulation games: Software market companies that primarily buy recreation programs say the acquisition outlook for this genre is increasing—a good sign for

Creating SubLogic's *Flight Simulator II* required painstaking attention to detail and the use of actual maps. *(SubLogic.)*

prospective authors. Most often cited as requirements for acceptance are accuracy in converting map data for the screen and full use of machine graphics and sound capabilities where appropriate.

Advancing technology, such as interactive video disks, is influencing the way microcomputer simulations will look in the near future. For example, Atari as well as Sega (the coin-operated games company that recently entered the home market) is experimenting with three-dimensional special effects for coin-op arcade simulations. One possibility now being researched for enhancing the feeling of realism is a video recorder—computer setup that reproduces the player's image, masks out the background, overlays it onto the video disk's frames, and synchronizes two representations so that they are one. In a sense, people no longer play the game—they enter the game and "live" it, watching themselves "walk" down the road, or "climb" a tree.

Another far out, yet not entirely improbable, development in the simulation arena extends beyond the realm of games. It's called "synthetic travel" or "travel by proxy" and may occur through developments in robotics. According to David Yates, a London computer scientist who is working on the scheme, you will enter a control module in, say, Buffalo, and take command of a robot in Brussels, say, peering through the machine's "eyes," and listening to live street sounds through its "ears" as you steer it through the local marketplaces. Early-model proxies might provide only visual and auditory information, Yates speculates, but later models would give participants a complete sensory experience, including taste.

Hobby and Leisure Time Programs

This subset of the entertainment market offers program designers an interesting and some-times offbeat opportunity for program sales. Among recent marketplace entrants in the hobby area are gardening "spreadsheets" for formulating feeding, planting, and watering schedules and other seasonal "must dos"; custom-tailored database managers for baseball card, coin, stamp, butterfly, and other collectors; computerized sewing and weaving patterns; proportional-scale drawing, artists' sketchpads, and other creative graphics tools; music composers; and more.

In the pure fun and novelty area, multiple-player party games and solitary pursuits such as *Movie Trivia* (Wizard), *Murder by the Dozen* (CBS Software), and *Biorhythms* (Orbyte) have drawn a solid following. To ensure universal appeal and usability, the subjects of these team or single-player games are purposely broad, including all kinds of trivia, IQ tests, science and word challenges, human relations quizzes (à la *Reader's Digest* or other maga-zines—how to communicate with your lover or spouse, etc.), and sexually oriented material (a strip poker disk is a steady seller, confides one marketing manager). Card games for one or more players are also good conversion possibilities. How do you acquire programming design skills in these areas? Practice makes perfect. Play lots of nonelectronic counterparts of the games you are thinking of emulating electronically to get a feel for formats and player interaction.

Warning: Most publishers prefer original submissions to those that propose computeriz-ing copyrighted material. Unless you own the copyright, using such material involves negotiating for permission to replicate logos and other trademarks subject to infringement and licensing the software marketing rights, which may add significantly to development costs.

Market outlook for hobby and leisure time programs: Just as the market for programs that make work speedier, easier, and more effective is blooming, directory respondents report a similar (although certainly smaller) demand for original diskettes and tapes that make people's free time more fun, productive, and perhaps more organized. Many of these applications may already be part of your own library; think about it. In fact, marketers advise looking first toward your favorite leisure interests for good program ideas. For exam-ple, if you're a puzzle freak, you might try for a computerized jigsaw or crossword series. For word and trivia games, a good grasp of the language and of your subject matter is essential.

Authors who can offer continuity—an ongoing series of programs—as well as ease of conversion to several machines are in a good position to strike up a steady, profitable relationship with a publisher of leisure time programs.

WHERE THE ACTION IS: EDUCATION

Education programs, designed for the home, classroom, or corporate training department, fall into five major subdivisions: drill and practice, interactive tutorials, learning games, simulations, and administration and teacher management. Although the market for software that helps people learn just about any subject imaginable (including how to run a computer) is experiencing excellent growth, many educational software suppliers, particularly those aiming at the school segment, have come under heavy criticism for offering expensive, poor-quality programs that don't always achieve desired or stated objectives. More recently, however, established publishers and newer entrants have redoubled their efforts to provide programs that offer sufficient learning value and user friendliness for both teacher and student. The market has improved also since traditional textbook publishers have entered, successfully adapting written material to the computer and supplementing product lines with original programs.

In both the classroom and the home segments, the user pie for education software can be sliced according to several age groups, starting with preschoolers and continuing with elementary, junior high, high school, college students, and, finally, adult learners. Education software made up 12 percent, or approximately $70 million, of the home micro market in 1982; by the end of the decade it will have grown to nearly $2 billion. So important is this area to consumers, says Egil Juliussen, a partner in Future Computing, a Dallas-based market research firm, that by 1987 fully 70 percent of all education programs will be written for home use rather than for classroom teaching. "It's a wide open segment with plenty of room for everyone," Juliussen speculates.

Many parents may not fully understand computers, but they do understand that kids growing up in an information age need more than a passing familiarity with the machines to master future job skills as well as basic societal functions that increasingly depend on computer-based knowledge (banking and library information retrieval, for example). For Mom and Dad, investing in a home computer is like buying the youngster an insurance policy against unemployment and social inadequacy. The home software segment has grown up around a powerful parental notion: Game playing is all well and good, but a computer should teach kids something besides how to improve *Space Invaders* scores.

Drill and Practice Programs

Just as in traditional skill drills, this software category ideally supplements classroom instruction by reinforcing the memorization of facts and concepts. The ever-patient computer-assisted drill program gives instant feedback and, so, encourages students to build on previously mastered material by practicing the newly acquired skills. Among the dozens of subject areas employing drill and practice are math, reading, foreign languages, geography, and history.

But whether they are conducted by humans or computers, drills of any nature can be deadly dull and boring, quickly turning a student off once the novelty of operating the computer is gone. However, such programs can be organized to maintain interest and even to be mildly entertaining, spurring students on to accomplish the tasks at hand. "It's a matter of motivation," explains Steve Pederson, president of Eduware, a major publisher of drill and practice as well as other educational programs. "If a kid's bored, he's not going to learn. Period. The program has got to focus on delivering instruction in such a way that the learning occurs as a natural outgrowth of the practice."

Other suppliers of drill and practice include McGraw-Hill, Random House, Harcourt

Brace Jovanovich, and Milliken's Edufun division—all traditionally involved in providing schools with textbooks and supplementary materials; also included are such third-party software publishers as Hayden, Developmental Learning Materials, Educational Activities, and Krell Software.

Market outlook for drill and practice programs: Stable to slightly declining, as indicated by directory respondents who view conventional drill software for both home and classroom as a necessary and important staple product, particularly in the area of standard test preparation (SAT, ACT, basic competency tests, etc.). Increasingly, however, other techniques, such as the interactive tutorial, incorporating skill drills (see below), are moving in to meet many of the same learning objectives in a less rigid manner.

Interactive Tutorials

These programs reinforce previously introduced concepts and principles that have not yet been thoroughly mastered. They may also be used to present new material in a self-instruction framework. Typically, a home learning tutorial is accompanied by an extensive syllabus, such as textbooks and other supplementary reading. Subjects suited to the format include formal disciplines (i.e., science, mathematics, grammar) as well as vocational training (i.e., computer programming, engine assembly, airplane maintenance). Adult continuing education is frequently presented in tutorial format—self-taught conversational Greek, for instance, or mastering piano for the left hand.

The most successful tutorials are highly interactive. Not only do they allow students to experience extensive computer feedback in terms of right or wrong answers, but also, through such techniques as branching, they foster a sense of cohesiveness and purpose and keep users moving in a progressive direction. "A tutorial worth its price enables users to see clearly where and why they've gone astray in the lesson," says Bruce Zweig, president of Lightning Software. "Branching should offer a remedial session so the user can get back on the progressive track." Zweig is the author of *Mastertype*, an enormously popular typing tutorial for all ages that masks its objective in a space game format. The program's success, he notes, lies in the software's "forgiving" characteristics. "Humans aren't computers. They are allowed to make mistakes. This is how people learn." Other popular programs from major tutorial suppliers are *Preparing for the SAT* (Harcourt Brace Jovanovich), *Algebra Series 1* (Edu-Ware), *Typing Tutor II* (Microsoft), and *Charles Goren's Bridge* (CBS Software).

Market outlook for interactive tutorials: Strong; a significant portion of educational SMD respondents cite an increasing demand for new programs, particularly in subjects for home self-instruction.

Learning Games

Covering a wide range of topics, programs that couch their learning goals and objectives in a "fun" environment have become increasingly important to the home market and, to a lesser extent, to the institutional consumer. "Edugames" or "edutainment," as they're

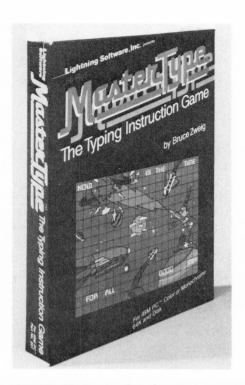

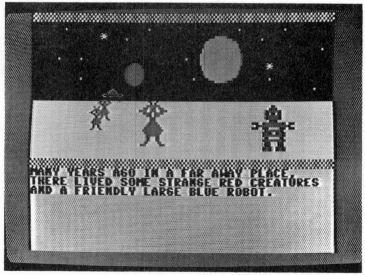

Mastertype masks its true education objective in a space game format, while *Kidwriter* lets children make up stories. *(Lightning Software; Spinnaker.)*

sometimes called, allow students to apply skills and concepts to a competitive situation: against the computer, against the individual's own record, or against peers or parents, for example. Team-oriented games foster cooperation and social interaction as players work together to achieve a common goal.

Learning games may seem easy to create at first glance, but there are numerous pitfalls. The most valuable programs make provisions for learning rules and developing and revising strategies to stick by those rules. Potentially good programs are marred or rendered ineffective by overuse of color (eye straining) and sound (nerve-wearing), too much negative feedback for wrong moves or answers (a few packages have been known to call children "dummies" for making a mistake—that's not quite conducive to effective learning), and more play than learning (e.g., adorning a wrong answer with flashy graphics or upbeat music encourages youngsters to make mistakes just to find out what will happen on screen).

"A learning game should offer the user plenty of entertainment," says Gerri Brioso, president of The Dovetail Group, Inc., an educational design company that has authored programs for CBS Software, Parker Brothers, and Milton-Bradley, among others. "However," she stresses, "the game shouldn't distract from the lesson objectives, which must be plainly in evidence. You don't have to be pedantic—you just have to make sure the kids are taking something away from the game besides pure fun." Dovetail's hits include *Sound Track Trolley* (Milton-Bradley) and the *Musical Learning and Performance Series* (CBS Software).

Among popular learning games and their publishers are *WizType* (Sierra On-Line, Sydney Development Corporation), *Stickybear ABC* (Xerox Education Publications), *Bumble Games* (The Learning Company), and *Rhymes and Riddles* (Spinnaker).

Market outlook for learning games: Excellent; a majority of recreation and education SMD respondents cite an increased acquisitions outlook for the category. Particularly needed are original, well-organized games emphasizing basic reading skills, spelling and grammar, math, and other elementary and high school–level lessons. In the college and adult segments, foreign languages, typing, computer literacy, and business games continue to offer good authoring opportunities.

Simulations

As in the games segment, educational simulations put users into a "make believe" environment, but for purposes of problem solving or providing better understanding of a situation that is otherwise inaccessible to users. Learners experience environments that may be too expensive, dangerous, remote, or complex for the classroom. The program allows students to make use of known skills and concepts to develop new problem-solving strategies. Simulations teach students how to make decisions, think logically, and understand concepts. Such exercises encourage learners to understand problem situations and help them consider alternative designs and relations among variables instead of applying a standard formula to quickly get the "right" answer.

The ability to achieve a sense of realism via the use of instructive graphics or sound is always a plus, but the most important in the development of educational simulations is the

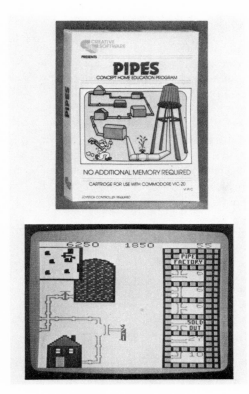

Creative Software's *Pipes*.

presentation of facts and information in a format that encourages logical thinking (i.e., outline subject's background, set the scene and present the problem, use branching to allow students one or more decision alternatives, etc.) In fact, many of the best simulations have been assembled entirely in text.

There's plenty of room in the genre for an active imagination, however. *Pipes*, for example, an award-winning home simulation published by Creative Software, teaches economic principles by asking players to construct a new house using the most cost-efficient building materials and construction methods. Eliot Dahan, Creative's vice president of product development, notes that such "concept education games" fill a niche between straight drill and practice and the tutorial. "Sometimes students will readily absorb the most important concepts in the act of play, when the pressure of being graded is absent," he says.

Simulations publishers making their mark on schools and homes nationwide include BrainBank (*The Skeletal System*), Micro-Ed (*The Atom*), and Creative Software (*In the Chips*).

Market outlook for education simulations: Very good; SMD respondents report an increased buying outlook for the category. Especially needed are science, business, and vocational training software.

Administration and Classroom Management

Programs that assist instructors and administrators in the tedious but necessary task of maintaining student records, scheduling classes, grading tests, and other "bookkeeping" chores are included in this group. A classroom management package may be simply a restructured file system or database manager that is tailored to fit school users. Or, as in the case of programs that help analyze students' progress or learning problems, packages may need to be developed along carefully established criteria.

An example of the latter case is the student evaluation package published by Southern Micro Systems for Educators. The program is geared especially to school psychologists and others involved in special education. Well-written user manuals and supplementary documentation are a must for assembling usable class management software, because the target group usually has little or no computer experience.

Market outlook for administration and classroom management: Fair; a small percentage of educational SMD respondents express increasing interest in the genre.

WHERE THE ACTION IS: BUSINESS AND PROFESSIONAL MANAGEMENT AND PERSONAL PRODUCTIVITY

Major software players in the world of office and small-business-oriented computing have divided applications into three generic areas: word processing (text editing), finance and spreadsheets, and database managers (electronic filing cabinets). Of secondary but growing importance are graphics packages for creating pie and bar charts and other illustrations that clarify business presentations. Applications using elements of one or more of the main categories include across-the-board programs for business and industrial activity: engineering, factory management, administrative management, accounting, inventorying and purchasing, etc. Custom-designed software serves the vertical markets—real estate, medicine, law, manufacturing, advertising and marketing, banking, publishing, to name a handful.

Software tailored to the single operator, home entrepreneur, or people who wish to organize their personal lives composes the personal productivity category. Although word processing, database management, spreadsheets, and graphics also form the basic categories for this group, applications may be further subdivided to include more specific packages, (e.g., loan amortization, tax preparation, household budgeting, figuring college costs, and home banking).

Market outlook for word processing: Nearly 40 percent of business customers buying a personal computer also buy a word processing program at the time of purchase. Winners in this field include MicroPRO's *WordStar,* Sierra On-Line's *Homeword,* Broderbund's *Bank Street Writer,* and Software Publishing's *pfs:write,* among others. The growth picture is expected to stabilize or increase only slightly in the years ahead, however, as the market-

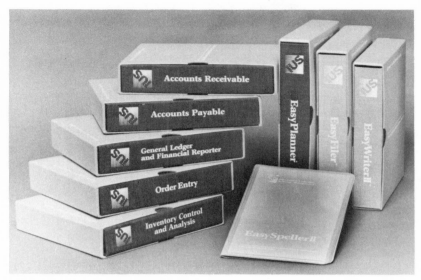

Business software publishers increasingly market uniformly packaged "families" of complementary products. *(Information Unlimited Software.)*

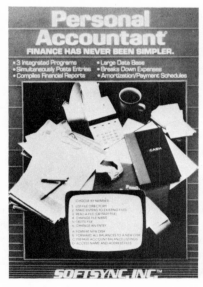
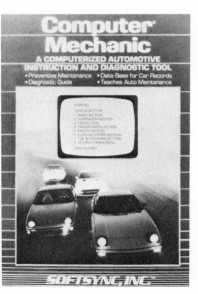

Personal productivity programs are geared to the home entrepreneur, as well as to anyone who wants to organize his or her personal life. *(Softsync.)*

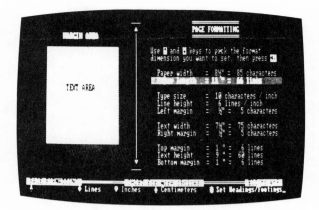

Late-generation word processing programs aim for simplified screens that resemble the typewritten page. *(Bruce & James; Software Publishing Corporation.)*

place for text editing programs becomes increasingly crowded. Best bets for authors involve creating new, innovative analytical tools—next-generation programs that take the task of editing a few steps further. Dictionaries, spelling checkers, and integrated software that allows users to switch back and forth between word processing and other applications such as graphing or financial modeling are examples of viable products.

Market outlook for financial spreadsheets: Almost 45 percent of new personal computer owners have purchased a spreadsheet program with their machines. Popular products include *VisiCalc* (VisiCorp.), *Lotus 1-2-3* (Lotus Development Corp.) and *PeachCalc* (Peachtree Software). The outlook for office-oriented spreadsheets is good, say directory respondents, while even greater opportunity lies ahead in the home-oriented segment. Emphasis for the latter group is on easy-to-use, flexible products with on-screen documentation able to "hold hands" with the novice user. At both office and home level, integration and the use of icons (i.e., programs offering on-screen "windows," each of which represents a separate task for the user to activate) play a growing role.

Market outlook for database managers (DBMs): DBMs have already proven their worth in the office market, where managers and administrative personnel have discovered multiple advantages of electronic filing. Best-sellers in the category include Ashton-Tate's *dBaseII* and *Friday,* Context's *MBA,* and Software Publishing's *pfs:file.* For home users, database managers are still largely a mystery, but the outlook is considered encouraging.

THE HIDDEN PROGRAM MARKETS

Sometimes it's not enough to come up with a general target audience (e.g., office workers or schoolteachers) for your prospective products; you must target the target group. For example, a Long Island, New York, program designer successfully aimed a house-painting package at suburban do-it-yourselfers and independent contractors. It features a mathematical formula that allows painters to estimate quickly and accurately how many gallons are needed for the job based on total area. A member of the New York chapter of the American Association for the Blind specializes in designing programs that aid both members of that handicapped group and their instructors. Another enterprising individual devised *Sports Secretary,* which helps baseball card and other memorabilia fans organize their collections.

Here are some additional ideas for further subdividing the markets:

- Recreation programs aimed specifically at men, women, children; the sports fan; the homebody; the do-it-yourselfer; etc.
- Personal productivity programs for the home entrepreneur (e.g., Tupperware sales representatives); the professional (dentist, doctor) who also manages real estate property as a sideline; the car or boat enthusiast; the community, parent, school, and religious organizer, Boy Scout leader, etc.
- Business and professional management programs for the restaurant owner, the sanitation service manager, the catering hall, the cemetery owner, etc.
- Classroom education programs for the adult and vocational training manager, the foreign language instructor, the college chemistry major, etc.

That's just the tip of the iceberg. The directory and your own market research efforts, including attendance at local computer shows (both consumer and trade), constant reading, and visits to retailers, will consistently reveal potential program ideas and, important, how large each program's potential audience is. Remember that target marketing also helps narrow your choice of publishers.

MISCELLANEOUS INCOME OPPORTUNITIES

Beginners with little or no published portfolio may wish to consider several starter markets which actively encourage independent contributions. In addition, note the following areas.

- **Computer magazines:**   Editors are always on the lookout for new programs (many even pay), usually brief games or useful miniprograms such as perpetual calendars or graphics utilities. To get started, peruse Section Six of the directory—a selection of periodicals and their submission guidelines. Before proposing a program, send for sample issues or go to your neighborhood newsstand, computer store, or public library and examine the program listings submitted by readers to the dozens of specialty magazines covering the industry.

- **Contests and competitions:**   Be on the lookout (via magazines and computer store bulletin boards) for companies that sponsor annual or ongoing contests. Broderbund, for example, holds a monthly competition for users of its *Arcade Machine* program. The best game designed each month wins a prize and the chance to be evaluated by Broderbund (or others) for possible publication and distribution. Atari Program Exchange, Wayne

Datasoft's "off-brand" Gentry division is devoted to publishing outside authors' programs. *(Datasoft.)*

Green Publications, and Alien Group are among the many organizations that host ongoing competitions for cash, prizes, and publication. Many a designer has launched a successful career through a contest; Fernando Herrera, president of First Star Software, for instance, got his start by winning an Atari Program Exchange annual best-program competition (see Herrera's profile, page 77).

- **Retail incentive development programs:** Stay in touch with your local computer stores. Often, software publishers ask key retailers to pass along the names of potential software authors.

- **Educational grants:** Hardware manufacturers such as Apple and IBM, in an attempt to introduce their brands into the schools, may encourage software development by qualified community groups, teachers, and students in exchange for equipment donations and the right of the authors to distribute programs developed through grants to their own school systems.

- **Low-priced offbeat brands:** Several major software publishers, including Atari (Atari Program Exchange), Datasoft (Gentry), and Rantom Software, maintain a line of inexpensive, plainly packaged products written almost exclusively by new independent authors with good program ideas of limited but still lucrative sales potential.

CHAPTER FOUR

Submitting Programs

This chapter shows you how to get off on the right foot with prospective software publishers: how to query a producer, how to protect your ideas, how to structure a software proposal, how to write a good cover letter. Included is a checklist for testing your program and brief guidelines for preparing documentation. Finally, we will touch on mailing procedures and following up.

THE SUBMISSIONS PROCESS

Unless you are asked for one, *never* send an unsolicited finished program or a detailed proposal. Even companies listed in the directory that say they will review unsolicited materials should be contacted first, either by letter (preferable) or by phone if the idea is extremely timely. The dangers of sending programs "blind" are real and often irrevocable. At the very least, your product can easily get lost and needlessly delayed in the shuffle. At worst, it could accidentally fall into the hands of people who wouldn't mind claiming it and circulating it as their own. You've worked much too long and hard to let that happen to your commercially viable creation. In addition, making contact with a software editor or acquisitions manager gives you an "in" over other authors who unwisely choose to send along unrequested disks or tapes. You become a known entity.

But wait—even before you query a company, be sure to send for a complete submission guidelines package, if one is available. This will tell you not only exactly how the company expects you to deliver a proposal but also some current program needs (and conversely, what is currently not needed), and whether a company accepts previously published programs in new formats, simultaneous submissions, and a host of important prequery information that can give you the jump on the competition.

THE QUERY

Consider the written query as a letter of introduction, representing both you and your project. It tells editors and acquisition managers whether you are fully knowledgeable about your product's and the publisher's target market. Because it's the first impression your potential publisher receives, the letter must grab the reader's attention at the outset or risk being pushed aside for better presentations.

Figure 4-1 is an example of a written query. The first paragraph immediately identifies the purpose of the program and its customers. The second paragraph explains its superiority to present (and possibly future) competition and the basic system requirements. The third paragraph reveals the project's stage of completion (proposal only; proposal, partial documentation, and partial sample disk, etc.) and gives an estimate of how much time you will need to deliver a finished product. The last part lists the author's credentials (perhaps indicating that a résumé is attached) and ends by reaffirming the program's match with the publisher's needs.

QUERY LETTER DOS AND DON'TS

DO: Address a person instead of a department or a title whenever possible. Use clear, straightforward language that comes to the point and demonstrates your ability to write clear program manual instructions.

DO: Include informal author's credentials if you have not been previously published. For example, if you wrote a program for your high school biology teacher that is now a permanent part of the school's computer library, that tells an editor something about your ability to write programs with enduring sales potential.

DO: Watch obvious mechanical details, i.e., type on standard, 8½ by 11-inch white bond paper, use a dictionary if you're not sure of spelling and a style book if you're not sure of grammar (Strunk and White's *Elements of Style* is recommended). Always include enough contact information—home address and phone, work address and phone (if possible), and hours during which you can be reached—to make the publisher's efforts to reach you as simple as possible.

DON'T: Try to be flip or funny, unless the subject unquestionably lends itself to humor. For example, for some game programs, you might be able to come up with a light, yet informative lead paragraph, e.g., "What's black and white and totally interactive? A simple-to-use children's riddles diskette that helps kids learn to read while they laugh. . . ."

DON'T: Flood editors with unwanted and unnecessary materials. For example, you might wish to enclose one or two writing samples with your letter, but more than that is overdoing it.

DON'T: Use worn-out typewriter or printer ribbons, dot matrix modes, or other difficult-to-read output that makes it easier for an editor to discard your letter than to struggle through an illegible mess. Similarly, avoid writing on programming or graphing paper; stick to white bond.

Jane Douglas
1919 Mockingbird Lane
Smallville, NY 10000

July 18, 1984

Atypical Software
209 West Avenue
Macon, TX 00001

Att.: Gary Lewis
Product Acquisitions

Dear Mr. Lewis,

What this country's puzzle devotees need—by the way, there are over 1 million of us, including men, women, and children, according to the June 1984 issue of *Puzzler Magazine*—is a good, computer-generated jigsaw program—in living color. I have just completed a draft version of such a program, which I call "*Jigsaw Rainbow*."

Unlike the few existing electronic puzzle makers from such suppliers as Buzy Bee, Inc., and Lazy Day Creations, which contain a predetermined, unchangeable number of scenes, *Jigsaw Rainbow* lets users create their own, three-dimensional pictures, backgrounds, and objects using the program's sophisticated color and graphics subroutines. In addition, programmed pictures may be stored on disk, either whole or broken apart into puzzle pieces for repeat play. This self-starting program, contained on a single floppy disk, requires no additional peripherals and no previous computer experience to operate, thanks to a simple set of "friendly" English commands. Running on the IBM PCjr with RGB color monitor, 64K RAM, one 360KB and the PC-DOS 2.3, and written in 8080 assembly language, *Jigsaw Rainbow* may be easily converted to other 8088-compatible micros, including the IBM PC. Further, I've included a copy-protect function that has been professionally tested and found to provide a 99.8 percent level of security.

Depending on your company's interest and given Atypical's history of marketing innovative entertainment software with mass audience appeal, I'd like to follow this letter with an exclusive proposal detailing the program and documentation, pricing and marketing options, and a sample diskette. The first draft of both program and documentation are already complete; I estimate being able to deliver a finished product to your office within 8 weeks of signing a licensing agreement.

In addition to working as a full-time systems analyst for XYZ Business Micros since 1981 (résumé attached), I've been a puzzle lover since my teens. I contribute original puzzle creations to fan magazines (see enclosed sample), and I have been developing this genre of game on my home computer for personal enjoyment.

I look forward to your feedback and to completing what I believe will be a valuable addition to Atypical's ZANY Games product line. From 9 a.m. to 5 p.m. on weekdays, I can be reached at (111) 555-0202; my home number is (112) 333-4949.

Sincerely,

Jane Douglas
Jane Douglas
att./

Figure 4-1   Sample query letter.

DON'T: Wait for publishers to ask for your actual proposal or sample disk before telling them that your query is out and around at a dozen or so competitors. That's the quickest way to end a publisher-author relationship before it starts. Simply state near the end of the query that you are communicating this idea to a select number of others.

The query letter is neither the time nor the place to bring up the subject of money—99 percent of the time. On rare occasions, royalties may be discussed in the first contact letter. Assume, for example, that you are holding a finished program that has been market-tested and proved salable in another format and now exactly suits a new publisher's needs for a different format. In this case, after describing the program and market for it, and stating that your offering is exclusive to that publisher, the letter should state that your product's production, marketing, and distribution rights (or whichever rights apply to the situation) are "available at the following suggested royalty rates" for a limited time (say, 30 to 45 days). In exchange for a fast response, the author's suggested rate is usually a few percentge points below what the publisher might normally expect to pay under other circumstances (i.e., if there were no time limit). The publisher is then free to accept the deal as is or request an extension of the decision deadline to review and test the program and to renegotiate the terms.

Beginners shouldn't attempt this tack; professionals must use discretion. Querying on a program that doesn't legitimately require instant action from the publisher is like crying wolf and is a surefire way to turn off editors.

Phone queries may be used primarily when a software idea or finished program is "hot" and time is of the essence. They also are used to establish communications with the appropriate editor or product manager. Although the same principles that apply to written queries apply to phone conversations, calls should always be followed up immediately in writing. Restate the gist of the conversation (e.g., "Dear Joe Jones, regarding our phone call this morning, August 13, I'd like to submit for your review and evaluation a color graphics subroutine I have developed for the IBM PC. . . .") and what conclusion was reached (e.g., "As we agreed on the phone, I'll send the detailed software proposal and an outline of the documentation to your attention next week. . . .")

THE NONDISCLOSURE AGREEMENT

Responses to queries vary. Some companies automatically invite interested designers to submit formal proposals or sample disks; others are more selective. No matter what the circumstances under which you are requested to send a proposal or a program, the easiest and most effective way to protect your ideas and samples during the submissions process is to include with your package a nondisclosure memo, which is either written by you or supplied by the company on request (or enclosed with its submission guidelines packet).

The nondisclosure agreement states (in varying language) that while your property is under the publisher's consideration, it will not be copied, distributed, or otherwise used for any reason other than to determine its marketability. It is signed by both author and publisher. Most major software producers include a standard agreement with their response to your query.

If an organization doesn't send you a document, it's to your ultimate benefit to write your own. Figure 4-2 is a sample included as a start; feel free to add such provisions as a reasonable deadline for completing evaluation—especially if you're submitting an exclusive proposal—returning rejected programs, etc.

In addition, publishers strongly suggest including your name (or your company's name) and the copyright notice on and in your program, the documentation, and all accompanying materials. Failure to do so means your program could unintentionally fall into the public domain—thus crushing any chances of commercial marketability.

If any publisher absolutely refuses to sign a nondisclosure memo, even after a reasonable period of negotiation, drop the company like a hot potato. Such agreements are universally accepted and encouraged; the scrupulous producer won't do business without one.

STRUCTURING THE COMPLETE PROPOSAL

Just like the fiction "slush piles" that inundate publishing houses, software departments must wade through dozens and dozens of submissions daily. As the number of authors

---

No-Nonsense Software Company may run and display the author's program on its own computers for purposes of evaluation only. In addition, we may run and display the author's program on the computers of those we designate as authorized reviewers. Further, we may make copies of the author's program for the express purposes of evaulation only. The author's copyright notice, if included in the original sent to us, will be included in any duplicates that we produce.

John King
John King
President

Al Lincoln
Al Lincoln
Author

Figure 4-2 Sample nondisclosure memo.

continues to grow, editors have begun to streamline the arduous sifting process by immediately discarding or returning proposals—unread—that overlook the most necessary points. Even if you've got the hottest idea around, it's obviously to your advantage to follow exactly outlines and suggestions set forth in author's guides. As one development manager puts it, "We're beginning to think it's hardly worth our time and trouble to solicit for outside talent when we have to go through a mound of garbage just to find the one diamond."

Chapter 2 discussed what publishers look for in a new submission and the evaluation process in detail. This section discusses how to organize your proposal if a publisher offers no established guidelines or specific format.

1. **Program description and purpose:**   One or two paragraphs that define the program, its objectives, and what makes it attractive to the prospective publisher.

2. **Customer base:**   One or two paragraphs about who will use the program and why; user characteristics; potential market size; expected market penetration.

3. **Competition:**   Three or four "analysis" paragraphs on who and what is now out there; how your proposed program differs and/or exhibits superior features; features, advantages, and disadvantages of competing programs; proposed pricing compared with that of the competition. This section requires thorough market research.

4. **Main menu contents and design features:**   A page or two that details menu items and how they interact with users (screen diagrams would aptly illustrate this); special features you're using (graphics, sound, etc.) and how they benefit the user; any anticipated design problems.

5. **System requirements:**   One paragraph that states programming language, machine, model, and DOS; number of bytes of memory required to operate program; required peripherals.

6. **Transportability:**   One paragraph that indicates how easily your program may be converted to other computers, possible conversion difficulties, suggested machines, etc.

7. **Marketing and packaging:**   Two or three pages that describe proposed documentation (size, length, content, etc.); possible physical package and outside art (include a sketch); elements of distribution and advertising campaigns.

8. **Program support:**   Three or four paragraphs that describe the nature of needed user support and how to accomplish it and possible revisions or updates to the program and how often these might be accomplished.

9. **Delivery:**   Reasonable estimate of completion of program sample, finished product, documentation, supplementary manuals, and other materials.

10. **Author's credentials:**   Attach a résumé or briefly describe previous design experience and why you're qualified to complete this proposal.

THE COVERING LETTER

Once your proposal is complete, and all supporting materials are ready to go, the cover note becomes the icing on your cake. It serves to headline your project to appropriate editors by refreshing their crowded memories about your topic. The letter should be brief and straightforward.

Figure 4-3 is a sample cover letter. Notice that the next-to-last paragraph contains

Jane Douglas
1919 Mockingbird La.
Smallville, NY 10000
August 12, 1984

Atypical Software
209 West Ave.
Macon, TX 00001

Att.: Gary Lewis, product acquisitions

Dear Gary,

Once again, it was a pleasure to speak with you regarding your interest in reviewing *Jigsaw Rainbow,* my full-color puzzle generator for the IBM PCjr.

As requested in Atypical's author submission kit, enclosed is the full program proposal, an outline of the documentation, a preview diskette, and two signed copies of the nondisclosure form. I've also included a rough sketch to illustrate the outside package. If the materials meet with the company's approval and a contract is offered, I would like to suggest a royalty rate of between 12 and 15 percent of net sales, based on a probable per package selling price of $34.95 suggested retail (PCjr disk version only).

I look forward to hearing from you in the near future.

Sincerely,

Jane Douglas
Jane Douglas
enc./

Figure 4-3 Sample cover letter.

specific rights the designer wishes to retain and a suggested royalty rate. This figure should be based not on the authors' needs but on careful research; it should be a knowledgeable estimate of what the your efforts are worth on the open market.

"I view the inclusion of a royalty figure as an important indication of whether the author really knows [the] marketplace and the competition," explains Jerry Gleason, editor in chief of McGraw-Hill's microcomputer unit. "Utilities, for example, generally earn a lower percentage of sales than certain categories of business software."

PROGRAM TESTING AND DOCUMENTATION

Other than ensuring that your software is as error-free as possible, what else can you do to pretest your ready-to-submit disk or tape? The following is a quick checklist of some factors you may want to explore before submitting the program.

- **Installation:** Are the start-up instructions easy to locate and follow?
- **Human factors:** Does the program provide enough human feedback? How long does it take for someone to master the program? How effective are screen, keyboard, and diskette interfaces? Are error messages and user prompts friendly and consistent?
- **Reliability:** Do all functions work? Can users restart the program easily? Can users easily correct errors?
- **Performance:** Are response and run times appropriate for the application and intended audience?

You can test for some of or all these factors by running your own focus group comprised of potential users (e.g., teachers, students, office workers). After a fair trial period (be sure your focus group samples contain the proper copyright notices), develop a little checklist sheet based on the above and have users write their comments—both pros and cons. Make the responses anonymous to encourage candor.

Although documentation nearly always goes through some rewriting and editing before reaching final form, the less a publisher has to rework your materials, the higher royalty you'll earn. Your version should be checked against the following criteria and any other formats specified by the publisher.

Is documentation complete and accurate?

Is it organized and easy to understand and use?

Is it appropriate for the target application and customer base?

Does the code contain appropriate comments and copyright notices?

MAILING AND FOLLOWING UP

Finally you are ready to send off the whole kit and caboodle. Make copies of everything, then use this checklist to assemble all necessary materials before mailing.

- Covering letter (signed)
- Neatly typed software proposal (including brief table of contents, appropriate copyright notices)
- Any sketches, screen diagrams, or other needed illustrations
- Sample files, diskettes, or tapes, requested source code or object code (labeled with your name, program's name and contents, and appropriate copyright notices)
- Nondisclosure memo (two signed copies, one to be returned to you with editor's signature; stamped, self-addressed envelope)
- Neatly typed documentation (outline or completed materials)
- Additional support materials, including results of your own market research, brochure, user's guide, etc.
- Author's credentials, résumé, writing samples

Written materials should be mailed either in a thick insular mailing envelope, or in a strong cardboard box (securely taped shut) or envelope such as the kind supplied by the post office. Remember that disks and tapes are sensitive magnetic media and are subject to easy erasure from airport security scanning equipment as well as to destruction from normal rough package handling. Put your media in an insulated mailer and send it separately from the written material or, if there's room, place it snugly inside the same package. Express mail isn't necessary unless you're on a deadline, but registering the package (return receipt requested) and insuring it against loss are both good ideas.

In addition, address one copy of the entire package to yourself, ask the post office to postmark it on the envelope seal, and mail it. When it comes back to you, put it in a safe place—*unopened*. If you ever discover that someone is illegally producing or distributing your idea, the sealed and dated copy can help prove actual ownership.

Most companies will send you a note letting you know your package has been received and is being reviewed by the appropriate editors. At the outset you should also receive your copy of the nondisclosure statement signed by the publisher. If you hear absolutely nothing after a week or two, call to make sure the package arrived; remember that companies have to sort through miles of mail and even the most efficient organizations get behind in correspondence. After that, it's a waiting game. Many major organizations take their time testing, criticizing, and otherwise handling your creations. If your program isn't subject to an extraordinary deadline, continue to work on other projects, write a novel, whatever— don't dwell on a single submission. You'll hear about its outcome soon enough.

If 2 months or more have passed without an encouraging (or discouraging) word from the publisher, a followup note to the appropriate editor as a reminder of your proposal and the date it was sent is in order. That should spur a response from most within a week or two; if not, call for information concerning the delay.

CHAPTER FIVE

Acceptance

Chapter 5 defines the major parts of the software license agreement (also called the "royalty contract" or similar term) and alerts you to the points that are likely to affect significantly the long-term publisher–program author relationship, with special emphasis on how marketplace factors influence the way your contract should be drafted. Specific royalty issues are addressed, including how much and how often monies should be paid; the advance; and compensation for supplementary services and materials, such as periodic updates and providing user instruction manuals. Reasons for seeking legal assistance, before as well as after a contract has been consummated, are given, and some steps to take in the case of an unsatisfactory arrangement or occurrence are offered. The last section of the chapter helps you survive—and conquer—the bad news of rejection with a few suggestions for reworking and resubmitting your proposal.

CONGRATULATIONS

It took awhile, but, thanks to your advanced "technoskills" and ace market research, the publisher you've set your sights on has offered to license, distribute, and market your software creation. Soon the whole computing world will be able to buy and benefit from your cherished labor of love.

What happens next? Typically, the company sends you a letter saying it is prepared to enter into a publishing agreement with you and that a contract is forthcoming. At the very moment that formidable document reaches your hands, the formal process of contract negotiation has begun. Don't take it lightly, but don't let the legalese or multiple clauses scare you, either. Above all, never "sign on the dotted line" without reading every inch of ink or, preferably, allowing a knowledgeable agent or attorney have a peek.

Because of a marketplace that is constantly in flux and because of its youth, there is no such thing in this industry as a standard contract (there probably never will be). Any publisher that tells you otherwise is lying, a fool, or both, as is any company that refuses to negotiate with you, even on minor points. Every sentence, phrase, and semicolon in a software agreement is subject to question and compromise.

Before discussing specifics, let's lay aside some of the possible unpleasantness and misunderstanding often associated with publishing agreements. Drawing up a contract is not tantamount to mounting an adversarial war. As you begin your negotiations, remember that this form is simply a convenient, organized method of creating a business relationship between two parties. Ideally, when the contract is signed, a relationship will be born that sows the seeds of a lasting, profitable harvest. Each side has something positive to offer the other: the program designer owns an important and valuable property; the publisher calls attention to it and makes it available to the user. Each side brings its own expertise and talent to the agreement, which establishes an equitable exchange for mutual benefit.

A note about verbal contract discussions: It's much better to set down all major issues in writing (sending a memo to follow up each phone conversation is also a good idea) than to rely on either party's memory.

MAJOR CONTRACT SECTIONS

Daniel Remer, attorney and author of *Legal Care for Your Software* (Addison-Wesley), a book that should be required reading for every software author, calls the licensing agreement the "ultimate validation of all those months of effort: someone values your creation enough to devote time, offer talent, and provide money to market it."

Marketing, as you realize by now, remains key throughout the process of creating commercially viable software, from the moment you input your first line of code to the moment an end user carries your boxed program home. The start-to-finish influence of the marketplace on contract negotiations is no exception. You are entitled, for example, to request a detailed outline of the publisher's proposed marketing strategy for your program and can even have that included in the contract so that there are no future misunderstandings. Keep in mind, though, that the publisher must have the flexibility to "go with the flow," changing plans as the market changes (i.e., adjusting pricing, promotion, and distribution policies). Many SMD respondents, for example, have profitably moved from specialty distribution channels such as computer stores to mass merchandisers and other broadbased outlets as consumers changed from hobbyists to those with little or no computer experience.

Deliverables

Just as you have set forth what you intend to furnish to the publisher in your original software proposal, the deliverables section of the contract specifies what the author is to provide (deliver) to the company. Among the items that become your responsibility are the actual program, any supporting documentation, the results of any market testing you have performed, the source code and the source code documentation. In addition, you may agree to provide supplementary users' manuals and other materials.

Delivery Schedule

The delivery schedule states an agreed-on (reasonable) date for handing over the above items to the publisher. If your proposal is based on an unfinished project, be sure to allow for plenty of debugging time and other possible delays. As a general rule of thumb, SMD respondents use a 3- to 8-month development timetable for games and less complex programs; 18 months to 24 months may be used as an approximate time frame for developing more complicated works.

Program Revisions, Updates, User Training

You and the publisher must iron out which side is responsible for providing program revisions or add-ons, fixing unexpected errors, and arranging for end user training, if necessary. Obviously, if you provide the company with the source code, you may not have to assume responsibility for maintenance. If you are expected to provide some maintenance, you may then wish to request reasonable additional compensation for doing so (e.g., you receive a flat fee if a problem needs more than a week or two of your attention).

In general, updates or add-ons are provided at no extra compensation to the author because enhancements extend a program's shelf life and improve its marketability. However, extraordinarily time-consuming updates and compensation for training users may be negotiated for separately.

Program Rights

Licensing any of and all the marketing and distribution rights to your program is a bit like allowing a publisher to select from a Chinese menu: You can let a company have everything or just a few key rights, or you can severely limit its marketing access to your work. Let's consider a few of the many choices available.

- **License length:** Most publishers justifiably want as long a time as possible to market the program, thus giving it the best possible chance to succeed and become a steady backlist seller.

- **Geographical rights:** Why give a company worldwide rights to sell your program when the company doesn't (and isn't likely to) have foreign distribution channels? Save worldwide or international rights for another publisher.

- **Market segmentation:** Consider dividing your program's marketing rights according to publishers' marketing specialties. For example, your home education program would also work well in a classroom, but it is to be published by a firm that has excellent mass market distribution and no school connections. You would do well to retain school rights so that another company with inroads to the nation's educational institutions could have a fair shot at the software.

- **Exclusive versus nonexclusive license:** There are several additional ways to divide up the rights to your program. If, for example, your publisher handles only one type of computer, you may want to retain the rights for other publishers to market your software on other systems by granting the company a nonexclusive license for, say, Apple II only. Hardware segmentation is becoming less of an issue, however, with most publishers selling software for the top three or four computer brands and operating systems. A nonexclusive distribution license may also be appropriate if you wish to continue to market your program through your own (noncompeting) channels (e.g., via direct mail to a segment of the target audience not otherwise served by the publisher's retail vehicles). Keep in mind, though, that many directory respondents say that their efforts to promote an author's program will be much more intense if they own an exclusive marketing license, including the rights to sublicense the package to other publishers.

Royalty Schedule

This, naturally, is every author's favorite section of the contract. However, the royalty schedule must be viewed as linked to the whole agreement and not as an entity unto itself. Again, the marketplace plays a key role in drafting the royalty agreement. For example, software authors will be compensated for their work in one of two basic ways. One is to receive a percentage of the total revenues generated by the program; the other is to receive a set amount of dollars per program sale. If the publisher wants to adjust the program's pricing according to market conditions, you probably will be paid by the first method, which allows the company maximum flexibility in setting the suggested retail price. Another twist on the percent-of-net-sales royalty, borrowed from the book publishing business, is to schedule a sliding royalty scale, e.g., 10 percent on the first 10,000 copies sold, 12 percent on the next 5000, and 15 percent on the next 5000.

In addition to negotiating the royalty schedule for the program, you may also be able to schedule separate royalties on documentation and other materials. Bear in mind that if the program needs little revision and modification by the publisher, you may be able to negotiate for a higher percentage.

Advances are also becoming a common part of the compensation section. Amounts may range from a few thousand dollars to a more substantial sum, depending on the nature of the project and the time needed to complete it.

The question of when royalties should be paid is usually a publisher's prerogative. Directory respondents report that quarterly or every 6 months is the norm. A longer stretch should be subject to negotiation (e.g., the company might provide a larger advance).

SOLVING CONTRACTUAL PROBLEMS

Disagreements between authors and publishers because of simple misunderstandings occur more frequently than one would suspect. Perhaps, in receiving a license to distribute your game program on ROM cartridge, your publisher believed it also had an implied right to produce it on disk. No, you insist, the rights to disk production belonged to the author all along. Thus, you now have the basis for a contract dispute.

Such minor problems may be solved easily, quickly, and painlessly, without rushing out to attorneys' offices and without building unnecessary enmity on both sides. A careful rereading of your contract may reveal areas that prove your point but that were initially overlooked by both parties. Failing that, friendly arbitration is another alternative. Above all, maintain open communications. In these instances of minor misunderstandings, it is far better to take one cautious step at a time than to risk destroying a hard-won business relationship for what was possibly a human (or computer!) error.

However, not every publisher honors its commitments; if you find that your publisher has seriously breached the contract (e.g., royalties aren't being paid on time or certain promotional promises have been broken), then you may have to bring in an attorney and start court proceedings. Be prepared for a drawn-out affair, however, which may result in your having to take your product elsewhere and begin the submissions process all over again.

For general information on contractual problems and legal issues such as infringement on software copyrights, patents, trademarks, and piracy, contact the Association for Computing Machinery in New York City or the Association of Data Processing Societies and Organizations (ADAPSO) in Arlington, Virginia. The Electronic Industries Association, in Washington, D.C., may also be able to help.

For individual legal assistance, engage an attorney who specializes in one or more of the above areas. The specialty of computer and communications law is becoming more widespread as the industry grows; ask a colleague to recommend a professional or call your local bar association office for a list of specialists in your area. In addition, we've listed names and addresses of trade associations and legal sources in Section Seven of the SMD. If these offices are not within your geographical or financial grasp, they may be able to recommend others who can meet your needs.

COPING WITH REJECTION

If bad news in the form of a rejection letter has just cast its shadow over your mailbox— again—don't despair. It happens to everyone. The important move is to get right back on the horse by analyzing what went wrong and then reworking and resubmitting your creation.

Occasionally, a company will allow an author whose program reveals particular promise but needs some modification to rewrite under its editorial guidance. In more extreme cases, however, most SMD respondents agree that rejections occur for one or more of the following reasons: (1) the proposal was unclear or insufficiently researched as to purpose and potential market of the program, (2) the program didn't deliver what was intended or contained too many errors, (3) the proposal was badly written or organized or was too sloppy to read, (4) the proposal or sample program was inappropriate for the particular publisher. Let's consider how you can remedy these situations should you find yourself facing one or more of them.

Just as there's no reason to hand in a badly written or disorganized proposal or documentation, there's also no excuse for a buggy program. It's the author's responsibility to pretest the software carefully and to eliminate as many problems as are encountered during a single pass. Inadequate market research can be licked by going back to industry sources such as trade magazines, product literature, and your own contacts and doing proper homework on your area of specialty. Submitting inappropriate programs can be prevented by studying the company's listing in the directory and by examining the company's current inventory of titles and comparing them with your own ideas. Finally, some publishers will gladly tell you why they turned down your (potentially good) program in the hopes of being able to work with you at a later date. Eagerly accept the criticism of professionals and learn from it.

A final point to keep in mind during the resubmittal process: Never take your freshly rejected program and promptly "mass mail" it to other publishers. As highlighted in the SMD every publisher is unique; each has a different set of market needs. Learn to distinguish a company by its business "personality"—advertising techniques, packaging, and other individual characteristics. By carefully segmenting your publisher and its audience, you'll soon have more acceptances than you'll be able to handle. Forward, march—and may the "FORTH" be with you!

CHAPTER SIX

Profiles

In Chapter 6 you'll find miniprofiles of a handful of the industry's countless stars and of a few of the major league players in the software editing, publishing, and polishing process. They are included to inform, advise, and, one would hope, inspire you to great achievement in your chosen area of expertise.

THE PUBLISHERS

International Business Machines (IBM)

Like the Marines, IBM is looking for a few good recruits. "Our standards are necessarily high," notes Joyce Wren, director of software publishing for the Entry Systems Division in Boca Raton, Florida. "We find that people expect far more from a product with the IBM logo, so we try very hard for quality."

With the release of the computer giant's littlest home-oriented offspring, PCjr, and with sales of PC, the older, business-style cousin, still going gangbusters, IBM's External Submissions Department, located in Armonk, New York, has never been busier. More than 100 queries and proposals pour into the suburban headquarters each week, says a spokesperson.

However, during the anxious 3- to 6-month wait endured by every program designer before receiving the company's yea or nay vote, it is Wren's department that ultimately decides the fate of each software proposal. Even after a finished product is actually unleashed on the marketplace, it undergoes constant reevaluation. Mondays, for example, are quality meeting days, when the department analyzes both hardware and software. (Among the most important analytical tools, Wren says, are the little user comment cards included in every piece of IBM software; many users' comments eventually end up in revisions or in new products.)

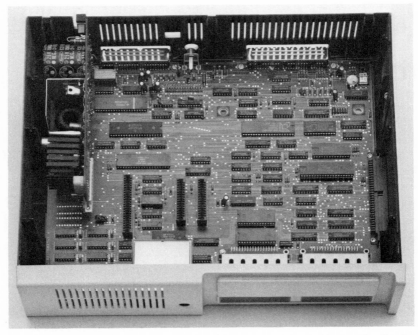

A bird's eye view of the PCjr's insides. IBM maintains an "open architecture" policy for independent authors. *(IBM.)*

IBM subscribes to an "open system" philosophy, providing potential authors (and hardware developers) with easy access to its computers' technical details. Resulting sales growth of IBM and compatible products have benefited consumers as well as program designers with bright ideas. Since the IBM Software Submissions program began in 1981, several individuals have achieved the $100,000 royalty mark. "The PC line will continue to be an open system," the director confirms. "The more good software available, the more applications there will be and the more sales."

Lifeboat Associates

Despite its reputation as the world's largest publisher of CP/M-based and other business, professional, and systems software, Lifeboat Associates believes the art of program development remains an effort of individuals. The best ideas and innovations will always be found not in the corporate planning suites but in the minds and basement micros of designers everywhere.

"Don't let anyone tell you the cottage industry is dead," Ed Currie, Lifeboat president says. "Far from it. With the numbers of successful individual authors increasing every year, cottage developers are alive and well, and there's no reason you can't be one of them."

The company likens itself to a book publisher, distributing and marketing over 350 packages for 175 different machines worldwide. However, unlike a traditional book publisher, Lifeboat must also continually support its end users with program updates, revisions, and customer training.

"We're very concerned that our authors maintain their products over their shelf life," he explains. "We also ask prospective contributors if they are willing and able to write add-on packages that give depth to the original product." Skill and the ability to adapt are necessary ingredients for succeeding in this business, Currie adds.

Lifeboat processes "in the neighborhood of" 1500 to 2000 new software submissions annually. More than 90 percent are rejected. "Poor quality, duplication of existing programs, and programs that don't serve the needs of our business audience are the primary reasons for rejection," Currie reports.

Of the authors who do gain access to the company's vast marketing pipeline, those who can prepare a series of related, broad-based applications are the most successful. "We're not saying our series authors become instant millionaires, although it's been known to happen," Currie says. "But it's not unrealistic to think in terms of $100,000 to $300,000 per annum for steadily selling products."

Sierra On-Line

Perhaps best known for its color graphics adventure epics such as *Time Zone* and *The Dark Crystal*, this top independent producer of home computer software has also become an important supplier of personal productivity and business-oriented products. Games are published under the SierraVenture and SierraVision labels, and the Sierra Business Products division markets, among others, *Homeword,* an innovative word processor for Apple, IBM, and other systems that employs icons at the screen bottom to help users with text creation, editing, and printing.

With the acquisition of several outside packages, including programs based on Johnny Hart's *Wizard of Id* and *BC* comic strip characters, Sierra has further branched into educational software development. "Our goal is to stay on top of the market," says Ken Williams, company chair, adding, "As a full-line software publisher, we have an obligation to maintain an aggressive policy for the acquisition of new products as well as back those products with extensive marketing and advertising programs and strong customer support."

Founded in 1980 by Williams and Roberta Williams, his wife, Sierra On-Line is headquartered in the tiny town of Coarsegold, California, right on the edge of Yosemite National Park. Although geographically isolated, the firm keeps close to its customers with an expertly managed telephone support system headed by its program designers and product managers.

Above all, Sierra On-Line seeks innovation and commitment from its outside authors. The Williamses constantly set an example of the dedication required: *Time Zone* took the couple more than a year to complete and resulted in 12 disk sides containing 39 intertwining scenarios. Producing the 1500 high-resolution graphic pages on disk meant developing a new form of compacting computer graphics so that more than 100 pictures instead of the usual 30 or 40 could be stored.

Software Guild authors' programs are uniformly packaged and documented for marketing under the Softsmith label. *(Softsmith.)*

The Software Guild

You've read their double-page, bold-headlined ads in popular computer magazines; you've
chatted with their friendly representatives at the big fairs. Perhaps you've even been solic-
ited by them. The Software Guild is to program authors what baseball scouts are to budding
major leaguers. Combing, sorting, rummaging through the acres of submissions received
weekly, the publisher selects exactly the right mix of mass market education, recreation,
and business packages for Apple, IBM, Atari, Commodore, and TRS-80 computers to
enhance its rapidly growing product lines. Currently, those lines consist of over 500 titles,
but the company's short-term goal is to carry a strong backlist of about 2000, according to
Regina Berdak, director of software development. "We buy more than 250 programs a
year," she reports, "That's about a 1 in 20 acceptance rate based on the numbers of
incoming proposals and programs."

Through Softsmith, the Guild's aggressive national marketing organization, authors' works
are given crucial brand name recognition: the Softsmith label, a distinctive silvery-blue box,

and a prominent place on a tall, hands-on display unit. The display appears in mass merchandisers, computer, and software specialty stores—even in toy stores and supermarkets—as well as in Softsmith's own franchised outlets.

"We take the author's product and enhance it to ensure salability," Durak explains. A Guild staff of programmers rewrites and polishes accepted programs, and an editorial group checks that documentation is crystal clear to the average user.

CBS Software

Tucked inconspicuously into a suite of offices behind the main reception area of the CBS Publications building in Greenwich, Connecticut, CBS Software operates much like the small design teams and individual authors who contribute to its expanding software library.

"We live the best of both worlds," says Ed Auer, president of CBS's youngest division. "We have the freedom to be entrepreneurs, but we also have the financial backing and worldwide marketing muscle of the parent organization behind us. It's a delightful way to introduce a business."

The division concentrates on the "nonhit" side of the business—home learning and continuing education for children and adults and personal enrichment and productivity—software that will survive in a competitive retail environment no matter how many fads or hot products come and go. "This philosophy represents the backbone of our submissions policy," Auer explains. "We look for products that satisfy a true need, that are value-enhanced by the computer, that may develop into a family of products, that appeal to all family members, and that are likely to live a long and healthy shelf life."

CBS has contracted with Children's Computer Workshop (a unit of Children's Television Workshop, producers of *Sesame Street*) for a line of "pro social" education games and with the Charles Goren organization for a bridge tutorial. In addition, many "unknowns" have joined the CBS lineup; *Success with Math*, for example, is a best-seller written by Microcomputer Workshops, Inc., a small group of educators based in Rye, New York. "We're signing new licenses all the time," the executive says. "Just as any traditional publisher, we're very comfortable working with independents to blend our marketing strengths with their creative talents."

THE AGENT: SYNERGISTIC SOFTWARE

"The software field has changed enormously since we got into it," says Mike Branham, manager of software development at Synergistic. Among the earliest independent publishers (marketing action games and home education), the company decided to redirect its goals by becoming an agent for talented programmers. "When we entered software publishing in 1978, you didn't need much money to package and market a product. Today, with the major book publishers and other well-financed corporations moving in, it's hard for a stand-alone software firm to compete. So we've decided to use our knowledge of the field in a way that would be most beneficial to us and to our authors—by selling their titles to other publishers."

Branham finds that although the players have changed, the market's needs remain much the same. "Recreation is still the most lucrative and desirable area, particularly games that have education value, as well as adventure and arcade programs."

As is the policy of most agents, Synergistic earns a percentage of an author's royalties as its fee for hooking up programmer and publisher. Although most agents take this percentage out of the author's regular royalty schedule, Branham's agency does it slightly differently. "We charge the publisher a certain number of percentage points above the contract which represents our commission so that the author really doesn't lose anything by working with us."

Branham warns potential authors not to be dazzled by huge royalty rates but rather to study companies' marketing channels carefully. "Royalties offered by the bigger companies may not be as high as those offered by smaller ones, but, in the long run, the author will make a lot more by going with a large concern, which has the sales force and marketing know-how it takes to get the programs sold," he says, adding, "It's better to have 5 percent or 10 percent of a huge pie than 20 percent of a small one."

THE AUTHORS

Activision's Alan Miller

He may not think of himself as a pioneer, but the label more than fits Alan Miller, Activision senior designer. In 1979, with three others, Miller cofounded Activision, the first independent producer of video games (and now computer games), just after a stint as senior design engineer at Atari, where he helped create the 400 and 800 home computers. Today he is a "technosuperstar," author of several best-selling cartridges, including *Tennis, Ice Hockey, StarMaster,* and *Robot Tank.*

"There are no instant success formulas," Miller cautions. "Sometimes you can spend weeks on a single idea and it still doesn't work out." The designer, who normally spends about 8 months completing a project, knows this all too well; once, he wasted 2 months trying to fashion a three-dimensional game using red- and green-tinted glasses. "I don't regret it," he says, "Trying something new makes it fun."

He does, however, regret his lack of formal training in art and music. "I majored in computer science and electrical engineering. But if I had it to do over again, I would have concentrated at least part of my studies in art and music because that's the direction computer games are going in—increasingly sophisticated use of graphics and sound." Moreover, he likens computer games design to playing an instrument. "Like a musician, you've got to be skilled, but you've also got to have talent."

For aspiring game designers, he advises: "Acquire a personal computer, learn BASIC right away—assembly will do too, although it's more difficult, and start writing. You'll get inspired. The ideas will come." The Atari 400 and 800, he adds, are good authoring systems because of their powerful graphics capabilities; those models also contain the same CPU as Apple and other popular 6502-based machines.

First Star's Fernando Herrera

An entire company born of a single product? That's hardly an extraordinary tale in the software industry, but the reason Fernando Herrera's firm, First Star Software, was founded is indeed unusual. In a business often characterized by kid whizzes, the designer became an aficionado of computers "late in life"—he was nearly 40 when he bought his first Apple for $2200. His initial effort, *My First Alphabet,* was devised to help his preschool-age son, Steve, born with severe cataracts that left him almost blind. The program taught Steve how to read and do simple arithmetic, and because it made life easier for the boy, Herrera sent it to the Atari Program Exchange (APX) so that it could aid others. To his utter surprise and delight, the package won a $25,000 first prize in APX's annual author's competition. Thus, the seed money materialized for Herrera's stab at business ownership.

With two partners, the designer launched First Star in 1982 to make and sell video and home computer games. Their first product, *Astro Chase,* featuring brilliant color graphics against Tchaikovsky's *1812 Overture* as background music, sold to Parker Brothers and soared to the top of the sales charts. Subsequently, the multimillion dollar company signed with Marvel Comics, among other licensed properties, to create games using well-known characters.

"All my life I've been a curious guy," Herrera says. "I'd take apart radios and calculators to see how they worked. I always was into gadgets and gimmicks. But when I bought a computer, my coworkers at my old job thought I was crazy. They said I should have bought a stereo."

As chief programmer of his growing concern, Herrera does his best creating at home, in the wee hours of the night.

Lotus Development's Mitchell Kapor

Once upon a time, Mitch Kapor wanted to change the world. A student at Yale in the late 1960s, he got caught up "in the frenzy of the times—war protests, recreational chemicals, 'Sergeant Pepper'." He studied linguistics and psychology. He resorted to mysticism. He became a disk jockey. He took up and even taught transcendental meditation.

Then in 1978 he "found himself" in an Apple. After running up tens of thousands of dollars in debts while programming in his spare time, he devised a statistical analysis tool that later formed the basis for two important VisiCorp programs, *VisiTrend* and *VisiPlot.* In late 1982, with $1.2 million in licensing fees from VisiCorp, another $500,000 in program royalties, and an additional $1 million in venture capital, Kapor started Lotus Development Corporation, makers of the widely used Lotus *1-2-3* integrated business package. The rest, as they say, is history. Today Lotus is a half-billion dollar company and climbing.

Could it happen all over again—to another single operator slavishly coding away every spare moment? "It's not like there are no windows of opportunity," Kapor told the *New York Times* recently. "It's like a funhouse, with windows opening and closing with tremendous rapidity." In the business market, he adds, intensifying competition means that authors—and publishers—must carefully define their target users and serve them well.

InfoSoft's Jerrold Koret

Designing the operating software and initial applications for Coleco's ADAM home computer was a tough assignment—maybe the toughest they every faced. But Jerry Koret and his partner, Richard Roth, aced it against a skin-of-the-teeth production deadline and despite a string of inevitable delays. Koret is president of InfoSoft Systems, Inc., a small, privately held development and consulting firm started in 1976 and located in Norwalk, Connecticut. With his partner, he is also the author of I/OS, ADAM's CP/M-compatible operating system, and a number of programming languages that may be used with the system.

"We are pleased to have played a role in developing the ADAM," Koret says. "This project made us the first software house to work with a major manufacturer of home computers in adapting business software for the consumer."

ADAM's built-in word processing package signals an important trend for producers and users alike, Koret believes. "With the advent of the ADAM, consumers will come to expect next-generation home computers that contain feature-packed software at reasonable prices." An accountant by trade and computer hobbyist by desire, Koret also forecasts tremendous advances in future operating software. For example, InfoSoft has developed a totally menu-driven communications package that reduces hardware dependency. "In 10 years nobody'll recognize the home computer as we now know it," he predicts.

CHAPTER SEVEN

How to Use the Software Marketplace Directory

For the reader's convenience, company listings in Part II, the Software Marketplace Directory, which follows this chapter, are divided into six major categories, each reflecting the industry's standard market classifications as outlined in previous chapters: (1) recreation, (2) personal productivity, (3) classroom education, (4) business and professional management, (5) systems, and (6) magazines. At the end of the directory is a name-and-address list of selected agents and legal resources.

Let's take a moment to step through a sample company listing (Figure 7-1) so that you can quickly interpret publishers' requirements to your best advantage:

- **Company contact:** Titles vary, but the name following the publisher's address and telephone number should be your first target. Typically, this person, after conferring with others in the organization, responds to your initial software suggestion, either with a complete submissions packet (and nondisclosure statement) and request for your full proposal and sample program or with a polite rejection letter. Obviously, before querying you should double-check that the name listed here is still active; people move fast and furiously in this business. Also, because of sheer volume of mail and because the initial selection process may be performed by many editors, some companies ask authors to address all first-time correspondence to a department rather than a person. Fear not— human contact is established soon afterward.

- **Year of founding:** This simply tells the author how long a company has been in business, which may or may not indicate how reputable it is. Remember that, because of this industry's youth, the majority of independent publishers and electronic publishing divisions are less than 5 years old.

Koala Technologies
4962 El Camino Real, Suite 125
Los Altos, CA 94022
(415) 964-2992
Nick Shain, director of marketing
Established 1982

COMPANY PROFILE

Computer tutorials, music and art, graphics tutorials. Also buys personal productivity, classroom education. **Micros; Operating Systems:** Apple II, Atari, Commodore 64 and Vic-20, IBM PC. **Recent Titles:** *The Micro Illustrator, The Dancing Bear, Spider Eater.* **Distribution Channels:** computer stores, consumer electronics stores, department stores, discount stores, mass merchandisers, software stores, supermarkets, toy stores, video stores. Buys 10 to 20 programs annually; buying outlook increasing.

SUBMISSION GUIDELINES

Preferred Medium: floppy disk. Complete documentation to be arranged between author and company. **Average Company Response Time:** 4 weeks; rejected programs not returned. Payment: 10 to 20 percent royalty paid on "milestone" basis or on outright purchase basis. **Distribution Rights:** exclusive. **Plugging In:** Koala software must showcase the KoalaPad Touch Tablet peripheral and demonstrate true educational value for children or adults. Author's guide available.

Figure 7-1 Sample Software Marketplace Directory listing.

- **Company profile:** Companies fully profiled within their respective categories are those that acquire software *primarily* of that genre. The first sentence of each listing describes the publisher's major market thrust. In our sample, for instance, Koala Technologies appears under "Recreation" because it is primarily interested in home learning and leisure activity products that enhance its KoalaPad Touch Tablet peripheral.

Where applicable, the second sentence of each listing represents the publisher's *secondary* preference for outside programs. These "Also buys" categories are markets into which the publisher has expressed a desire to expand or which the company already carries to supplement its primary product line. For example, Koala views classroom education and personal productivity applications as natural extensions of its home learning line. Pay careful attention to the secondary interests of software publishers—they are open invitations to authors with marketable ideas.

- **Micros; operating systems:**   In examining the machines and systems supported by the publisher, note that some companies list specific manufacturers' models and others simply list a manufacturer's name to cover all models within a brand. Companies that list major suppliers such as Apple and IBM are usually open to compatible machines. (Still, it's a good idea to check with an individual publisher before submitting a query.) In this category, all the computers a publisher supports are given first; at the end of the list any operating systems the publisher supports are shown.

- **Recent titles:**   This gives the potential author a jumping-off point for researching software that the company has already deemed acceptable for publication. It also further defines company interests and markets. Go out and study some packages. (In rare instances, a respondent is so new to the business that its first titles were still in development at press time.)

- **Distribution channels:**   Notice which firms distribute primarily through specialty stores and which stick mainly to mass merchants. That tells you something about the customer base.

- **Number of programs bought annually:**   We asked publishers to tell us how many programs they acquire from outside authors yearly and to project that buying outlook a bit into the future. Where "No annual buying limit" appears in place of a figure, you can assume that the publisher buys as many good programs as come in "over the transom" in a 12-month period ("good" can mean as few as 3 or as many as 100, according to respondents). In addition, because of the number of start-up divisions and organizations and because many older companies have only recently turned to outside sources, some entries state, "Has yet to buy any outside programs; company is now actively soliciting."

- **Submission guidelines:**   Use this part of the company listing to verify a publisher's basic program evaluation policy and method of payment. But remember that personnel and policies change more than occasionally; you should always call or write a prospective publisher prior to sending any materials to determine their interest and to request a complete submissions packet, if available. Except for a handful of respondents, the vast majority of publishers require a written or phone query before they will consider your finished project. We've noted the exceptions as they occur.

- **Preferred media:**   Although your program may eventually appear in any number of formats, including ROM cartridge, database network, and hard-copy printout, this designates the medium on which your review sample should be delivered.

- **Documentation:**   "Complete documentation required" means the author should submit program instructions and any supplementary user materials in a form that is essentially finished. (Most companies say they will edit anyway, but the less editing needed, the higher the compensation.) If "initial" documentation is requested, then the publisher only wants a rough draft or outline and is prepared to finish materials in house or assist the author in completing documentation. The same approach should be taken when a listing states "Complete documentation to be arranged between author and the company."

- **Average company response time:**   This rough estimate of the time it takes a company to accept or reject your submission should be treated as such. Add 6 to 8 weeks before you camp out in front of the editor's office. Also, most companies will automatically return rejected programs to protect themselves, but it is plain good manners to provide a self-addressed, stamped envelope (SASE) for their use. (If a firm states that it does not return programs, the SASE may ensure that they do.)
- **Payment:**   Practically everything is negotiable in this business, but those stating specific terms give authors some indication of what to expect from their efforts.
- **Distribution rights:**   Although most companies want exclusive rights to your program, many will negotiate if they believe the product would be a valuable addition to their line. This portion of the listing can help you determine what marketing rights you may be able to retain for future use.
- **Plugging in:**   We've saved the best for last. This section is straight from the source's mouth, telling you exactly what's actively needed for which market or customer base and how to make your submission stand out from the crowd.

THE CROSS-REFERENCE

In your travels through the SMD, you may wish to target a "hot" proposal for as many potential publishers as possible. So that you can easily spot both the *primary* and *secondary* acquisition interests of each company, the last pages of every market category contain a special cross-referenced "minidirectory." Behind recreation, for example, you'll find the four other directory headings, personal productivity, classroom education, business and professional management, and systems, under which is listed every publisher that also buys recreation products. If you want to explore one of these secondary entries further, you need only turn to its proper market category for a full company description.

COMPANIES THAT WON'T BUY YOUR SOFTWARE

Some publishers are just too big or too popular to ignore. Apple is a great example. Only a short time ago that firm was a major force in software development. Then management looked around and saw hundreds of others making software for its machines. Apple's acquisitions department, as *Variety* likes to say, went "foldo." Noting well-known or important companies that do not actively solicit for outside programs can save time and headaches. However, a phone call to determine if the organization has changed its policy certainly will not hurt.

ABOUT THE SMD SURVEY

After interviewing nearly 1000 software companies and selected computer magazines by telephone and direct-mail questionnaire, we weeded out responses that simply didn't suit the purpose of this book: for example, small companies that function strictly as authoring teams rather than publishers or firms that develop all programs internally or that consider outside authors' work so seldom that a listing would not benefit readers. Other perfectly viable markets didn't make it because they were established after the directory deadline; we will attempt to include them in future editions. The results of our weeding process has yielded the cream of the crop—more than 300 active sources for independent program authors.

DISCLAIMER NOTICE

A listing in the SMD does not constitute our endorsement or guarantee of any organization. Your valuable program should be adequately protected before it is submitted to a potential publisher.

PART TWO
The Software Marketplace Directory

Recreation

Aardvark Software
P.O. Box 26505
Milwaukee, WI 53213
(414) 289-9988
Does not actively solicit.

Activision, Inc.
Drawer no. 7286
Mountain View, CA 94039
(415) 960-0410
Hugh Bowen, director of software development
and acquisition
Established 1979

COMPANY PROFILE

Action, adventure, sports games. **Micros; Operating Systems:** Atari VCS 2600 and home computers, Intellivision. **Recent Titles:** *Enduro, Kaboom, Robot Tank, River Raid.* **Distribution Channels:** bookstores, computer stores, consumer electronics stores, department stores, mass merchandisers, software stores, supermarkets, toy stores, video stores. No annual buying limit.

SUBMISSION GUIDELINES

Preferred Media: floppy disk or ROM cartridge. Complete documentation required. **Average Company Response Time:** 3 to 5 weeks; re-jected programs returned. **Payment:** negotiable royalty. **Distribution Rights:** exclusive. **Plugging In:** Company wants programs written in assembly language only. Send résumé and any previous design credits or pertinent background information with submission. "We stress original concepts, innovative use of animation, color, graphics, and music."

Addison-Wesley Publishing Company
6 Jacob Way
Reading, MA 01867
(617) 944-3700, ext. 2438
Ed Kelly, director of software development and
acquisitions
Established 1980

COMPANY PROFILE

Home education, computer tutorials. Also buys personal productivity, classroom education. **Micros; Operating Systems:** Apple II, II +, and IIe, Atari 800 and 1200, Commodore 64, IBM PC. **Recent Titles:** *Super Strategies for the SAT, Teach Yourself Apple BASIC, Apple Visions.* **Distribution Channels:** bookstores, catalogs, computer stores, consumer electronics stores, department stores, direct mail, software stores, toy stores. Buys 5 to 25 programs annually; buying outlook increasing.

SUBMISSION GUIDELINES

Preferred Medium: floppy disk. Complete documentation required. **Average Company Response Time:** varies; rejected programs returned. **Payment:** negotiable royalty. **Distribution Rights:** negotiable.

Adventure International, division of Scott
   Adams, Inc.
P.O. Box 3435
Longwood, FL 32750
(305) 862-6917
Mark Sprague, software acquisitions and
   development manager
Established 1978

COMPANY PROFILE

Action, adventure games and simulations. Also buys personal productivity, classroom education, business and professional management, systems. **Micros; Operating Systems:** Apple, Atari, Coleco's ADAM, Commodore 64, IBM PC, Northstar Horizon and Advantage, TI Professional, TRS-80 I, III, IV, and Color Computer; CP/M. **Recent Titles:** *Saigon: The Final Days, Earthquake-San Francisco 1906, Preppie II.* **Distribution Channels:** bookstores, catalogs, computer stores, direct mail, discount stores, mass merchandisers, software stores, supermarkets, video stores. Buys 100 programs annually; buying outlook increasing.

SUBMISSION GUIDELINES

Preferred Medium: floppy disk. Complete documentation required. **Average Company Response Time:** 2 to 4 weeks; rejected programs returned with SASE. **Payment:** negotiable royalty paid monthly. **Distribution Rights:** exclusive. **Plugging In:** Adventure International's first question when looking at a new submission is, "Does it have mass market possibilities?" "We are *not* looking for highly specialized programs, but for those with general appeal. Currently, one of the most popular types of program is the arcade game for the micro. If this type of game is your forte, send us a program written in machine language (so it's fast) with good sound and good graphics. A multiplayer option and the

ability to save the top 10 scores to disk are good features to include, too. Be careful about infringing on arcade game audiovisual rights. We would much rather see something original than another arcade copy. Any game, household program, utility, or business application program will certainly be considered if it has mass market appeal. Whatever the subject, we are looking for quality. Make sure the program you submit does the job (or executes the game) in the best manner possible." Adventure also needs conversion authors. Author's guide available.

Alien Group
27 W. 23rd St.
New York, NY 10010
(212) 741-1770
Mike Matthews, president
Established 1982

COMPANY PROFILE

Firm manufactures speech synthesizer dubbed "The Voice Box" and seeks entertainment software that uses the peripheral. Also buys classroom education. **Micros; Operating Systems:** Apple II, II +, and IIe, Atari, Commodore 64. **Recent Titles:** in development. **Distribution Channels:** computer stores, software stores. Buys three programs annually; buying outlook increasing.

SUBMISSION GUIDELINES

Preferred Medium: floppy disk. Complete documentation required. **Average Company Response Time:** 3 weeks; rejected programs not returned. **Payment:** negotiable royalty or outright purchase. **Distribution rights:** exclusive. **Plugging In:** Company is looking for "fun programs with speech capabilities."

Amiga Corporation
3350 Scott Blvd., Bldg. No. 7
Santa Clara, CA 95051
(408) 748-0222
Att.: director of software development
Established 1982

COMPANY PROFILE

Sports games. **Micros; Operating Systems:** Atari 800 and VCS 2600, ColecoVision. **Recent Title:** *Mogul Maniac.* **Distribution Channels:** department stores, mass merchandisers, toy stores, video stores. Buys one program annually; buying outlook increasing.

SUBMISSION GUIDELINES

Preferred Medium: floppy disk. Initial documentation required. **Average Company Response Time:** varies; rejected programs returned. **Payment:** negotiable royalty or outright purchase. **Distribution Rights:** exclusive. **Plugging In:** "Send us your program if you think it would work well with one of our peripherals, such as our Joyboard."

Artificial Intelligence Research Group
921 N. La Jolla Ave.
Los Angeles, CA 90046
(213) 656-7368
Steve Grumette, director of software
    development
Established 1981

COMPANY PROFILE

Artificial intelligence. Also buys personal productivity, classroom education. **Micros; Operating Systems:** Apple II, IBM PC; CP/M. **Recent Title:** *ELIZA.* **Distribution Channels:** computer stores, consumer electronics stores, direct mail, software stores. Buys one program annually; buying outlook the same.

SUBMISSION GUIDELINES

Preferred Medium: floppy disk. Initial documentation required. **Average Company Response Time:** 3 weeks; rejected programs returned. **Payment:** 15 to 25 percent royalty. **Distribution Rights:** exclusive. **Plugging In:** "Take a lead from our company's name. We're open to any idea provided it allows the computer to simulate the human mental process."

Artworx Software Company, Inc.
150 N. Main St.
Fairport, NY 14450
(800) 828-6573
Arthur Walsh, director of software development
    and acquisitions
Established 1981

COMPANY PROFILE

Action, adventure, and simulation games. Also buys personal productivity, classroom education. **Micros; Operating Systems:** Apple, Atari, Commodore, VIC. **Recent Titles:** *Gwendolyn, Hazard Run, Strip Poker.* **Distribution Channels:** catalogs, computer stores, department stores, mass merchandisers, software stores, video stores. Buys 12 programs annually; buying outlook same.

SUBMISSION GUIDELINES

Preferred Medium: floppy disk. Complete documentation required. **Average Company Response Time:** 2 weeks; rejected programs returned. **Payment:** 10 to 15 percent royalty paid monthly. **Distribution Rights:** exclusive. **Plugging In:** Company sponsors annual award for programming excellence. Write for details.

Atari, Inc.
1265 Borregas Ave.
P.O. Box 427
Sunnyvale, CA 94086
(408) 745-2000
John Peeke-Vout, director of external software
    development
Established 1979

COMPANY PROFILE

Home education, arcade games. Also buys personal productivity, classroom education, business and professional management, systems. **Micros; Operating Systems:** Apple, Atari VCS, 5200, and home computers, Commodore 64 and VIC-20, IBM PC, TI-99/4A. **Recent Titles:** *Mickey in the Great Outdoors, Hangman, Juggles' House, My First Alphabet, Star Raiders, E.T. Phone Home.* **Distribution Channels:** computer stores, consumer electronics stores, department stores, discount stores, mass merchandisers, software stores, toy stores, video stores. Has no annual buying limit.

SUBMISSION GUIDELINES

Preferred Medium: floppy disk. Complete documentation required. **Average Company Response Time:** varies; rejected programs not returned. **Payment:** negotiable royalty paid quarterly or outright purchase. **Distribution Rights:** exclusive.

Atari Program Exchange (APX)
P.O. Box 3705
Santa Clara, CA 95055
(800) 558-1862
Jack Perron, acting manager
Established 1982

COMPANY PROFILE

Home education, strategy, arcade games. Also buys personal productivity, classroom education, business and professional management, systems. **Micros; Operating Systems:** Atari. **Recent Titles:** *Dandy Home Loan Analysis, Video Kaleidoscope, Smasher, The Bean Machine.* **Distribution Channels:** computer stores, consumer electronics stores, department stores, direct mail, mass merchandisers, software stores, video stores. Buys 60 programs annually; buying outlook increasing.

SUBMISSION GUIDELINES

Preferred Media: floppy disk, cassette tape. Complete documentation required. **Average Company Response Time:** 4 to 6 weeks; rejected programs returned. **Payment:** 10 percent royalty (on gross receipts) paid quarterly. **Distribution Rights:** nonexclusive. **Plugging In:** All programs accepted by APX automatically become contestants in the company's quarterly contest. Categories are entertainment and personal development, home management, learning, and systems and telecommunications. The judges consider user interface and overall design, originality, ease of use, implementation, documentation, and interest level. Author's guide available (includes contest information).

Avalon Hill Microcomputer Games
4517 Hartford Rd.
Baltimore, MD 21214
(301) 254-9200
Michael G. Cullum, new products director
Established 1980

COMPANY PROFILE

Adventure games. Also buys classroom education. **Micros; Operating Systems:** Apple II+ and IIe, Atari VCS and home computers, Commodore 64, TI 99/4A, Timex Sinclair, TRS-80 I, III, and Color Computer. **Recent Titles:** *Legionnaire, Telengard, Paris in Danger.* **Distribution Channels:** bookstores, catalogs, computer stores, consumer electronics stores, department stores, mass merchandisers, software stores, toy stores, video stores. Buys five programs annually; buying outlook the same.

SUBMISSION GUIDELINES

Preferred Media: floppy disk, paper printout. Complete documentation required. **Average Company Response Time:** 3 weeks; rejected programs returned. **Payment:** negotiable royalty paid biannually or outright purchase. **Distribution Rights:** exclusive. **Plugging In:** Avalon Hill wants the programmer to submit programs prepared for the "ultimate consumer." "Send the program only when you have extensively playtested it and feel it is your best effort."

Avant-Garde Creations, Inc.
P.O. Box 30160
Eugene, OR 97403
(503) 345-3043
Mary Carol Smith, acquisitions director
Established 1979

COMPANY PROFILE

Arcade games, simulations, and novelty. Also buys personal productivity, classroom education, business and professional management, systems. **Micros; Operating Systems:** Apple II and IIe, Atari 800, Commodore 64, IBM PC (and compatibles), TI-99/4A, Timex Sinclair. **Recent Titles:** *Jump Jet, Amperfinesse, Trompers.* **Distribution Channels:** bookstores, catalogs, computer stores, consumer electronics stores, department stores, direct mail, discount stores, mass merchandisers, software stores, toy stores, video stores. Buys 20 programs annually; buying outlook increasing.

SUBMISSION GUIDELINES

Preferred Medium: floppy disk. Complete documentation required. **Average Company Response Time:** 6 weeks; rejected programs returned. **Payment:** 2 to 20 percent royalty paid semiannually. **Distribution Rights:** exclusive. **Plugging In:** Company wants programs to be "state-of-the-art in terms of both graphics and user-friendliness." Technical and educational programs should be researched by experts.

Blue Chip Software
19818 Ventura Blvd., Suite 204
Woodland Hills, CA 91364
(213) 881-8288
Bob Slapin, marketing director
Established 1982

COMPANY PROFILE

Adventure, historical games. Also buys classroom education. **Micros; Operating Systems:** Apple, Atari, DEC, IBM PC, Kaypro, Osborne, TI Professional; CP/M. **Recent Titles:** *Millionaire, Squire, Tycoon*. **Distribution Channels:** bookstores, catalogs, computer stores, consumer electronics stores, department stores, direct mail, distributors, mass merchandisers, software stores. Buys 10 programs annually; buying outlook increasing.

SUBMISSION GUIDELINES

Preferred Medium: floppy disk. Complete documentation to be arranged between author and company. **Average Company Response Time:** 6 weeks; rejected programs returned. **Payment:** negotiable royalty paid monthly. **Distribution Rights:** exclusive. **Plugging In:** "We want a couple of programmers with a good background in graphics. We want our games to have a socially redeeming value. Authors with games should have a series in mind. Our target audience is 10-year-olds to adults, including business-oriented people."

Boston Educational Computing
78 Dartmouth St.
Boston, MA 02116
(617) 536-5116
Phil Degnon, director of software development
and acquisitions
Established 1983

COMPANY PROFILE

Math, language arts skills for children. Also buys classroom education. **Micros; Operating Systems:** Atari, Commodore 64. **Recent Titles:** *Alpha-BECi, Number-BECi*. **Distribution Channels:** computer stores, department stores, direct mail, discount stores, distributors, software stores, video stores. Has not yet bought any outside programs; company is now actively soliciting.

SUBMISSION GUIDELINES

Preferred Media: floppy disk, cassette tape. Complete documentation to be arranged between author and company. **Average Company Response Time:** 2 weeks; rejected programs returned. **Payment:** outright purchase. **Distribution Rights:** exclusive. **Plugging In:** Boston Educational Computing requires color graphics and that "everything on the screen should be large. Each segment should take up one-sixth of the screen while it is being viewed. No test matter, unless it is for reading skills programs. Software should motivate kids to learn, but we don't want the two hundredth version of *Hangman*."

Broderbund Software, Inc.
17 Paul Dr.
San Rafael, CA 94903
(415) 479-1170
Gary Carlston, vice president of development
Established 1980

COMPANY PROFILE

Adventure and skill games. Also buys personal productivity, business and professional management. **Micros; Operating Systems:** Apple, Atari, Commodore 64 and VIC-20, IBM PC. **Recent Titles:** *Choplifter!, David's Midnight Magic, Lode Runner*. **Distribution Channels:** catalogs, computer stores, department stores, direct mail, manufacturers' representatives, software stores. Has not yet bought outside programs; company is now actively soliciting.

SUBMISSION GUIDELINES

Preferred Medium: floppy disk. Complete documentation required. **Average Company Response Time:** 1 week; rejected programs returned. **Payment:** negotiable royalty paid monthly. **Distribution Rights:** exclusive.

———————

BudgeCo
428 Pala Ave.
Piedmont, CA 94611
(415) 658-8141
Does not actively solicit.

———————

CBS Electronics
41 Madison Ave.
New York, NY 10010
(212) 481-6400
Richard Eckerstrom, director of product
    acquisition
Established 1982

COMPANY PROFILE

Arcade games. **Micros; Operating Systems:** Apple, Atari VCS, 2600, 5200, home computers, ColecoVision, Commodore, IBM PC, Mattel Intellivision. **Recent Titles:** *Solar Fox, Tunnel Runner, Mountain King.* **Distribution Channels:** catalogs, computer stores, consumer electronics stores, department stores, direct mail, discount stores, mass merchandisers, software stores, toy stores, video stores. Buys 12 to 15 programs annually; buying outlook the same.

SUBMISSION GUIDELINES

Preferred Medium: floppy disk. Complete documentation required. **Average Company Response Time:** 8 weeks; rejected programs not returned. Payment: negotiable. **Distribution Rights:** exclusive.

———————

CBS Software
One Fawcett Pl.
Greenwich, CT 06836
(203) 622-2620
Robert Lovler, director of product development
Established 1982

COMPANY PROFILE

Simulations, games, and home education. Also buys classroom education, personal productivity, business and professional management. **Micros; Operating Systems:** Apple, Atari, Commodore 64, IBM PC and PCjr. **Recent Titles:** *Match-Wits, Mystery Master: Murder by the Dozen, Success with Math Series.* **Distribution Channels:** bookstores, catalogs, computer stores, consumer electronics stores, department stores, discount stores, mass merchandisers, software stores, video stores. Buys 35 programs annually; buying outlook increasing.

SUBMISSION GUIDELINES

Preferred Medium: floppy disk. Initial documentation required. **Average Company Response Time:** 8 weeks; rejected programs returned. **Payment:** negotiable royalty or outright purchase. **Distribution Rights:** negotiable. **Plugging In:** Call product development department to discuss current needs.

———————

Chalk Board, Inc.
3772 Pleasantdale Rd.
Atlanta, GA 30340
(404) 496-0101
Margee Walsh, vice president of product
    development
Established 1983

COMPANY PROFILE

Children's educational games and tutorials in music, math, and a variety of other subjects. Also buys classroom education. **Micros; Operating Systems:** Apple, Atari, IBM, Commodore VIC-20 and 64. **Recent Titles:** *Micro Maestro, Logic Master, Music Math.* **Distribution Channels:** catalogs, computer stores, consumer electronics stores, department stores, discount stores, mass merchandisers, software stores, toy stores, video stores. Has not yet bought outside programs; company is now actively soliciting.

SUBMISSION GUIDELINES

Preferred Media: floppy disk, cassette tape. Initial documentation required. **Average Company Response Time:** "several weeks"; rejected programs returned. **Payment:** negotiable royalty. **Distribution Rights:** nonexclusive. **Plugging In:** "The first question we ask potential developers is, 'Do you care about kids?' because furthering the education and skills of children is the most important objective of this company. Home education products that utilize our touch-sensitive Powerpad tablets are a priority."

Children's Computer Workshop, division of
  Children's Television Workshop
One Lincoln Pl.
New York, NY 10023
(212) 595-3456
Does not actively solicit.

Cload Publications, Inc.
P.O. Box 1448
Santa Barbara, CA 93102
(805) 962-6271
Established 1978

COMPANY PROFILE

Three monthly magazines sold on disk or tape: *CLOAD Magazine*, *Chromasette Magazine*, and *SilverWare*. Prints several games per issue. Also buys personal productivity, classroom education, systems. **Micros; Operating Systems:** *CLOAD* is for TRS-80 models I, III, and IV. *Chromasette* is for TRS-80 Color Computer. *SilverWare* is for TRS-80, 100, and 150. **Recent Titles:** *Balloons* (*Chromasette*, May 1983), *Pennypede* (*Chromasette*, April 1983), *Lazerblitz* (*CLOAD*, May 1983). **Distribution Channels:** catalogs, computer stores, direct mail, software stores. Buys 150 programs annually; buying outlook same.

SUBMISSION GUIDELINES

Preferred Media: floppy disk, cassette tape. Complete documentation to be arranged between author and company. **Average Company Response Time:** 2 weeks to 2 months; rejected programs returned. **Payment:** outright purchase; rates vary widely from $50 or more for a front cover to $300 for a well-coded program. Average program accepted falls into $125 to $175 range. **Distribution Rights:** negotiable. **Plugging In:** CLOAD says it does not like to see "ripped off codes—we really get upset over this," and programs with "just a few bugs left in." However, CLOAD likes to see "instructions that are humorous, informative, usable, spelled correctly; practical programs, educational programs, interactive games, and good-quality cassettes." Author's guide available.

Coleco Industries, Inc.
Coleco Corporate Center
999 Quaker Lane S.
West Hartford, CT 06110
(203) 725-6420
Al Kahn, director of marketing
Established 1976 (electronics division)

COMPANY PROFILE

Arcade, action, strategy, children's games, home education, leisure time, self-improvement. Also buys personal productivity. **Micros; Operating Systems:** Atari VCS, Coleco's ADAM and ColecoVision; also plans to offer software for other "major home computers." **Recent Titles:** *ADAM's Early Learning Series*, *Buck Rogers Planet of Zoom*, *ColorForms Electronic Crayons*, *Donkey Kong Junior*, *SmartFiler*, *Time Pilot*. **Distribution Channels:** catalogs, consumer electronic stores, department stores, discount stores, mass merchandisers, toy stores, video stores. No annual buying limit.

SUBMISSION GUIDELINES

Preferred Media: floppy disk, cassette tape, video tape (VHS), storyboards. Initial documentation required. **Average Company Response Time:** 4 weeks; rejected programs returned. **Payment:** negotiable royalty or outright purchase. **Distribution Rights:** exclusive. **Plugging In:** Company, which manufacturers Coleco-Vision, ADAM Family Computer System and a line of peripherals, actively seeks educational and home application software. Most Coleco games, however, are arcade adaptations, and company feels that unless your idea "is so fantastic, it's really hard to market it, since no one has ever heard of it."

ColorQuest, division of Softlaw Corporation
9072 Lyndale Ave. S.
Minneapolis, MN 55420
(612) 881-2777
Dave Nelson, director of software development
   and acquisitions
Established 1981

COMPANY PROFILE

Adventure games. Also buys systems. **Micros; Operating Systems:** Commodore 64, TRS-80 Color Computer. **Recent Titles:** *Beyond the Cimeeon Moon, Adventure Trilogy, Super Color Writer II.* **Distribution Channels:** computer stores, direct mail, software stores. Buys five to six programs annually; buying outlook increasing.

SUBMISSION GUIDELINES

Preferred Medium: floppy disk. Complete documentation to be arranged between author and company. **Average Company Response Time:** 4 weeks; rejected programs returned. **Payment:** negotiable royalty paid quarterly. **Distribution Rights:** nonexclusive. **Plugging In:** Machine language only. "No knockoffs—we don't want *PAC-MAN* look-alikes." Author's guide available.

Comm*Data Computer House, Inc.
320 Summit
Milford, MI 48042
(313) 685-0113
Larry Jones, president
Established 1979

COMPANY PROFILE

Home educational games. Also buys personal productivity, classroom education, business and professional management, systems. **Micros; Operating Systems:** all Commodore machines. **Recent Titles:** *Supercuda, BASIC Tools, Primary Math Tutor.* **Distribution Channels:** bookstores,

catalogs, computer stores, consumer electronics stores, department stores, mass merchandisers, multilevel marketing companies, software stores, supermarkets, toy stores, video stores. Buys 36 programs annually; buying outlook the same.

SUBMISSION GUIDELINES

Preferred Media: floppy disk or cassette tape. Initial documentation required. **Average Company Response Time:** 3 weeks; rejected programs not returned. **Payment:** negotiable royalty paid monthly or outright purchase. **Distribution Rights:** exclusive. **Plugging In:** Author's guide available.

Commodore, Computer Systems Division
1200 Wilson Dr.
West Chester, PA 19380
(215) 431-9100
Larry Ercolino, approved products manager
Established 1982

COMPANY PROFILE

Home education, action games, novelty programs. Also buys classroom education, personal productivity. **Micros; Operating Systems:** Commodore. **Recent Titles:** *Know Your Personality, Know Your Own I.Q., Starpost.* **Distribution Channels:** bookstores, catalogs, computer stores, consumer electronics stores, department stores, direct mail, mass merchandisers, software stores, video stores. No annual buying limit.

SUBMISSION GUIDELINES

Preferred Media: floppy disk, cassette tape. Complete documentation required. **Average Company Response Time:** 8 to 16 weeks; rejected programs not returned. **Payment:** negotiable royalty. **Distribution Rights:** exclusive. **Plugging In:** "Commodore is always interested in quality software in any area. Your submitted software should be original, complete, and fully operational. The product should be easy to use and highlight the capabilities of the Commodore computer. Preference is given to programs already running on Commodore machines." Author's guide available.

CompuServe, Inc.
5000 Arlington Centre Blvd.
Columbus, OH 43220
(614) 457-8600
Att.: database manager, consumer division
Established 1979

COMPANY PROFILE

Broad range of action, arcade, adventure, other games; leisure and home education programs. Also buys personal productivity, classroom education, business and professional management, systems. **Micros; Operating Systems:** all popular brands, any configuration capable of becoming a dumb terminal. **Recent Title:** *Mail List.* **Distribution Channel:** online software exchange. No annual buying limit.

SUBMISSION GUIDELINES

Preferred Medium: floppy disk. Initial documentation required. **Average Company Response Time:** approximately 8 weeks; rejected programs returned. **Payment**: negotiable, fixed dollar amount of per package price. **Distribution Rights:** nonexclusive. **Plugging In:** "If the program is successfully evaluated, it becomes part of our On-Line Program Exchange. Of course, we prefer downloadable submissions, however, we also mail customers disk programs. Any category of software is welcome." Author's guide available.

———————

Computer-Advanced Ideas, Inc. (recently changed to Advanced Ideas, Inc.)
1442A Walnut St., Suite 341
Berkeley, CA 94709
(415) 526-9100
Geoff Zawolkow, vice president of software development
Established 1982

COMPANY PROFILE

Home educational games. Also buys classroom education. **Micros; Operating Systems:** Apple, IBM, Commodore 64 and VIC-20, and other "popular micros." **Recent Titles:** *Master Match, Wizard of Words, Tic Tac Show, The Game Show.* **Distribution Channels:** bookstores, catalogs, computer stores, consumer electronics stores, department stores, direct mail, discount stores, mass merchandisers, software stores, toy stores, video stores. Company buys 10 programs annually; buying outlook increasing.

SUBMISSION GUIDELINES

Preferred Medium: floppy disk. Complete documentation to be arranged between author and company. **Average Company Response Time:** 2 weeks; rejected programs returned upon request. **Payment:** negotiable royalty paid quarterly or outright purchase. **Distribution Rights:** exclusive. **Plugging In:** Firm is committed to the idea that "computers should make sense to people." Programs submitted should be easy to use.

———————

Continental Adventures
4975 Brookdale
Bloomfield Hills, MI 48013
(313) 645-2140
Ralph Hoag, director of software development and acquisitions
Established 1981

COMPANY PROFILE

Adventure games. **Micros; Operating Systems:** Atari. **Recent Titles:** *Safe-Guard, Safe-Guard Plus, Ghost Tower.* **Distribution Channels:** bookstores, computer stores, direct mail. Buys fewer than 10 programs annually; buying outlook decreasing.

SUBMISSION GUIDELINES

Preferred Medium: floppy disk. Complete documentation required. **Average Company Response Time:** "several" weeks; rejected programs returned. **Payment:** 5 to 10 percent royalty paid quarterly. **Distribution Rights:** exclusive.

———————

Cornsoft Group, Inc.
6008 N. Keystone
Indianapolis, IN 46220
(317) 257-3227
Tom Harleman, director of software development and acquisitions
Established 1981

COMPANY PROFILE

Arcade games. Also buys personal productivity, classroom education. **Micros; Operating Systems:** TRS-80 Color Computer, Timex Sinclair 1000 and 2000. **Recent Titles:** *Frogger, Crazy Painter, Bounceoids.* **Distribution Channels:** bookstores, computer stores, consumer electronics stores, department stores, discount stores, mass merchandisers, software stores, toy stores, video stores. Buys six programs annually; buying outlook increasing.

SUBMISSION GUIDELINES

Preferred Medium: floppy disk. Initial documentation required. **Average Company Response Time:** 3 weeks; rejected programs returned. **Payment:** 10 to 40 percent royalty paid quarterly. **Distribution Rights:** exclusive. **Plugging In:** Cornsoft is looking for contract programmers to do conversions of arcade games and other licenses for all home computers.

Creative Software
230 E. Caribbean Dr.
Sunnyvale, CA 94089
(408) 745-1655
Elliot Dahan, director of software development
and acquisitions
Established 1978

COMPANY PROFILE

Action and arcade games and home education. Also buys personal productivity. **Micros; Operating Systems:** Commodore 64 and VIC-20, IBM PCjr, TI-99/4A. **Recent Titles:** *In the Chips, Moondust!, Save New York, Rat Hotel.* **Distribution Channels:** bookstores, consumer electronics stores, department stores, mass merchandisers, software stores, toy stores, video stores. Has not yet bought outside programs; company is now actively soliciting.

SUBMISSION GUIDELINES

Preferred Media: floppy disk, cassette tape. Complete documentation to be arranged between author and company. **Average Company Response Time:** 2 weeks; rejected programs re-

turned. **Payment:** negotiable. **Distribution Rights:** negotiable. **Plugging In:** "We advocate 'concept' education programs—learning programs that retain entertaining elements so kids don't realize they're learning. No drill and practice!"

Databar Corporation
10202 Crosstown Circle
Eden Prairie, MN 55344
(612) 944-5700
Stan Strong, director of software development
and acquisitions
Established 1983

COMPANY PROFILE

Home education for children. Also buys personal productivity, classroom education, business and professional management. **Micros; Operating Systems:** Atari, Commodore, Timex Sinclair, TI-99/4A, TRS-80. **Recent Titles:** in development. **Distribution Channels:** Army PXs, bookstores, catalogs, computer stores, consumer electronics stores, department stores, direct mail, discount stores, drugstores, mass merchandisers, software stores, supermarkets, toy stores, video stores. Buys 150 programs annually; buying outlook increasing.

SUBMISSION GUIDELINES

Preferred Media: floppy disk, paper printout. Complete documentation required. **Average Company Response Time:** 2 weeks; rejected programs returned. **Payment:** 10 percent royalty paid monthly. **Distribution Rights:** negotiable. **Plugging In:** Databar programs must utilize the company's optical character reader peripheral. Author's guide available.

Datamost, Inc.
8943 Fullbright Avenue
Chatsworth, CA 91311
(213) 709-1202
Gary Koffler, director of new product
development
Established 1981

COMPANY PROFILE

Action and adventure games. Also buys personal productivity. **Micros; Operating Systems:** Apple II, Atari home computers, Commodore 64 (diskette and cartridge). **Recent Titles:** *Aztec, Snack Attack, Swashbuckler.* **Distribution Channels:** bookstores, catalogs, computer stores, department stores, direct mail, discount stores, mass merchandisers, software stores, toy stores. Buys 50 to 75 programs annually; buying outlook increasing.

SUBMISSION GUIDELINES

Preferred Medium: floppy disk. Initial documentation required. **Average Company Response Time:** 2 weeks; rejected programs returned (on request). **Payment:** 5 percent royalty on cartridges, 20 percent royalty on cassettes and disks paid quarterly, or outright purchase. **Distribution Rights:** negotiable. **Plugging In:** Datamost prefers programs that are written in machine language and are at least 75 percent complete. Author's guide available.

Datasoft, Inc.
9421 Winnetka Ave.
Chatsworth, CA 91311
(213) 701-1980
Stewart Bloom, director of product development
Established 1980

COMPANY PROFILE

Action and adventure games. Also buys personal productivity, classroom education, business and professional management, systems. **Micros; Operating Systems:** Atari 400, 800, and 1200, Apple II, IIe, and II+, Commodore 64 and VIC-20, IBM PC, Texas Instruments, TRS-80 Color Computer. **Recent Titles:** *Zaxxon.* **Distribution Channels:** bookstores, catalogs, computer stores, consumer electronics stores, department stores, direct mail, discount, mass merchandisers, software stores, toy stores, video stores. Buys twenty programs annually; buying outlook decreasing.

SUBMISSION GUIDELINES

Preferred Medium: floppy disk. Complete documentation required. **Average Company Re-**

sponse Time: 1 week; rejected programs returned. **Payment:** negotiable royalty. **Distribution Rights:** exclusive. **Plugging In:** Datasoft's recently launched, low-cost Gentry software line is stocked exclusively with outside author's material. Recent Gentry titles include *Starbase Fighter, Magneto Bugs,* and *Maniac Miner.* For either line, Datasoft analyzes the following elements: Will the program sell? Is it user-friendly? Does it use the maximum capabilities of the system for which it has been designed? In addition, "Will our consumers be impressed and want to play it, use it over a long period of time; is it a classic?" Phone queries encouraged. Author's guide available.

Dilithium Press
8285 S.W. Nimbus, Suite 151
Beaverton, OR 97005
(503) 646-2713
Gary Swanson, software editor
Established 1982

COMPANY PROFILE

BASIC games and home education. Also buys personal productivity, classroom education, business and professional management, systems. **Micros; Operating Systems:** Apple, Atari, Commodore 64, PET, and VIC-20, IBM PC. **Recent Titles:** *More Than 32 BASIC Programs for the Commodore 64, More Than 32 BASIC programs for the VIC-20.* **Distribution Channels:** bookstores, catalogs, computer stores, direct mail, software stores, video stores. No annual buying limit.

SUBMISSION GUIDELINES

Preferred Media: floppy disk, cassette tape. Complete documentation required. **Average Company Response Time:** 2 to 3 weeks; rejected programs returned. **Payment:** 10 to 25 percent royalty paid semiannually or outright purchase. **Distribution Rights:** *exclusive.* **Plugging In:** Author's guide available.

Don't Ask Computer Software, Inc.
2265 Westwood Blvd., Suite B-150

Los Angeles, CA 90064
(213) 477-4514
Samuel Cohon, new products coordinator
Established 1981

COMPANY PROFILE

Word skills games, simulations. Also buys class-room education, systems. **Micros; Operating Systems:** Albert, and other Apple compatibles, Apple II, II+, and IIe, Atari 400, 800, and XL, Commodore 64. **Recent Titles:** *Wordrace, POK-ERSCAM, TeleTari.* **Distribution Channels:** book-stores, catalogs, computer stores, consumer electronics stores, department stores, direct mail, discount stores, mass merchandisers, software stores, toy stores, video stores. Buys 18 programs annually; buying outlook increasing.

SUBMISSION GUIDELINES

Preferred Media: floppy disk, cassette tape. Complete documentation required. **Average Company Response Time:** 3 weeks; rejected programs returned. **Payment:** 20 to 25 percent royalty (depending on level of development) paid quarterly or outright purchase. **Distribution Rights:** exclusive. **Plugging In:** Don't Ask wants "complete, polished software. Innovative, original programs preferred—especially those that expand the capabilities of the microcomputer. Please make certain to supply complete and readable documentation with all submissions." Author's guide available.

———————

Doubleday, Inc.
245 Park Ave.
New York, NY 10017
(212) 953-4561
Does not actively solicit.

———————

Electronic Arts
2755 Campus Dr.
San Mateo, CA 94403
(415) 571-7171
Stephanie Barrett, director of software
   development and acquisitions
Established 1982

COMPANY PROFILE

Arcade games (some user-modifiable) with emphasis on graphics and sound effects. Also buys personal productivity, classroom education. **Micros; Operating Systems:** Apple II, Atari, Commodore 64, IBM PC. **Recent Titles:** *Pinball Construction Set, Hard Hat Mack, Archon.* **Distribution Channels:** catalogs, computer stores, consumer electronic stores, department stores, record stores, software stores, video stores. Buys the "10 best programs" annually; buying outlook increasing.

SUBMISSION GUIDELINES

Preferred Medium: floppy disk. Complete documentation required. **Average Company Response Time:** 4 weeks; rejected programs returned. **Payment:** negotiable royalty paid quarterly (with advances during development). **Distribution Rights:** exclusive. **Plugging In:** Firm believes that "excellence in software is achieved by working with and providing support for independent software designers. Our structure is similar to that of the music recording industry. The talent department includes producers and talent development resources. Our research and development arm works on long-range programs to provide software development tools for creative artists from both inside and outside traditional computer fields."

———————

Epyx, Inc.
1043 Kiel Court
Sunnyvale, CA 94089
(408) 745-0700
Randy Glover, manager of product development
Established 1979

COMPANY PROFILE

Arcade, adventure, home education games. **Micros; Operating Systems:** Apple, Atari, Commodore 64 and VIC-20, IBM PC and PCjr. **Recent Titles:** *Jumpman, Jumpman Junior, Temple of Apshai, Oil Barons.* **Distribution Channels:** computer stores, consumer electronics stores, department stores, discount stores, mass merchandisers, software stores, toy stores. Buys 15 programs annually; buying outlook increasing.

SUBMISSION GUIDELINES

Preferred Medium: floppy disk. Complete documentation required. **Average Company Reponse Time:** 4 weeks; rejected programs returned. **Payment:** 5 to 15 percent royalty paid quarterly or outright purchase. **Distribution Rights:** exclusive. **Plugging In:** Include loading instructions, computer requirements, and any additional notes and comments with your submissions.

First Star Software
22 E. 41st St.
New York, NY 10017
(212) 532-4666
Marc E. Jaffe, vice president of business affairs.
Established 1982

COMPANY PROFILE

Action and adventure games with sharp color graphics. **Micros; Operating Systems:** Atari, Apple IIe, Commodore 64 and VIC-20, TRS-80. **Recent Titles:** *Astro Chase, Panic Button, Soap Suds.* **Distribution Channels:** computer stores, consumer electronics stores, department stores, direct mail, software stores, video stores. Buys four programs annually; buying outlook increasing.

SUBMISSION GUIDELINES

Preferred Media: floppy disk, cassette tape. Complete documentation required. **Average Company Response Time:** 2 weeks; rejected programs returned. **Payment:** 5 to 15 percent royalty paid quarterly. **Distribution Rights:** negotiable.

Funtastic, Inc.
5–12 Wilde Ave.
Drexel Hill, PA 19026
(215) 622-5716
Dan Illowsky, president
Established 1982

COMPANY PROFILE

Arcade, maze games. Also buys classroom education. **Micros; Operating Systems:** Apple II, II+, IIe, and III, IBM PC. **Recent Titles:** *Master Miner, Cosmic Crusader, Snack Attack II.* **Distribution Channels:** bookstores, catalogs, computer stores, consumer electronics stores, department stores, direct mail, discount stores, mass merchandisers, software stores, toy stores. Buys 5 to 10 programs annually; buying outlook increasing.

SUBMISSION GUIDELINES

Preferred Medium: floppy disk. Initial documentation required. **Average Company Response Time:** 2 weeks; rejected programs returned. **Payment:** negotiable royalty. **Distribution Rights:** exclusive. **Plugging In:** Funtastic's greatest need is arcade games for the IBM PC, although the company will review programs in other categories.

Gamestar, Inc.
1302 State St.
Santa Barbara, CA 93101
(805) 963-3487
Scott S. Orr, president
Established 1982

COMPANY PROFILE

Sports simulation games. **Micros; Operating Systems:** Atari 400, 800, and 1200, Commodore 64. **Recent Titles:** *Baja Buggies, Starbowl Football, Star League Baseball.* **Distribution Channels:** bookstores, catalogs, computer stores, consumer electronics stores, department stores, direct mail, discount stores, mass merchandisers, software stores, toy stores. No annual buying limit.

SUBMISSION GUIDELINES

Preferred Medium: floppy disk. Initial documentation required. **Average Company Response Time:** 2 weeks; rejected programs returned. **Payment:** negotiable royalty paid quarterly or outright purchase. **Distribution Rights:** exclusive. **Plugging In:** Gamestar insists submitted programs meet the following conditions: game must be sports-oriented and written in assembly; animation must be extensive; game must allow for solo and two-player action; Atari-compatible games must not exceed 32K. Furthermore, a "sports game must be a cut above to become a Gamestar product." Author's guide available.

Gessler Educational Software, division of Gessler Publishing
900 Broadway
New York, NY 10003
(212) 673-3113
Seth Levin, president
Established 1982

COMPANY PROFILE

Games and tutorials designed to teach foreign languages. Also buys classroom education. **Micros; Operating Systems:** Apple, Atari, Commodore 64, IBM PC, TRS-80. **Recent Titles:** *Type-Writer, Poker Pari,* and *Anagrams Hispano-americanos.* **Distribution Channels:** bookstores, catalogs, computer stores, consumer electronic stores, department stores, mass merchandisers, software stores. Buys 12 to 20 programs annually; buying outlook increasing.

SUBMISSION GUIDELINES

Preferred Medium: floppy disk. Initial documentation required. **Average Company Response Time:** 3 to 5 weeks; rejected programs returned. **Payment:** negotiable royalty. **Distribution Rights:** negotiable, depending on firm's level of involvement in developing the program. **Plugging In:** "We're looking for educational programs that make learning a foreign language enjoyable and easy. Programs can be games, drill and practice, review, tutorials, or any other educational application." Current programs teach French, Spanish, German, Italian, Latin, English as a second language, and others. Author's guide available.

The Great Game Company
450 North Park Rd.
Hollywood, Fl 33021
(305) 966-8520
Eugene B. Settler, president
Established 1982

COMPANY PROFILE

Games based on television game shows. **Micros; Operating Systems:** ColecoVision and ADAM (is looking into other major home computers). **Recent Titles:** *Family Feud, Price Is Right, Jeopardy, Password.* **Distribution Channels:** bookstores, catalogs, computer stores, consumer electronics stores, department stores, direct mail, mass merchandisers, software stores, supermarkets, toy stores, video stores. Buys eight programs annually; buying outlook the same.

SUBMISSION GUIDELINES

Preferred Media: floppy disk, storyboards, cassette tape. Complete documentation required. **Average Company Response Time:** 2 weeks; rejected programs returned (send SASE to ensure return). **Payment:** negotiable royalty or outright purchase. **Distribution Rights:** exclusive. **Plugging In:** Although the company started its line with games derived exclusively from well-known television game shows, firm is open to any entertainment idea that has "merit and will appeal to the family-oriented buyer."

Hayden Software Company
600 Suffolk St.
Lowell, MA 01853
(617) 937-0200
Scott Marshall, marketing manager
Established 1981

COMPANY PROFILE

Strategy, arcade, and adventure games. Also buys personal productivity, classroom education, business and professional management, systems. **Micros; Operating Systems:** Apple and compatibles, Atari, Commodore 64, DEC Rainbow and Mate II, IBM PC and compatibles. **Recent Titles:** *Championship Golf, Final Conflict, Go, Bellhop, Crime Stopper, Piewriter for Apple, General Ledger, Factor Blast, Programmer's Workshop.* **Distribution Channels:** bookstores, catalogs, computer stores, consumer electronics stores, department stores, direct mail, mass merchandisers, software stores, video stores. No annual buying limit.

SUBMISSION GUIDELINES

Preferred Media: floppy disk, cassette tape. Initial documentation required. **Average Company Response Time:** varies; rejected programs returned. **Payment:** Negotiable royalty or outright purchase. **Distribution Rights:** negotiable. **Plugging In:** Company is open to programs on home finance, word processing, educational material for ages 4 and up. Author's guide available.

HESWARE (Human Engineered Software)
150 N. Hill Dr.
Brisbane, CA 94005
(415) 468-4111
Jay Balakrishnan, director of product acquisition
Established 1982

COMPANY PROFILE

Adventure, strategy, and arcade games and home education. Also buys personal productivity, business and professional management, systems. **Micros; Operating Systems:** Apple, Atari, Commodore 64, IBM PC and PCjr. **Recent Titles:** *HESwriter, Turtle Toyland Junior, Attack of the Mutant Camels, Retro Ball.* **Distribution Channels:** bookstores, computer stores, consumer electronic stores, department stores, mass merchandisers, software stores, toy stores. Buys 12 programs annually; buying outlook increasing.

SUBMISSION GUIDELINES

Preferred Media: floppy disk, cassette tape. Initial documentation required. **Average Company Response Time:** 3 weeks. **Payment:** negotiable royalty (according to program category) paid quarterly. **Distribution Rights:** exclusive. **Plugging In:** Company prefers authors to send in programs with nondisclosure agreement initially instead of making contact via mail or phone. "We want to see programs, not proposals. Time is of the essence in the software business, and we can boot up and evaluate a running program faster than we can read through a letter and hope the program meets expectations. We're looking for new applications for computer technology and innovative variations on existing themes, for example, a database manager for the Commodore 64."

Imagic
981 University Ave.
Los Gatos, CA 95030
(408) 399-2200
Does not actively solicit.

Infocom
55 Wheeler St.
Cambridge, MA 02138
(617) 492-1031
Michael Berlyn, senior software designer
Established 1979

COMPANY PROFILE

Text-based adventure games. **Micros; Operating Systems:** Apple, Atari, Commodore, DEC Rainbow and RI-11, IBM PC and PCjr, NEC, Osborne, TI Professional, TRS-80 I and III. **Recent Titles:** *Zork Series, Deadline, Witness.* **Distribution Channels:** bookstores, computer stores, consumer electronics stores, department stores, record stores, software stores, video stores. Has not yet bought outside programs; company is now actively soliciting.

SUBMISSION GUIDELINES

Preferred Medium: floppy disk. Complete documentation required. **Average Company Response Time:** 2 to 6 weeks; rejected programs not returned. **Payment:** negotiable royalty. **Distribution Rights:** exclusive. **Plugging In:** Company uses a unique interactive technology on all its programs and will work closely with the author to use that format.

Inhome Software
2485 Dunwin Dr., Unit 8
Mississauga, Ontario, Canada L5L 1T1
(416) 828-0775
Peter Scholes, secretary-treasurer
Established 1981

COMPANY PROFILE

Arcade-style games and home education. Also buys classroom education. **Micros; Operating Systems:** Apple, Atari, Commodore 64. **Recent**

Titles: *Baseball, Captain Beeble.* **Distribution Channels:** bookstores, computer stores, direct mail, software stores. Buys seven to eight programs annually; buying outlook increasing.

SUBMISSION GUIDELINES

Preferred Medium: floppy disk. Complete documentation required. **Average Company Response Time:** 2 weeks.; rejected programs returned. **Payment:** Negotiable royalty of no more than 10 percent paid quarterly. **Distribution Rights:** exclusive.

Insoft, Inc.
10175 S.W. Barbur Blvd., Suite 202B
Portland, OR 97219
(503) 244-4181
Michael D. Brown, director of software
    development and acquisitions
Established 1981

COMPANY PROFILE

Arcade games. Also buys business and professional management, systems. **Micros; Operating Systems:** Apple II, IIe, and III, IBM PC. **Recent Titles:** *Grapple, Spider Raid, Zargs.* **Distribution Channels:** bookstores, catalogs, computer stores, consumer electronics stores, department stores, direct mail, discount stores, mass merchandisers, software stores. Buys three programs annually; buying outlook the same.

SUBMISSION GUIDELINES

Preferred Medium: floppy disk. Complete documentation required. **Average Company Response Time:** 4 to 6 weeks; rejected programs returned. **Payment:** negotiable royalty paid quarterly or outright purchase. **Distribution Rights:** exclusive. **Plugging In:** Insoft wants software that has a large potential market, fills a specific customer need, and is user-friendly. Author's guide available.

Instant Software, Inc., division of Wayne Green, Inc.
Route 101 & Elm St.

Peterborough, NH 03458
(603) 924-9471
David M. Rowell, director of software
    development and acquisitions
Established 1978

COMPANY PROFILE

Home education, games, simulations, music. Also buys personal productivity, classroom education, business and professional management. **Micros; Operating Systems:** Apple, Atari, Commodore 64 and VIC-20, IBM PC, Panasonic JR-200, TI-99/4A, Timex Sinclair 1000, TRS-80, Zenith Z-90 series. **Recent Titles:** *Space Shuttle, English Olympics, Math Voyager.* **Distribution Channels:** bookstores, catalogs, computer stores, consumer electronics stores, department stores, direct mail, mass merchandisers, software stores. Buys 12 programs annually; buying outlook the same.

SUBMISSION GUIDELINES

Preferred Media: floppy disk, cassette tape. Complete documentation to be arranged between author and company. **Average Company Response Time:** 2 weeks; rejected programs returned. **Payment:** negotiable royalty paid quarterly or outright purchase. **Distribution Rights:** exclusive. **Plugging In:** Company wants programmers to "give us their forte, not merely what they think will sell. Write where your interest and skills lie. The program should not only meet the competition but offer more—something better—such as more features, better graphics, or faster, easier use. Author's guide available.

Intelligent Statements (Screenplay)
P.O. Box 3558
500 Eastowne Office Park, Suite 212
Chapel Hill, NC 27514
(919) 493-8596
Pam Reading, assistant director of marketing
Established 1982

COMPANY PROFILE

Adventure and arcade games, hobbies and leisure time programs under the Screenplay label. Also buys personal productivity. **Micros; Operating**

Systems: Apple, Atari, Commodore 64, Fortune 32 and 16, IBM PC and PCjr, Osborne, TRS-80; CP/M. **Recent Titles:** *The Warriors of Ra, Asylum, Ken Uston's Professional Blackjack, Togo Joe.* **Distribution Channels:** computer stores, consumer electronic stores, direct mail, mass merchandisers, software stores. No annual buying limit.

SUBMISSION GUIDELINES

Preferred Medium: floppy disk. Initial documentation required. **Average Company Response Time:** 4 weeks; rejected programs returned. **Payment:** negotiable royalty or outright purchase. **Distribution Rights:** exclusive. **Plugging In:** "We are devoted to acquiring, creating, and distributing only the most sophisticated and entertaining pieces of software product for personal computers that fit the mold we call 'Grown-up Gameware,' products that express the new maturity of the field—in terms of both hardware and user interests." Author's guide available.

International Publishing & Software, Inc.
3948 Chesswood Dr.
Downsview, Ontario, Canada M3J 2W6
(416) 636-9409
Robert Fraser, production manager
Established 1982

COMPANY PROFILE

Arcade, maze, word, board games. Also buys personal productivity, classroom education, business and professional management, systems. **Micros; Operating Systems:** Commodore 64 and VIC-20, Timex Sinclair. **Recent Titles:** *Packrabbit, Battleship, Slots.* **Distribution Channels:** catalogs, computer stores, consumer electronics stores, direct mail, software stores, video stores. Buys 100 programs annually; buying outlook increasing.

SUBMISSION GUIDELINES

Preferred Medium: cassette tape. Initial documentation required. **Average Company Response Time:** 2 to 3 weeks; rejected programs returned. **Payment:** negotiable royalty paid quarterly. **Distribution Rights:** exclusive. **Plugging**

In: Company is particularly interested in adventure and fantasy games. In other areas, engineering, financial planning, budgeting, programming aids, education for all grade levels ("preschoolers to Ph.D.s") and novelty applications. Author's guide available.

JMG Software International
710 Upper James
Hamilton, Ontario L9C 2Z8
(416) 389-6086
George Geczy, acquisitions director
Established 1982

COMPANY PROFILE

Arcade-style games and simulations, Also buys personal productivity, business and professional management, systems. **Micros; Operating Systems:** Apple, Commodore 64, IBM PC, TRS-80 I, III, IV, and Color Computer. **Recent Titles:** *Supreme Ruler Plus, Exterminate!* **Distribution Channels:** catalogs, computer stores, direct mail, software stores. Has not yet bought outside programs; company is now actively soliciting.

SUBMISSION GUIDELINES

Preferred Media: floppy disk, cassette tape. Complete documentation to be arranged between author and company. **Average Company Response Time:** 1 to 4 weeks; rejected programs returned. **Payment:** Negotiable royalty or outright purchase. **Distribution Rights:** exclusive. **Plugging In:** "We look for *quality;* we are willing to look at new ideas in any field, as well as more commonplace programs."

Koala Technologies
4962 El Camino Real, Suite 125
Los Altos, CA 94022
(415) 964-2992
Nick Shain, director of marketing
Established 1982

COMPANY PROFILE

Computer tutorials, music and art, graphics tutorials. Also buys personal productivity, classroom education. **Micros; Operating Systems:** Apple II, Atari, Commodore 64 and VIC-20, IBM PC. **Recent Titles:** *The Micro Illustrator, The Dancing Bear, Spider Eater.* **Distribution Channels:** computer stores, consumer electronics stores, department stores, discount stores, mass merchandisers, software stores, supermarkets, toy stores, video stores. Buys 10 to 20 programs annually; buying outlook increasing.

SUBMISSION GUIDELINES

Preferred Medium: floppy disk. Complete documentation to be arranged between author and company. **Average Company Response Time:** 4 weeks; rejected programs not returned. **Payment:** 10 to 20 percent royalty paid on "milestone" basis or outright purchase. **Distribution Rights:** exclusive. **Plugging In:** Koala software must showcase the KoalaPad Touch Tablet peripheral and demonstrate true educational value for children or adults. Author's guide available.

The Learning Company
545 Middlefield Rd.
Menlo Park, CA 94025
(415) 328-5410
Carol Dilfer, director of software development
  and acquisitions
Established 1970

COMPANY PROFILE

Home educational games for younger children. Also buys classroom education. **Micros; Operating Systems:** Apple II, II+, and IIe, Atari, TRS-80 Color Computer. **Recent Titles:** *Juggles' Rainbow, Bumble Games, Rocky's Boots.* **Distribution Channels:** bookstores, catalogs, computer stores, consumer electronics stores, department stores, direct mail, mass merchandisers, software stores, toy stores. No annual buying limit.

SUBMISSION GUIDELINES

Preferred Medium: floppy disk. Initial documentation required. **Average Company Response Time:** 2 weeks; rejected programs returned. **Payment:** negotiable royalty. **Distribution Rights:** negotiable.

Lightning Software, Inc., subsidiary of
  Scarborough Systems
P.O. Box 11725
Palo Alto, CA 94306
(415) 327-3280
Bruce Zweig, director of software development
  and acquisitions
Established 1981

COMPANY PROFILE

Home education. Also buys personal productivity, classroom education. **Micros; Operating Systems:** Apple, Atari, Commodore 64, IBM PC. **Recent Title:** *MasterType.* **Distribution Channels:** bookstores, catalogs, computer stores, consumer electronics stores, department stores, direct mail, discount stores, mass merchandisers, sales representatives, software stores, toy stores, video stores. Has not yet bought outside programs; company is now actively soliciting.

SUBMISSION GUIDELINES

Preferred Media: floppy disk, ROM cartridge. Complete documentation required. **Average Company Response Time:** 4 weeks; rejected programs returned. **Payment:** negotiable royalty. **Distribution Rights:** negotiable. **Plugging In:** Company's main interest is in "educational software with a whimsical or game-like flavor. We are also considering home utility packages." Author's guide available.

Matrix Software
315 Marion Ave.
Big Rapids, MI 49307
(616) 796-2483
Doug Pierce, sales manager and programmer
Established 1978

COMPANY PROFILE

Astrology, astronomy, and biorhythms. **Micros; Operating Systems:** Apple, Commodore, IBM, TRS-80. **Recent Titles:** *M-65: Astrological Chart Service & Research System, M-30: Natal Astrology Package, M-90: Horoscope Interpreter* (report writer). **Distribution Channels:** bookstores, catalogs, sales representatives, software stores. No annual buying limit.

SUBMISSION GUIDELINES

Preferred Medium: floppy disk. Complete documentation to be arranged between author and company. **Average Company Response Time:** 3 weeks. **Payment:** minimum 20 percent royalty. **Distribution Rights:** negotiable.

Mattel Electronics
5150 Rosecrans Ave.
Hawthorne, CA 90250
(213) 978-5150
Does not actively solicit.

Microcomputers Corporation
34 Maple Ave.
Armonk, NY 10504
(914) 273-6480
Jerald Greenberg, director of software
    development and acquisitions
Established 1979

COMPANY PROFILE

Logic and home education games. Also buys personal productivity, classroom education, business and professional management, systems. **Micros; Operating Systems:** Commodore 64 and VIC-20, TI 99/4A. **Recent Titles:** *Jotto, Powwow & Cornerbound, Addition.* **Distribution Channels:** bookstores, catalogs, computer stores, consumer electronics stores, department stores, direct mail, discount stores, mass merchandisers, software stores, supermarkets, toy stores, video stores. Buys 40 programs annually; buying outlook increasing.

SUBMISSION GUIDELINES

Preferred Media: cassette tape, paper printout. Complete documentation required. **Average Company Response Time:** 4 weeks; rejected programs returned. **Payment:** 5 to 10 percent royalty paid annually or outright purchase. **Distribution Rights:** exclusive.

MicroLab, Inc.
2699 Shokie Valley Rd.

Highland Park, IL 60035
(312) 433-7550
Michael Hatlak, vice president of product
    development
Established 1980

COMPANY PROFILE

Adventure games. Also buys personal productivity, classroom education, business and professional management, systems. **Micros; Operating Systems:** "all popular systems." **Recent Titles:** *Miner 2049'er, Hi Rise, Death in the Caribbean.* **Distribution Channels:** bookstores, catalogs, computer stores, consumer electronics stores, department stores, direct mail, discount stores, mass merchandisers, record stores, software stores, supermarkets, toy stores, video stores. Buys 25 to 50 programs annually; buying outlook decreasing.

SUBMISSION GUIDELINES

Preferred Medium: floppy disk. Initial documentation required. **Average Company Response Time:** 2 weeks; rejected programs returned. **Payment:** negotiable royalty paid monthly or outright purchase. **Distribution Rights:** exclusive.

Milton-Bradley Company
111 Maple St.
Springfield, MA 01101
(413) 525-6411
Does not actively solicit.

Muse Software, Inc.
347 N. Charles St.
Baltimore, MD 21201
(301) 659-7212
Eric Ace, director of software development and
    acquisitions
Established 1978

COMPANY PROFILE

Arcade and adventure games, computer tutorials. Also buys personal productivity, classroom education, business and professional management.

Micros; Operating Systems: Apple II, II+, and IIe, Atari 400, 800, and 1200, Commodore 64; IBM PC-DOS 2.1 and 2.2. **Recent Titles:** *Titan Empire, Castle Wolfenstein, Know Your Apple.* **Distribution Channels:** computer stores, direct mail, discount stores, mass merchandisers, software stores, video stores. Buys five programs annually; buying outlook increasing.

SUBMISSION GUIDELINES

Preferred Medium: floppy disk. Complete documentation required. **Average Company Response Time:** 4 weeks; rejected programs returned. **Payment:** negotiable royalty paid quarterly. **Distribution Rights:** exlcusive.

N.A.P. Consumer Electronics Corporation
   (Magnavox/Odyssey)
I40 & Straw Plains Pike
Knoxville, TN 37914
(615) 521-4316
Does not actively solicit.

Not-Polyoptics
13721 Lynn St., Suite 15
Woodbridge, VA 22191
(703) 491-5543 and 549-4622
Michael V. Capobianco, program development
   director
Established 1981

COMPANY PROFILE

Action, adventure, and strategy games, flight simulation. Also buys personal productivity, business and professional management. **Micros; Operating Systems:** TI 99/4 and 99/4A. **Recent Titles:** *Treasure Trap, 99 'Vaders, Waldoball.* **Distribution Channels:** bookstores, catalogs, computer stores, consumer electronics stores, direct mail, software stores, video stores. Buys 5 to 10 programs annually; buying outlook increasing.

SUBMISSION GUIDELINES

Preferred Media: floppy disk, cassette tape. Complete documentation required. **Average Company Response Time:** 2 to 3 weeks; rejected programs returned. **Payment:**

"minimum" 30 percent royalty paid quarterly. **Distribution Rights:** exclusive. **Plugging In:** Firm is initiating a "Program Author Co-Op" to "reward programmers who create exceptional software for the TI computers. Our company began as the union of three programmers who had designed game programs for the 99/4A and joined together to bring this software before the public. From the beginning, the profits were shared by the programmers in proportion to sales of their games. Programming is still the highest priority with us. Make your program as versatile and original as possible. Please include SASE." Author's guide available. Company may be diversifying because of Texas Instruments' decision to leave the home computer market.

Odesta
930 Pitner Ave.
Evanston, IL 60202
(312) 498-5615
Mike Collins, national sales manager
Established 1980

COMPANY PROFILE

Classic board games using artificial intelligence. Also buys business and professional management. **Micros; Operating Systems:** Apple, Atari, Commodore 64, IBM PC. **Recent Titles:** *Chess 7.0, Checkers 2.1, ODIN, Backgammon 5.0, How about a Nice Game of Chess?* **Distribution Channels:** bookstores, catalogs, computer stores, department stores, direct mail, mass merchandisers, software stores. Buys one program annually; buying outlook increasing.

SUBMISSION GUIDELINES

Preferred Medium: floppy disk. Initial documentation required. **Average Company Response Time:** 2 to 4 weeks; rejected programs returned. **Payment:** negotiable royalty. **Distribution Rights:** exclusive. **Plugging In:** "Our programs are known for extensive features. In one package alone we have 27 different functions including 17 skill levels, 'advice,' 'look ahead,' 'demonstration,' and 'tutorial'. All programs submitted must also feature problem-solving techniques."

Parker Brothers
50 Dunham Rd.
Beverly, MA 01915
(617) 927-7600
Does not actively solicit.

Passport Designs, Inc.
116 N. Cabrillo Highway
Half Moon Bay, CA 94019
(415) 726-0280
David Kusek, president
Established 1981

COMPANY PROFILE

Music programs designed for use with company's "Soundchaser" keyboard, interface card, and Mountain Computer's MusicSystem. Also buys personal productivity, classroom education, business and professional management, systems. **Micros; Operating Systems:** Apple DOS. **Recent Titles:** *Chopin, Notewriter, Turbo-Traks, Kaleido-Sound.* **Distribution Channels:** computer stores, consumer electronics stores, direct mail, music stores, software stores. Buys 5 to 10 programs annually; buying outlook "dramatically" increasing.

SUBMISSION GUIDELINES

Preferred Medium: floppy disk. Initial documentation required. **Average Company Response Time:** 4 to 8 weeks; rejected programs returned. **Payment:** negotiable royalty or outright purchase. **Distribution Rights:** negotiable.

Penguin Software, Inc.
830 N. 4th Ave.
Geneva, IL 60134
(312) 232-1984
Dave Albert, director of software development
    and acquisitions
Established 1981

COMPANY PROFILE

Adventure games with a humorous angle. Also buys personal productivity, classroom education, business and professional management, systems.

Micros; Operating Systems: Apple II + and IIe, Atari 400, 800, 600XL, 800XL, 1200XL, 1400XL, and 1450XL, Commodore 64, IBM PC. **Recent Titles:** *Minit Man, Pensate, Spy's Demise.* **Distribution Channels:** bookstores, catalogs, computer stores, consumer electronics stores, department stores, direct mail, mass merchandisers, software stores, video stores. Buys 20 programs annually; buying outlook increasing.

SUBMISSION GUIDELINES

Preferred Medium: floppy disk. Complete documentation required. **Average Company Response Time:** 2 to 4 weeks rejected programs returned with SASE. **Payment:** 20 to 30 percent gross and 8.4 to 12.6 percent royalty paid monthly. **Distribution Rights:** negotiable. **Plugging In:** Author's guide available.

Phoenix Software, Inc.
64 Lake Zurich Dr.
Lake Zurich, IL 60047
(312) 438-4850
Judith Wessel, general manager
Established 1981

COMPANY PROFILE

Text and graphic adventure games. Also buys business and professional management, systems. **Micros; Operating Systems:** Apple, Atari, IBM PC. **Recent Titles:** *Sherwood Forest, Forms Foundry, MAD RAT.* **Distribution Channels:** bookstores, catalogs, computer stores, consumer electronics stores, department stores, direct mail, discount stores, mass merchandisers, software stores, video stores. Buys five programs annually; buying outlook decreasing.

SUBMISSION GUIDELINES

Preferred Medium: floppy disk. Complete documentation required. **Average Company Response Time:** 3 to 4 weeks; rejected programs returned. **Payment:** 20 to 25 percent royalty paid monthly. **Distribution Rights:** exclusive. **Plugging In:** Phoenix is looking for "original arcade games for Apple or Atari."

Piccadilly Software
89 Summit Ave.
Summit, NJ 07901
(201) 277-1020
Dennie Tolley, president
Established 1981

COMPANY PROFILE

Action and arcade games. Also buys classroom education, business and professional management. **Micros; Operating Systems:** Apple, Atari IBM, TRS-80. **Recent Titles:** *Martian Soil, Falcons, Invasion of Everything, The Mole* (education game). **Distribution Channels:** computer stores, department stores, direct mail, software stores. Buys six programs annually; buying outlook increasing.

SUBMISSION GUIDELINES

Preferred Medium: floppy disk. Complete documentation required. **Average Company Response Time:** 4 weeks; rejected programs returned. **Payment:** negotiable royalty. **Distribution Rights:** exclusive. **Plugging In:** "We hope to increase our acquisitions to at least 12 programs a year. We're looking for what sounds obvious but is difficult to achieve—games that are entertaining, challenging, and that offer a high level of interest and originality." Author's guide available.

Prentice-Hall, Inc.
Englewood Cliffs, NJ 07632
(201) 592-2000/2170
Ernest C. H. Hursh, director of marketing
    software
Established 1981

COMPANY PROFILE

Computer tutorials, home education. Also buys personal productivity, classroom education, business and professional management, systems. **Micros; Operating Systems:** Apple, Atari, Commodore 64 and VIC-20, IBM PC. **Recent Titles:** *Paint, Multiploy, Teach Yourself VisiCalc.* **Distribution Channels:** bookstores, catalogs, computer stores, consumer electronics stores, department stores, direct mail, discount stores,

mass merchandisers, software stores, toy stores, video stores. Buys 150 to 200 programs annually; buying outlook increasing.

SUBMISSION GUIDELINES

Preferred Medium: floppy disk. Complete documentation required. **Average Company Response Time:** 2 weeks; rejected programs returned. **Payment:** negotiable royalty paid semiannually or outright purchase. **Distribution Rights:** negotiable.

Program Design, Inc. (PDI)
95 E. Putnam Ave.
Greenwich, CT 06830
(203) 661-8799
John Victor, director of software development
    and acquisitions
Established 1978

COMPANY PROFILE

Computer tutorials, home education, and adventure games. **Micros; Operating Systems:** Apple II, II +, and IIe, Atari 400 and 800, Commodore 64 and PET, TI 99/4A. **Recent Titles:** *New Step by Step, Preparing for the SAT, Sammy the Sea Serpent.* **Distribution Channels:** bookstores, catalogs, computer stores, direct mail, mass merchandisers, software stores, toy stores, video stores. Buys six programs annually; buying outlook increasing.

SUBMISSION GUIDELINES

Preferred Media: floppy disk, cassette tape. Complete documentation required. **Average Company Response Time:** "several weeks"; rejected programs returned. **Payment:** negotiable royalty paid quarterly. **Distribution Rights:** nonexclusive. **Plugging In:** Author's guide available.

Quality Software
6660 Reseda Blvd., Suite 105
Reseda, CA 91355
(213) 344-6599
Robert Christiansen, director of software
    development and acquisitions
Established, 1978

COMPANY PROFILE

Arcade, adventure, and card games. Also buys personal productivity, systems. **Micros; Operating Systems:** Apple II, II+, and IIe, Atari 400 and 800, IBM PC. **Recent Titles:** *Meteoroids in Space, Ali Baba and the Forty Thieves, Pro Poker.* **Distribution Channels:** catalogs, computer stores, direct mail, software stores. Buys five programs annually; buying outlook increasing.

SUBMISSION GUIDELINES

Preferred Medium: floppy disk with accompanying paper printout. Initial documentation required. **Average Company Response Time:** 2 weeks; rejected programs returned. **Payment:** negotiable royalty paid quarterly or monthly. **Distribution Rights:** negotiable. **Plugging In:** "We would like to see an actual program, but the program does not need to be in its final finished state. Good programming is an important asset, but marketability depends on many other factors. The concept and approach are most important. If your program is incomplete, indicate the ways in which you intend to add to it or improve it. If we are interested at all, we may agree with your ideas and/or suggest other improvements."

_____

Quark, Inc.
2525 West Evans, Suite 220
Denver, CO 80219
(303) 934-2211
Does not actively solicit.

_____

Rainbow Computing, Inc.
9719 Reseda Blvd.
Northridge, CA 91324
(213) 349-0300
Tina Day, assistant marketing manager
Established 1976

COMPANY PROFILE

Arcade and strategy games, drawing, hobby, and leisure time programs. Also buys personal productivity, classroom education, business and professional management, systems. **Micros; Operating Systems:** Apple II+ and IIe, Digital Rainbow 100, IBM PC. **Recent Titles:** *Poor*

Man's Graphics Tablet, Bat-Stat, Statistics with Daisy. **Distribution Channels:** computer stores, direct mail, software stores. Buys one to two programs annually; buying outlook increasing.

SUBMISSION GUIDELINES

Preferred Medium: floppy disk. Complete documentation required. **Average Company Response Time:** 4 to 6 weeks; rejected programs returned. **Payment:** 5 to 25 percent royalty (on gross sales) paid quarterly. **Distribution Rights:** negotiable.

_____

Ranco Software Games, Inc.
4 Bartlett Ave.
Roanoke, AL 36274
(205) 863-4718
Charles Jordan, director of product development
Established 1982

COMPANY PROFILE

Sports, action games. Also buys personal productivity, classroom education, business and professional management, systems. **Micros; Operating Systems:** Apple II+, Commodore 64 and VIC-20, Franklin Ace 1000, Orange, TRS-80. **Recent Titles:** *Command Strategy Football.* **Distribution Channels:** computer stores, direct mail, mass merchandisers, software stores, video stores. Buys 5 to 20 programs annually; buying outlook increasing.

SUBMISSION GUIDELINES

Preferred Media: floppy disk, cassette tape. Complete documentation required. **Average Company Response Time:** 1 to 2 weeks; rejected programs returned. **Payment:** 10 to 15 percent royalty paid quarterly or outright purchase. **Distribution Rights:** exclusive.

_____

Rantom Software
Box 5480
Avon, CO 81620
(303) 949-6646
Thomas J. Richards, director of software
  development
Established 1982

COMPANY PROFILE

Action, adventure games. Also buys personal productivity, classroom education, business and professional management, systems. **Micros; Operating Systems:** Apple, Atari, Commodore 64 and VIC-20, TRS-80. **Recent Titles:** *Thrax Lair, Sherlock, Trust.* **Distribution Channels:** bookstores, catalogs, computer stores, consumer electronics stores, department stores, direct mail, discount stores, mass merchandisers, software stores, video stores. Buys 10 programs annually; buying outlook the same.

SUBMISSION GUIDELINES

Preferred Media: floppy disk, cassette tape, paper printout; submit source code if possible. Initial documentation required. **Average Company Response Time:** 1 week; rejected programs not returned. **Payment:** 30 to 50 percent royalty paid monthly. **Distribution Rights:** exclusive. **Plugging In:** Rantom publishes a full-color, boxed product line for outstanding programs. Company also publishes an APX-type line with over 15 new titles which generally sell for under $19.95. "This allows us to evaluate many different types of products which otherwise may not have been published." Author's guide available.

RB Robot Corporation
18301 W. 10th Ave., Suite 310
Golden, CO 80401
(303) 279-5525
Deborah Waldo, marketing manager
Established 1982

COMPANY PROFILE

Games, novelty, home education programs designed for use with company's robot. Also buys personal productivity, classroom education, business and professional management. **Micros; Operating Systems:** Apple IIe, IBM PC; Robot Control language (Tiny BASIC). **Recent Titles:** *Spin the Robot, R2D2.* **Distribution Channels:** catalogs, computer stores, direct mail, software stores. Company buys 10 to 15 programs annually; buying outlook increasing.

SUBMISSION GUIDELINES

Preferred Media: floppy disk. Initial documentation required. **Average Company Response Time:** 8 weeks; rejected programs not returned. **Payment:** 12 percent royalty (based on suggested retail price) paid quarterly. **Distribution Rights:** exclusive. **Plugging In:** Company is searching for programs that will enable their home robot to do a variety of tasks, including functional household work, promotional and commercial uses (security, store openings, etc.). No program may violate Isaac Asimov's three laws of robotics: (1) Robot cannot break the law or harm humans through action or inaction. (2) Robot may not bring harm to itself (unless it violates law 1). (3) Robot must seek to maintain and preserve itself (unless doing so violates law 1 and 2). Author's guide available.

Reston Publishing Company, Inc.
11480 Sunset Hills Rd.
Reston, VA 22090
(703) 437-8900
Nikki Hardin, editor

COMPANY PROFILE

Home art education and computer tutorials for children, math skills games, arcade games. Also buys classroom education. **Micros; Operating Systems:** Apple, Atari, Commodore, TI, Timex Sinclair. **Recent Titles:** *Multiploy, Cyberlogo Turtle, Apple Graphics.* **Distribution Channels:** bookstores, catalogs, computer stores, direct mail, software stores, video stores. No annual buying limit.

SUBMISSION GUIDELINES

Preferred Media: floppy disk, cassette tape. Complete documentation required. **Average Company Response Time:** 4 to 8 weeks; rejected programs returned. **Payment:** negotiable royalty. **Distribution Rights:** negotiable. **Plugging In:** Author's guide available.

Ritam Corporation
P.O. Box 921

Fairfield, IA 52556
(515) 472-8262
Jonathan Isbit, vice president
Established 1979

COMPANY PROFILE

Games based on popular board games. **Micros; Operating Systems:** Apple II, IIe, and II+, TRS-80. **Recent Titles:** *Monty Plays Scrabble, Monty Plays Monopoly.* **Distribution Channels:** computer stores, consumer electronics stores (Radio Shack), software stores. Has not yet bought outside programs; company is now actively soliciting.

SUBMISSION GUIDELINES

Preferred Medium: floppy disk. Complete documentation required. **Average Company Response Time:** 2 weeks; rejected programs returned. **Payment:** negotiable royalty. **Distribution Rights:** exclusive.

Roklan Software
3335 N. Arlington Heights Rd.
Arlington Heights, IL 60004
(312) 392-2525
Jim Gonzalez, vice president of marketing and
  sales
Established 1974

COMPANY PROFILE

Arcade games. Also buys personal productivity, business and professional management. **Micros; Operating Systems:** Apple, Atari, Commodore 64, TI 99/4A, TRS-80; CP/M. **Recent Titles:** *Lifespan, Wizard of Wor, Gorf.* **Distribution Channels:** bookstores, catalogs, computer stores, consumer electronics stores, department stores, discount stores, mass merchandisers, software stores, toy stores, video stores. Buys 20 or more programs annually; buying outlook increasing.

SUBMISSION GUIDELINES

Preferred Medium: floppy disk. Initial documentation required. **Average Company Response**

Time: 4 weeks; rejected programs returned.
Payment: negotiable royalty. **Distribution Rights:** negotiable.

Royal Software/COMPUTER PALACE
2160 W. 11th Ave.
Eugene, OR 97402
(503) 683-5361
Don Marr, owner
Established 1982

COMPANY PROFILE

Arcade and other games. Also buys personal productivity, classroom education, business and professional management, systems. **Micros; Operating Systems:** Atari 400 and 800. **Recent Titles:** *Meteor Storm, Super Mailer.* **Distribution Channels:** computer stores, direct mail, mass merchandisers, software stores. Has not yet bought outside programs; company is now actively soliciting.

SUBMISSION GUIDELINES

Preferred Medium: floppy disk. Complete documentation required. **Average Company Response Time:** 1 to 4 weeks; rejected programs returned. **Payment:** negotiable royalty. **Distribution Rights:** exclusive.

Sentient Software, Inc.
P.O. Box 4929
Aspen, CO 81612
(303) 925-9293
Larry Gottlieb, vice president of software
  acquisitions
Established 1981

COMPANY PROFILE

Action, adventure games. Also buys personal productivity, business and professional management. **Micros; Operating Systems:** Apple II, II+, and IIe, Atari 800 and 1200XL, Commodore 64, IBM PC. **Recent Titles:** *Cyborg, Gold Rush, Congo.* **Distribution Channels:** bookstores, catalogs, computer stores, consumer electronics stores, department stores, direct mail, discount stores, mass merchandisers, software stores, toy stores. Has not yet bought outside programs; company is now actively soliciting.

SUBMISSION GUIDELINES

Preferred Medium: floppy disk. Initial documentation required. **Average Company Response Time:** 2 weeks; rejected programs not returned. **Payment:** 10 to 20 percent royalty paid quarterly. **Distribution Rights:** exclusive.

Sierra On-Line, Inc.
Sierra On-Line Bldg.
Coarsegold, CA 93614
(209) 683-6858
David Siri, manager of product development
Established 1980

COMPANY PROFILE

Action, adventure, and role-playing games with "imaginative twists," home education. Also buys personal productivity, business and professional management. **Micros; Operating Systems:** Apple, Atari, Coleco's ADAM, Commodore 64 and VIC-20, IBM PC and PCjr. **Recent Titles:** *Apple Cider Spider, Lunar Leeper, Ultima II.* **Distribution Channels:** bookstores, catalogs, computer stores, consumer electronics stores, department stores, direct mail, discount stores, mass merchandisers, software stores, toy stores, video stores. Buys 10 to 15 programs annually; buying outlook increasing.

SUBMISSION GUIDELINES

Preferred Media: floppy disk, cassette tape. Initial documentation required. **Average Company Response Time:** 2 weeks; rejected programs returned. **Payment:** negotiable royalty paid monthly or outright purchase. **Distribution Rights:** exclusive. **Plugging In:** Sierra will accept submissions "not quite completed or 'as is,' and offer recommendations toward completion." Author's guide available.

Sim Computer Products, Inc.
1100 E. Hector St.

Whitemarsh, PA 19428
(215) 825-4250
Leland J. Ancier, product manager
Established 1982

COMPANY PROFILE

Home education games. Also buys personal productivity, classroom education. **Micros; Operating Systems:** Atari, Commodore 64, TI 99/4A. (Company may add Apple, Coleco's ADAM, IBM PC and PCjr, and Timex Sinclair). **Recent Titles:** *Colorcraft, Homecalc, Kentucky Derby.* **Distribution Channels:** bookstores, catalogs, computer stores, consumer electronics stores, direct mail, discount stores, software stores, video stores. Buys four to eight programs annually; buying outlook increasing.

SUBMISSION GUIDELINES

Preferred Medium: floppy disk. Initial documentation required. **Average Company Response Time:** 8 weeks; rejected programs not returned. **Payment:** 5 to 25 percent royalty paid monthly. **Distribution Rights:** negotiable. **Plugging In:** Firm needs BASIC programs for its *Inside BASIC* series for all machines. These programs are intended to teach the users the workings of well-designed programs so that users can create their own.

Simon and Schuster, Electronic Publishing Group
1230 Avenue of the Americas
New York, NY 10020
(212) 245-6400
Jim Korenthal, vice president of technical
    services
Established 1983

COMPANY PROFILE

Game, entertainment, and home education software based on popular books and characters. Also buys personal productivity, classroom education. **Micros; Operating Systems:** Apple, Atari, Commodore 64, IBM PC, TRS-80. **Recent Titles:** *Star Trek, Hitchhiker's Guide to the Galaxy, Henson's Muppets.* **Distribution Channels:** bookstores, computer stores, consumer electronics stores, mass merchandisers, software stores, toy stores. No annual buying limit.

SUBMISSION GUIDELINES

Preferred Media: floppy disk, cassette tape. Initial documentation required. **Average Company Response Time:** 6 to 8 weeks; rejected programs returned. **Payment:** negotiable royalty (with "moderate advance"). **Distribution Rights:** negotiable. **Plugging In:** Prefers to review submissions sent by knowledgeable agents. Author's guide available.

Sinclair Research, Ltd.
50 Stanford St.
Boston, MA 02114
(617) 742-4826
Does not actively solicit.

Sirius Software, Inc.
10364 Rockingham Dr.
Sacramento, CA 95827
(916) 366-1195
Ernest Brock, director of software development
Established 1980

COMPANY PROFILE

Action and adventure games with original themes. Also buys classroom education. **Micros; Operating Systems:** Apple II, Atari home computers, Commodore 64, VIC-20, and IBM PC. **Recent Titles:** *Type Attack, Bandits, Buzzard Bait.* **Distribution Channels:** bookstores, catalogs, computer stores, consumer electronics stores, department stores, discount stores, mass merchandisers, software stores, toy stores, video stores. Buys 12 programs annually; buying outlook the same.

SUBMISSION GUIDELINES

Preferred Medium: floppy disk. Initial documentation required. **Average Company Response Time:** 2 weeks; rejected programs returned. **Payment:** 3 to 21 percent royalty paid quarterly. **Distribution Rights:** exclusive. **Plugging In:** Sirius is "only interested in entertainment software—fast action and adventures. Programs must

be in machine language and have good graphics, sound effects, and playability." Author's guide available.

Sir-tech Software, Inc.
6 Main St.
Ogdensburg, NY 13669
(315) 393-6633
Robert Sirotek, director of software development

COMPANY PROFILE

Arcade, adventure, simulation games. Also buys personal productivity, classroom education, business and professional management. **Micros; Operating Systems:** Apple II, II +, and IIe, IBM PC. **Recent Titles:** *Wizardry, Police Artist, Galactic Attack.* **Distribution Channels:** bookstores, computer stores, direct mail, software stores. No annual buying limit.

SUBMISSION GUIDELINES

Preferred Medium: floppy disk. Complete documentation preferred. **Average Company Response Time:** 3 to 5 weeks; rejected programs returned. **Payment:** 10 to 30 percent royalty on gross sales (depending on application) paid monthly or outright purchase. **Distribution Rights:** negotiable. **Plugging In:** Sir-tech places a premium on good documentation. "User friendliness is a must; be precise but not overinvolved." Also, if your program was rejected by another company, tell Sir-tech why and what you think you can do to overcome previous objections or why you think the previous assessment of your program was wrong. Author's guide available.

Soft Images
200 Rte. 17
Mahwah, NJ 07430
(800) 526-9042/(201) 529-1440
Norman J. Wazaney, Jr., director
Established 1982

COMPANY PROFILE

Adult-oriented party games. **Micros; Operating Systems:** Apple II, II +, IIe, and III, Atari 400 and 800, IBM PC and PCjr, TRS-80 I, II, III, and IV. **Recent Titles:** *Pandemonium, Black Jack Strategy, Single's Night at Molly's.* **Distribution Channels:** bookstores, catalogs, computer stores, consumer electronics stores, department stores, direct mail, discount stores, mass merchandisers, software stores, toy stores, video stores. Buys 15 programs annually; buying outlook increasing.

SUBMISSION GUIDELINES

Preferred Medium: floppy disk. Initial documentation required. **Average Company Response Time:** 1 week; rejected programs returned. **Payment:** escalating royalty paid quarterly. **Distribution Rights:** exclusive. **Plugging In:** Company wants software of "an intelligent nature."

Softsel Computer Products, Inc.
8295 South La Cienega Blvd.
Inglewood, CA 90301
(213) 412-1700
Scott Hillman, vice president of product services
Established 1980

COMPANY PROFILE

World's largest distributor of third-party microcomputer software in all categories (primarily recreation). Also evaluates personal productivity, classroom education, business and professional management, systems. **Micros; Operating Systems:** all popular computers. **Distribution Channels:** bookstores, catalogs, computer stores, consumer electronics stores, department stores, direct mail, discount stores, mass merchandisers, software stores, toy stores, video stores. Company doesn't acquire software but reviews previously published submissions in any category for possible inclusion in its catalog or for recommending unpublished but promising packages to appropriate third-party producers for further consideration. Evaluates "hundreds" of submissions weekly.

SUBMISSION GUIDELINES

Preferred Media: floppy disk, cassette tape. Complete documentation required. **Average Company Response Time:** varies; rejected programs returned. **Payment:** not applicable. **Dis-**

tribution Rights: nonexclusive. **Plugging In:** Authors are more than welcome to send us completed programs, but we do not develop and publish software; we are basically for authors who also want to be their own publishers and distributors."

Softside Magazine
10 Northern Blvd.
Northwood Executive Park
Amherst, NH 03031
(603) 882-2555
Att.: software editor
Established 1978

COMPANY PROFILE

Disk- and cassette-based magazine issued monthly, containing a broad range of games, simulations, and home education programs. Also buys personal productivity, classroom education, business and professional management, systems. **Micros; Operating Systems:** Apple, Atari, Commodore, IBM PC and PCjr, TRS-80. **Recent Titles:** *ST-80 DOC* (telecommunications), *Draw 7 Plus, Psychedellics, Character Set Creator.* **Distribution Channels:** direct mail, newsstand sales, the Source (online database). Buys approximately 40 programs annually in each machine format for SoftSide DV (disk version) and SoftSide CV (cassette version); buying outlook the same.

SUBMISSION GUIDELINES

Preferred Medium: floppy disk. Complete documentation preferred (the more complete, the higher the payment). **Average Company Response Time:** within 6 weeks; rejected programs returned with SASE. **Payment:** $85 to $2500 outright purchase, plus a 25 percent royalty for translation of your program to another computer system; an additional payment of half the original amount is made for reprints. "On rare occasions, if we decide not to publish a program after it has been accepted, you'll receive a 20 percent kill fee in lieu of a publication fee." **Distribution Rights:** nonexclusive; buys one-time publication rights, or "sometimes we buy full rights to a program, depending on its value. You retain ownership of the program, but you may not sell it to anyone else for 3 months following pub-

lication." **Plugging In:** "SoftSide is always looking for well-written, original programs for each of
the microcomputers we support. Normally, we try
to publish programs that would interest a wide
spectrum of our readers, but we love to see truly
original and creative programs, so don't hesitate
to submit something a little offbeat. Translations
of previously published programs are also welcome. If translation interests you, be sure to send
for our list of translation needs." Author's guide
available.

Softsync, Inc.
14 E. 34th St.
New York, NY 10016
(212) 685-2080
Ken Coach, director of marketing
Established 1981

COMPANY PROFILE

Leisure time programs, arcade games. Also buys
personal productivity, classroom education, business and professional management. **Micros; Operating Systems:** Apple, Atari, Commodore,
IBM PC, Timex Sinclair. **Recent Titles:** *Cosmic
Gorilla, Model Diet, Computer Mechanic.* **Distribution Channels:** bookstores, catalogs, computer stores, consumer electronics stores, department stores, direct mail, discount stores, mass
merchandisers, software stores, toy stores, video
stores. Buys 25 programs annually; buying outlook the same.

SUBMISSION GUIDELINES

Preferred Medium: floppy disk. Initial documentation required. **Average Company Response
Time:**   3 weeks; rejected programs returned on
request. **Payment:**   10 percent royalty of gross
paid quarterly or outright purchase. **Distribution
Rights:**   exclusive.

The Software Guild
2935 Whipple Rd.
Union City, CA 94587
(415) 487-5900
Regina Berdak, director of software development
Established 1981

COMPANY PROFILE

Home education, learning games, leisure time
programs. Also buys personal productivity, classroom education, business and professional management, systems. **Micros; Operating Systems:** Apple, Atari, Commodore, IBM, TRS-80.
Recent Titles: *Pollywog, Touch Typing Tutor,
Drinks on a Disk.* **Distribution Channels:**
bookstores, computer stores, consumer electronics stores, department stores, discount stores,
mass merchandisers, software stores, supermarkets, toy stores, video stores, company-leased
Softsmith franchises. To promote brand recognition among consumers, the Guild markets all software under the Softsmith label. Buys 250 programs annually; buying outlook increasing.

SUBMISSION GUIDELINES

Preferred Media: floppy disk, cassette tape.
Complete documentation required. **Average
Company Response Time:**   8 to 12 weeks; rejected programs returned. **Payment:**   20 percent
royalty on net sales up to $200,000; 15 percent
royalty on net sales between $200,000 and
$400,000; 10 percent royalty on net sales in ex-
cess of $400,000, paid monthly. **Distribution
Rights:**   negotiable. **Plugging In:**   The Software
Guild says it approaches affiliated authors and
publishers as "business partners. We are moti-
vated to maximize each program's visibility, distribution, and sales." Author's guide available.

Source Telecomputing Corporation
1616 Anderson Rd.
McLean, VA 22102
(703) 734-7500
Jeana Entwisle, manager of product acquisition
Established 1976 (online 1979)

COMPANY PROFILE

Database network offering consumer information
and programs (including games, hobbies, music,
art, home education, and self-improvement) to
subscribers. Also buys personal productivity,
classroom education, business and professional
management, systems. **Micros; Operating Systems:**   all popular computers; any computer

configuration that can act as a dumb terminal. **Recent Titles:** *Data ESP, Data Games, Play I-Ching, Wine, Play Vegas.* **Distribution Channels:** computer stores, direct mail, software stores. No annual buying limit.

SUBMISSION GUIDELINES

Preferred Media: floppy disk, paper printout. Complete documentation required. **Average Company Response Time:** 4 to 6 weeks; rejected programs returned. **Payment:** variable royalty (based on subscriber usage) paid monthly or quarterly or outright purchase. **Distribution Rights:** exclusive. **Plugging In:** Individuals can offer their software through the Source in two ways: (1) *Private sector services:* If you are an organization or individual with information for a limited or "private" audience, you can create a private network on the services. For example, if you managed an association which desires to distribute electronically a newsletter or legislative updates, you may input your data on your own service. *You* control the updating and editing of your information, as well as maintaining a list of people you have authorized to access your data. (2) *User publisher:* If you are an organization or individual with information for a "public" audience, the Source may approve your database for access by all of its subscribers. You still maintain responsibility for editing and updating your information in a format consistent with the Source's editorial standards. The Source master index lists over 600 subjects covered, and the company seeks subjects not yet fully serviced. Constantly updated offerings are preferred because they encourage repeat access. Author's guide available.

Spectral Associates
3418 S. 90th St.
Tacoma, WA 98409
(206) 581-6938
Cindy Shackleford, manager
Established 1981

COMPANY PROFILE

Arcade, adventure games. Also buys classroom education, systems. **Micros; Operating Systems:** Dragon Data, TDP System 100, TRS-80 Color Computer. **Recent Titles:** *Defense, An-*

droid Attack, Color Zap. **Distribution Channels:** bookstores, catalogs, computer stores, consumer electronics stores, direct mail, software stores. Buys 20 programs annually; buying outlook increasing.

SUBMISSION GUIDELINES

Preferred Medium: cassette tape. Complete documentation required. **Average Company Response Time:** 2 weeks; rejected programs returned. **Payment:** 25 percent royalty paid quarterly. **Distribution Rights:** exclusive.

SpectraVideo Inc.
39 W. 37th St.
New York, NY 10018
(212) 869-7911
Paul Hodara, director of software development
Established 1983

COMPANY PROFILE

Arcade games, leisure time, music, home education, and self-improvement. Also buys personal productivity, classroom education. **Micros; Operating Systems:** SpectraVideo SV-318 (home) and SV-328 (personal); CP/M 2.2, CP/M 3.0, MSX. **Recent Titles:** *Super Cross Force, Spectra Diary, Introduction to BASIC.* **Distribution Channels:** computer stores, consumer electronics stores, department stores, discount stores, mass merchandisers, software stores, toy stores. Buys 15 programs annually; buying outlook increasing.

SUBMISSION GUIDELINES

Preferred Media: floppy disk, cassette tape. Initial documentation required. **Average Company Response Time:** 2 to 3 weeks; rejected programs returned. **Payment:** negotiable royalty (only for hit game adaptations) or outright purchase. **Distribution Rights:** exclusive. **Plugging In:** Company is primarily interested in accomplished programmers who have already created software and worked on other micros. Current need is for educational games for all ages (young children to college level). Author's guide available.

Spinnaker Software Corporation
215 First St.
Cambridge, MA 02142
(617) 868-4700
Nancy Evans, public relations
Established 1982

COMPANY PROFILE

Home education for young children, teaching basic math, grammar, and reading skills. **Micros; Operating Systems:** Apple, Atari, Coleco's ADAM, Commodore 64, and VIC-20. **Recent Titles:** *Story Machine, Face Maker, Trains.* **Distribution Channels:** bookstores, catalogs, computer stores, consumer electronics stores, department stores, direct mail, mass merchandisers, software stores, toy stores. Buys eight programs annually; buying outlook increasing.

SUBMISSION GUIDELINES

Preferred Media: floppy disk, cassette tape. Initial documentation required. **Average Company Response Time:** 2 weeks; rejected programs returned. **Payment:** negotiable royalty or outright purchase. **Distribution Rights:** exclusive. **Plugging In:** In addition to children's titles, company has just begun an adult education line and needs programs for that group.

_____

Starpath Corporation
2005 De La Cruz Blvd.
Santa Clara, CA 95050
(408) 970-0200
Does not actively solicit.

_____

Sterling Swift Publishing Company
7901 South IH-35
Austin, TX 78744
(512) 282-6840
Sterling Swift, director of software development
Established 1975

COMPANY PROFILE

Home education. Also buys classroom education, personal productivity. **Micros; Operating Systems:** primarily Apple II + and IIe and IBM PC, also Atari, Commodore, TI, TRS-80. **Recent Titles:** *Super Quiz II, Discover BASIC, The Arithmetic Classroom.* **Distribution Channels:** bookstores, catalogs, computer stores, direct mail, software stores. No annual buying limit.

SUBMISSION GUIDELINES

Preferred Medium: floppy disk. Complete documentation required. **Average Company Response Time:** 2 to 3 weeks; rejected programs returned. **Payment:** negotiable royalty. **Distribution Rights:** negotiable.

_____

Strategic Simulations, Inc.
465 Fairchild Dr., 108
Mountain View, CA 94043
(415) 964-1353
Chuch Krogel, research and development
     director
Established 1980

COMPANY PROFILE

Sophisticated war games simulations, sports games. Also buys classroom education. **Micros; Operating Systems:** Apple, Atari, Commodore 64, IBM PC. **Recent Titles:** *Broadsides, Combat Leader, Fortress, Professional Tour Golf.* **Distribution Channels:** computer stores, direct mail, software stores. Buys 14 programs annually (80 percent of all programs marketed); buying outlook increasing.

SUBMISSION GUIDELINES

Preferred Medium: floppy disk. Initial documentation required. **Average Company Response Time:** 2 weeks; rejected programs returned. **Payment:** 10 to 20 percent royalty paid monthly. **Distribution Rights:** exclusive. **Plugging In:** "We don't want any arcade games and nothing for children. All our programs emphasize real life simulations. We are now going into simulations applicable for high school use." Author's guide available.

_____

SubLogic Corporation
713 Edgebrook Dr.

Champaign, IL 61820
(217) 359-8482
Does not actively solicit.

Sydney Development Corporation
103 Fourth Ave.
Ottawa, Canada K1S 2L1
(613) 232-7168
Michael Bate, director of design graphics
Established 1979

COMPANY PROFILE

Games and home education featuring characters from *The Wizard of Id* comic strip. **Micros; Operating Systems:** Apple, Atari, Coleco's ADAM and ColecoVision, Commodore 64, IBM PC and PCjr; MSX. **Recent Titles:** *Quest for Tires, Wiz Type, Wiz Math, Wiz Spell.* **Distribution Channels:** computer stores, department stores, mass merchandisers, software stores, toy stores. Has not yet bought outside programs; company is now actively soliciting.

SUBMISSION GUIDELINES

Preferred Media: floppy disk, paper printout, or storyboard. Complete documentation required. **Average Company Response Time:** 4 weeks; rejected programs returned. **Payment:** negotiable royalty or outright purchase. **Distribution Rights:** exclusive. **Plugging In:** "We seek entertainment-oriented programs with good graphics and animation. Submission need not have an educational bent nor be based on the *Wizard of Id* character."

Synapse Software
5221 Central Ave.
Richmond, CA 94804
(415) 527-7751
Ihor Wolosenko, director of software
   development
Established 1981

COMPANY PROFILE

Adventure games. Also buys personal productivity, classroom education, systems. **Micros; Operating Systems:** Apple II and IIE, Atari 400,

800, 1200, 600XL, 800XL, 1450XL, and 5200, Commodore 64 and VIC-20, IBM PC, TRS-80 Color Computer. **Recent Titles:** *Necromancer, Shamus, Filemanager+.* **Distribution Channels:** bookstores, catalogs, computer stores, consumer electronics stores, department stores, direct mail, discount stores, mass merchandisers, software stores, toy stores, video stores. Buys 10 programs annually; buying outlook increasing.

SUBMISSION GUIDELINES

Preferred Medium: floppy disk. Initial documentation required. **Average Company Response Time:** varies; rejected programs returned. **Payment:** negotiable royalty paid quarterly. **Distribution Rights:** negotiable. **Plugging In:** "Most submissions require substantial modification to meet Synapse play and application standards. Authors should be open-minded and willing to modify as needed. About 80 percent of Synapse products are conceived in house."

Terrapin, Inc.
380 Green St.
Cambridge, MA 02139
(617) 492-8816
John McClees, president
Established 1977

COMPANY PROFILE

Home education using LOGO. Also buys classroom education. **Micros; Operating Systems:** Apple, Commodore 64. **Recent Titles:** *Terrapin LOGO for Apple II, Commodore 64 LOGO.* **Distribution Channels:** bookstores, catalogs, computer stores, consumer electronics stores, department stores, direct mail, mass merchandisers, software stores, toy stores. Has not yet bought outside programs; company is now actively soliciting.

SUBMISSION GUIDELINES

Preferred Medium: floppy disk. Initial documentation required. **Average Company Response Time:** 4 weeks; rejected programs returned on request. **Payment:** negotiable royalty or outright purchase. **Distribution Rights:** negotiable. **Plugging In:** "We do not want spin-off or improved programs based on already existing software. We are only looking for extremely original educational applications of LOGO.''

TG Products
1104 Summit Ave., Suite 110
Plano, TX 75074
(214) 424-8568
Don R. Geyer, vice president of marketing
Established 1983

COMPANY PROFILE

Arcade, maze, adventure games. Also buys personal productivity, classroom education. **Micros; Operating Systems:** Apple, Atari, Commodore 64 and VIC-20, IBM PC. **Recent Titles:** *Nightstrike, Droids, Ozzy's Orchard, Abracadabra.* **Distribution Channels:** bookstores, computer stores, consumer electronics stores, department stores, discount stores, mass merchandisers, software stores, toy stores. Buys 24 to 30 programs annually; buying outlook increasing.

SUBMISSION GUIDELINES

Preferred Medium: floppy disk. Initial documentation required. **Average Company Response Time:** 6 to 8 weeks; rejected programs returned. **Payment:** negotiable royalty paid monthly or outright purchase. **Distribution Rights:** exclusive. **Plugging In:** Company has a special interest in ''arcade-style'' games that will complement firm's line of joysticks and trackballs. The company will also consider business applications.

THORN EMI Home Video
1370 Avenue of the Americas
New York, NY 10019
(212) 977-8990
Jay Press, director of market development
Established 1982

COMPANY PROFILE

Action, adventure, sports, games. Also buys personal productivity. **Micros; Operating Systems:** Apple, Atari 400, 800, and 1200, Commodore 64 and VIC-20, IBM PC, TI 99/4A.

Recent Titles: *Submarine Commander, Fourth Encounter, Orc Attack.* **Distribution Channels:** computer stores, consumer electronics stores, department stores, software stores, video stores. No annual buying limit.

SUBMISSION GUIDELINES

Preferred Medium: cassette tape. Complete documentation required. **Average Company Response Time:** ''several weeks''; rejected programs returned. **Payment:** outright purchase. **Distribution rights:** negotiable.

Tiger Electronic Toys, Inc.
909 Orchard
Mundelein, IL 60060
(312) 949-8100
Ron Taylor, software development
Established 1979

COMPANY PROFILE

Arcade and adventure games. **Micros; Operating Systems:** Atari, Commodore 64 and VIC-20, TI 99/4A. **Recent Titles:** *Miner 2049er, Polaris.* **Distribution Channels:** computer stores, department stores, discount stores, mass merchandisers, software stores, toy stores, video stores. Buys five programs annually; buying outlook increasing.

SUBMISSION GUIDELINES

Preferred Media: floppy disk, cassette tape. Complete documentation required. **Average Company Response Time:** 2 to 4 weeks; rejected programs returned. **Payment:** negotiable royalty or outright purchase. **Distribution Rights:** negotiable. **Plugging In:** ''Due to all the sophisticated games already on the market, any program submitted must be novel or unique and have superior graphics and sound.''

TMQ Software
626 S. Wheeling Rd.
Wheeling, IL 60090
(312) 520-4440
Tod Zipnick, chief executive officer
Established 1980

COMPANY PROFILE

Arcade games and home education. Also buys personal productivity, classroom education. **Micros; Operating Systems:** Apple, Atari, Commodore 64, IBM PC and PCjr. **Recent Titles:** *File-Fax, Rat Patrol, PigPen.* **Distribution Channels:** computer stores, department stores, original equipment manufacturers, software stores. No annual buying limit.

SUBMISSION GUIDELINES

Preferred Media: floppy disk, cassette tape, paper printout. Initial documentation required. **Average Company Response Time:** 1 to 3 weeks; rejected programs returned. **Payment:** negotiable royalty or outright purchase. **Distribution Rights:** negotiable. **Plugging In:** Company does a lot of programming for other publishers (20 percent of all Atari cartridges are done by TMQ). Firm has a large need for programmers who can do game conversions (for a one-time fee). For original software, company seeks "unique" games and low-end business applications.

Tom Mix Software
3424 College N.E.
Grand Rapids, MI 49505
(616) 364-4791
Tom Mix, president
Established 1981

COMPANY PROFILE

Arcade games, flight simulation. Also buys personal productivity, classroom education, systems. **Micros; Operating Systems:** TRS-80 Color Computer. **Recent Titles:** *Donkey King, Trapfall, Buzzard Bait.* **Distribution Channels:** catalogs, computer stores, consumer electronics stores, department stores, direct mail, software stores, video stores. Buys 30 to 50 programs annually; buying outlook increasing.

SUBMISSION GUIDELINES

Preferred Media: floppy disk, cassette tape. Complete documentation required. **Average Company Response Time:** 2 weeks; rejected programs not returned. **Payment:** 25 to 35 percent royalty paid monthly or outright purchase.

Distribution Rights: exclusive. **Plugging In:** Tom Mix cites a constant need for new software. "We feel we pay top royalties."

Tom Snyder Productions, Inc.
123 Mt. Auburn St.
Cambridge, MA 02138
(617) 876-4433
Richard D. Abrams, vice president
Established 1980

COMPANY PROFILE

Home education teaching youngsters basic math, grammar, and reading skills. **Micros; Operating Systems:** Apple, Atari, Commodore 64, IBM PC and PCjr. **Recent Titles:** *The Search Series, Snooper Troops, Fraction Fever, In Search of the Most Amazing Thing.* **Distribution Channel:** major software publishers (Scholastic, Spinnaker, etc.). No annual buying limit.

SUBMISSION GUIDELINES

Preferred Medium: floppy disk. Complete documentation required. **Average Company Response Time:** 1 week; rejected programs returned. **Payment:** outright purchase. **Distribution Rights:** exclusive. **Plugging In:** Company is primarily interested in programmers who can translate already developed games to other systems for a flat fee.

Tronix Publishing, Inc.
8295 S. La Cienega Blvd.
Inglewood, CA 90301
(213) 215-0529
Frank Mullin, director of software development
Established 1982

COMPANY PROFILE

Arcade, action, self-improvement, and home education with mass market appeal. Also buys personal productivity, systems. **Micros; Operating Systems:** Apple, Atari, Commodore 64 and VIC-20, IBM PC and PCjr. **Recent Titles:** *Dollars & Sense, Chatterbee, Juice, Waterline, Suicide Strike.* **Distribution Channels:** computer stores, consumer electronics stores, department stores, discount stores, mass merchandisers, software stores, toy stores, video stores. No annual buying limit.

SUBMISSION GUIDELINES

Preferred Media: floppy disk, cassette tape. Initial documentation required. **Average Company Response Time:** 1 to 4 weeks; rejected programs returned. **Payment:** negotiable royalty or outright purchase (author's preference). **Distribution Rights:** exclusive. **Plugging In:** Company markets games under the Tronix label and personal productivity under the Monogram banner; home education and utilities are packaged for Don't Ask Software. All programs must be "home"-oriented. In the games area, company reviews completed submissions that have a definite advertising and marketing hook. "Many of the games we see play okay, but they just have nothing to hang an ad campaign on. We're looking for titles that lend themselves to an immediately recognizable ad theme." Tronix also wants home education games. Author's guide available.

United Microware Industries, Inc. (UMI)
3503-C Temple Ave.
Pomona, CA 91768
(714) 594-1351
David Lundberg, technical director
Established 1981

COMPANY PROFILE

Adventure and simulation games. Also buys personal productivity, classroom education, business and professional management, systems. **Micros; Operating Systems:** Commodore 64 and VIC-20, Atari 400 and 800. **Recent Titles:** *Motor Mania, Pennant Drive, Grand Master.* **Distribution Channels:** bookstores, catalogs, computer stores, consumer electronics stores, department stores, mass merchandisers, software stores, toy stores. Buys 15 to 20 programs annually; buying outlook increasing.

SUBMISSION GUIDELINES

Preferred Medium: floppy disk. Complete documentation required. **Average Company Response Time:** 2 weeks; rejected programs returned. **Payment:** negotiable royalty paid quarterly. **Distribution Rights:** exclusive. **Plugging In:** United Microware says "each submission is considered on its merits." Author's guide available.

Victory Software Corporation
1410 Russell Rd.
Paoli, PA 19301
(215) 296-3787
Bruce Robinson, president
Established 1982

COMPANY PROFILE

Adventure, arcade games. **Micros; Operating Systems:** Commodore 64 and VIC-20, Texas Instruments, Timex Sinclair. **Recent Titles:** *Bounty Hunter, Creator's Revenge.* **Distribution Channels:** catalogs, computer stores, consumer electronics stores, department stores, direct mail, distributors, mass merchandisers, software stores, video stores. Buys 12 programs annually; buying outlook increasing.

SUBMISSION GUIDELINES

Preferred Media: floppy disk or cassette tape. Complete documentation to be arranged between company and author. **Average Company Response Time:** 2 to 6 weeks (fall is company's busiest season; authors are urged to submit programs during the slower, midsummer period); rejected programs returned. **Payment:** usually monthly negotiable royalty but company may purchase programs outright. **Distribution Rights:** exclusive. **Plugging In:** Arcade games must have some machine code or they "won't go fast enough. Put copyright notice on and in the program before showing it around (even to friends) to avoid letting it slip into the public domain. Also, be sure to put your name and address on the disk's label. You'd be surprised at how many tapes we get with no identification." Don't send a query letter or other inquiry because "it clogs things up."

Walt Disney Telecommunications & Non-
   Theatrical Company
Computer Software Division
500 South Buena Vista St.
Burbank, CA 91521
(213) 840-1574
Does not actively solicit.

Warlock Software, division of Tylos, Inc.
1900 Emery St., Suite 318

Atlanta, GA 30318
(404) 352-1015
Issam N. Haddad, software author
Established 1983

COMPANY PROFILE

Novelties. Also buys classroom education. **Micros; Operating Systems:** Apple II, II +, and IIe; Apple DOS 3.3. **Recent Title:** *Soothsayer—The Electronic I Ching.* **Distribution Channels:** direct mail, software stores. Has not yet bought outside programs; company is now actively soliciting.

SUBMISSION GUIDELINES

Preferred Medium: floppy disk. Complete documentation required. **Average Company Response Time:** 4 to 5 weeks; rejected programs returned. **Payment:** negotiable. **Distribution Rights:** negotiable. **Plugging In:** Warlock requires that authors submit a summary of program objectives and functions and system environment and test results if applicable.

Warner Software
666 Fifth Ave.
New York, NY 10103
(212) 484-3129
Richard Sarnoff, director of software
   development and acquisitions
Established 1982

COMPANY PROFILE

Home education, leisure time, games. Also buys personal productivity. **Micros; Operating Systems:** Apple II, Atari, Commodore 64, IBM PC. **Recent Titles:** in development. **Distribution Channels:** bookstores, catalogs, computer stores, consumer electronics stores, department stores, direct mail, discount stores, mass merchandisers, software stores, supermarkets, toy stores, video stores. Has not yet bought outside programs; company is now actively soliciting.

SUBMISSION GUIDELINES

Preferred Medium: floppy disk. Initial documentation required. **Average Company Response Time:** 1 week; rejected programs returned with

SASE. **Payment:** 10 to 20 percent royalty paid quarterly or outright purchase. **Distribution Rights:** negotiable. **Plugging In:** "Author should submit résumé, clear explanation of his or her software, and an indication of the target market. Additional or background materials are usually helpful. High-quality, innovative software submissions are encouraged. Each arrangement is individually tailored as appropriate."

Windcrest Software, Inc.
P.O. Box 423
Waynesboro, PA 17268
(717) 794-2191
Kevin Burton, software product manager
Established 1982

COMPANY PROFILE

Action games and simulations. Also buys personal productivity, classroom education, business and professional management, systems. **Micros; Operating Systems:** Apple, Atari, Commodore 64, IBM PC, Timex Sinclair 1000 and 2000, TRS-80 I, III, and Color Computer. **Recent Titles:** *Baseball's Best, Analogies, Panzer War.* **Distribution Channels:** bookstores, catalogs, computer stores, consumer electronics stores, direct mail, software stores. Buys 24 programs annually; buying outlook increasing.

SUBMISSION GUIDELINES

Preferred Medium: floppy disk. Complete documentation required. **Average Company Response Time:** 2 weeks; rejected programs returned. **Payment:** 15 percent royalty paid semiannually (with cash advance). **Distribution Rights:** exclusive. **Plugging In:** "With your submission, indicate expected target audience and price range." Author's guide available.

Window, Inc.
469 Pleasant St.
Watertown, MA 02172
(617) 923-9147
Henry Olds, Jr., publisher
Established 1982

COMPANY PROFILE

Disk-based magazine published monthly that focuses on learning applications; includes feature programs, games, articles, and reviews of software under development. Also buys personal productivity, classroom education. **Micros; Operating Systems:** Apple. **Recent Cover Stories:** "Window-on-BASIC" (*Window,* vol. 1.1), "Notebook" (*Window,* vol. 1.2), "Mini-Songwriter" (*Window,* vol. 1.3). **Distribution Channel:** direct mail. Buys approximately 100 programs annually; buying outlook increasing.

SUBMISSION GUIDELINES

Preferred Medium: floppy disk. Initial documentation required. **Average Company Response Time:** 2 weeks; rejected programs returned. **Payment:** negotiable outright purchase. **Distribution Rights:** nonexclusive.

––––––––––

Wizard Video Games
948 N. Fairfax Ave.
Los Angeles, CA 90046
(213) 859-0034
Alison E. Frankley, director of software
  development and acquisitions
Established 1982

COMPANY PROFILE

Games based on movies. Also buys classroom education. **Micros; Operating Systems:** Atari VCS 2600, 400, 800, and 1200, Commodore 64 and VIC-20. **Recent Titles:** *Texas Chainsaw Massacre, Halloween, Movie Trivia Quiz.* **Distribution Channels:** computer stores, consumer electronics stores, department stores, direct mail, mass merchandisers, software stores, video stores. Buys 6 to 10 programs annually; buying outlook increasing.

SUBMISSION GUIDELINES

Preferred Medium: floppy disk. Complete documentation required. **Average Company Response Time:** varies; rejected programs returned. **Payment:** negotiable royalty or outright purchase. **Distribution Rights:** negotiable. **Plugging In:** "We are looking to acquire educational games for home computers."

––––––––––

Xerox Education Publications, Computer
  Software Division
245 Long Hill Rd.
Middletown, CT 06457
(203) 347-7251
Fritz J. Luecke, manager of computer software
Established 1983

COMPANY PROFILE

Arcade-style home education for ages 3 to 6 featuring the "Stickybear" character. Also buys classroom education. **Micros; Operating Systems:** Apple II and II + ; Apple DOS 3.3. **Recent Titles:** *Stickybear Bop, Stickybear ABC, Stickybear Numbers, Old Ironsides.* **Distribution Channels:** bookstores, catalogs, computer stores, consumer electronics stores, department stores, direct mail, mass merchandisers, software stores. No annual buying limit (all programs bought outside).

SUBMISSION GUIDELINES

Preferred Medium: floppy disk. Initial documentation required. **Average Company Response Time:** 6 to 8 weeks; rejected programs returned. **Payment:** negotiable royalty or outright purchase. **Distribution Rights:** negotiable.

––––––––––

CROSS-REFERENCES—RECREATION

The following companies also buy recreation software. Their complete listings may be found under the major headings shown.

PERSONAL PRODUCTIVITY

Acorn Software, division of Banbury Books
Alphanetics Software
Computerized Management Systems
Computer Software Associates, Inc.
Digital Marketing Corporation
Dynacomp, Inc.
Harper & Row Electronic and Technical Publishing
Hoyle and Hoyle Software, Inc.
Orbyte Software
Pacific TriMicro
PC Disk Magazine
Powersoft, Inc.
The Quick Brown Fox Company
Reader's Digest Services, Inc.
Sams Software, division of Howard W. Sams, Inc.
Scarborough Systems, Inc.
Silicon Valley Systems, Inc.
Software Publishing Corporation
T&F Software

CLASSROOM EDUCATION

Bertamax, Inc.
BrainBank, Inc.
Cybertronics International
DesignWare, Inc.
Developmental Learning Materials
Discovery Games
Edu-Ware Services, Inc. (an MSA Company)
Electronic Courseware Systems, Inc.
Houghton Mifflin Company
Innovative Programming Associates, Inc.
Krell Software Corporation
McGraw-Hill Book Company
Micro-Ed, Inc.
Micro Power & Light Company
Milliken Publishing Company

Random House School Division
RockRoy, Inc.
Scholastic, Inc.
Science Research Associates, Inc.
SouthWest EdPsych Services
Teach Yourself by Computer Software
T.H.E.S.I.S.
John Wiley & Sons

BUSINESS AND PROFESSIONAL MANAGEMENT

Alternative Software, Inc. (formerly Lens Masterson & Associates)
Eagle Software Publishing, Inc.
Epson America, Inc.
Hewlett-Packard, Personal Computer Division
IBM External Submissions
Manhattan Software
MMG Micro Software
NEC Home Electronics USA
Peachtree Associates, Inc.
Pioneer Software
Resource Software International, Inc.
Sensible Software, Inc.
Sunrise Software, Inc.

SYSTEMS

Alpha Software Corporation
Apparat, Inc.
Aurora Software
Digital Research, Inc. Computer Products Division
InfoSoft Systems, Inc.
The Micro Works, Inc.
MicroSPARC, Inc.
The Software Toolworks
Southeastern Software
Southwestern Data Systems

Personal Productivity

Acorn Software, division of Banbury Books
7655 Leesburg Pike
Falls Church, VA 22182
(703) 893-0868
Daphne Schor, president
Established 1979

COMPANY PROFILE

Financial management. Also buys recreation, business and professional management. **Micros; Operating Systems:** Atari 400 and 800, IBM PC, TRS-80 III and IV. **Recent Titles:** *Evasion, Money Manager.* **Distribution Channels:** bookstores, computer stores, direct mail, software stores. No annual buying limit (all programs bought outside).

SUBMISSION GUIDELINES

Preferred Medium: floppy disk. Complete documentation required. **Average Company Response Time:** 4 to 6 weeks; rejected programs returned with SASE. **Payment:** negotiable royalty paid quarterly. **Distribution Rights:** exclusive. **Plugging In:** "We don't want look-alikes of what is already on the market. Study the field carefully. We want something different." Author's guide available.

Alphanetics Software
P.O. Box 339
Forestville, CA 95436
(707) 887-7237
Mark Davis, director of software development
　　and acquisitions
Established 1976

COMPANY PROFILE

Personal scheduling, portfolio management. Also buys recreation, classroom education, business and professional management. **Micros; Operating Systems:** IBM PC and XT. **Recent Titles:** *Business Pac I, Auto Dialer, BASIC Instruction Course.* **Distribution Channels:** direct mail, software stores. Buys six programs annually; buying outlook increasing.

SUBMISSION GUIDELINES

Preferred Medium: floppy disk. Complete documentation to be arranged between author and company. **Average Company Response Time:** 1 week; rejected programs returned. **Payment:** outright purchase. **Distribution Rights:** exclusive. **Plugging In:** Alphanetics is "looking for engineering programs and is open to new programs involving personal and business management, education, entertainment, or any original idea."

Arlington Software + Systems
97 Bartlett Ave.
Arlington, MA 02174
(617) 641-0290
Peter Brajer, president
Established 1981

COMPANY PROFILE

Home management. Also buys business and professional management, systems. **Micros; Operating Systems:** PC DOS. **Recent Titles:** *PCHMS—Personal Computer Home Management System, PCAT—Personal Computer Automated Telemarketing System.* **Distribution Channels:** catalogs, computer stores, direct mail, software stores. No annual buying limit.

SUBMISSION GUIDELINES

Preferred Medium: floppy disk. Initial documentation required. **Average Company Response Time:** 2 to 6 weeks; rejected programs returned. **Payment:** 10 to 30 percent royalty paid quarterly or outright purchase. **Distribution Rights:** exclusive. **Plugging In:** Author's guide available.

———————

Artsci
5547 Satsuma
North Hollywood, CA 91601
(213) 985-5763
William Smith, chief executive officer
Established 1977

COMPANY PROFILE

Personal finance, spreadsheet, and other productivity packages aimed at the first-time computer user. Also buys business and professional management. **Micros; Operating Systems:** Apple and compatibles. **Recent Titles:** *MAGICALC, MAGIC WINDOW, MAGIC MEMORY.* **Distribution Channels:** computer stores, direct mail, software stores. Buys three programs annually; buying outlook increasing.

SUBMISSION GUIDELINES

Preferred Medium: floppy disk. Complete documentation required. **Average Company Re-**

sponse Time: 4 to 6 weeks; rejected programs returned. **Payment:** negotiable royalty paid monthly or quarterly. **Distribution Rights:** exclusive.

———————

Best Programs
5314 Leesburg Pike
Alexandria, VA 22302
(703) 931-1300
Jim Peterson, director of software development
    and acquisitions
Established 1982

COMPANY PROFILE

Personal finance. Also buys business and professional management. **Micros; Operating Systems:** IBM PC, TI Professional, Wang. **Recent Titles:** *Personal Computer/Personal Finance Program, Personal Computer/Fixed Asset System, Personal Computer/Professional Finance Program.* **Distribution Channels:** bookstores, catalogs, computer stores, consumer electronics stores, department stores, discount stores, mass merchandisers, software stores. Buys seven programs annually; buying outlook increasing.

SUBMISSION GUIDELINES

Preferred Medium: floppy disk. Complete documentation required. **Average Company Response Time:** 1 week; rejected programs returned. **Payment:** negotiable royalty or outright purchase. **Distribution Rights:** negotiable.

———————

Bluebird's Computer Software
P.O. Box 339
Wyandotte, MI 48192
(313) 285-4455
Does not actively solicit.

———————

Bruce & James Program Publishers, Inc.
Wharfside Bldg.
680 Beach St., Suite 354
San Francisco, CA 94109
(415) 775-8500
Does not actively solicit.

———————

Computer Software Associates, Inc.
50 Teed Dr.
Raldolph, MA 02368
(617) 961-5700
Sandow S. Ruby, president
Established 1982

COMPANY PROFILE

Spreadsheets. Also buys recreation, classroom education, business and professional management. **Micros; Operating Systems:** Apple IIe, Commodore 64 and VIC-20. **Recent Titles:** *PractiCalc 64, Sprint Typer, Zeppelin*. **Distribution Channels:** bookstores, catalogs, computer stores, consumer electronics stores, department stores, discount stores, mass merchandisers, software stores, toy stores, video stores. Buys 10 to 15 programs annually; buying outlook increasing.

SUBMISSION GUIDELINES

Preferred Medium: floppy disk. Complete documentation to be arranged between author and company. **Average Company Response Time:** varies; rejected programs returned with SASE. **Payment:** negotiable. **Distribution Rights:** negotiable. **Plugging In:** Along with disk, send program title and a one- to two-paragraph description of the program's function, features, and operating instructions.

Computerized Management Systems
1039 Cadiaz Dr.
Simi, CA 93065
(805) 526-0151
Dennis Jarvis, director of software development
Established 1981

COMPANY PROFILE

Accounting and household chore management programs. Also buys recreation, classroom education, business and professional management. **Micros; Operating Systems:** Apple, Atari, Commodore 64, IBM PC and PCjr, TRS-80. **Recent Titles:** *Basic Accountant, Electronic Checkbook, Grocery List*. **Distribution Channels:** company markets all software through third-party publishers such as McGraw-Hill,

Reader's Digest, and Simon and Schuster. No annual buying limit.

SUBMISSION GUIDELINES

Preferred Media: floppy disk, cassette tape. Complete documentation to be arranged between author and company. **Average Company Response Time:** varies; rejected programs returned. **Payment:** negotiable royalty of up to 35 percent or outright purchase. **Distribution Rights:** negotiable. **Plugging In:** Company seeks "genuinely useful software for the home" but does not want games. Will also assist authors in packaging and marketing their own programs.

Continental Software
11223 S. Hindry Ave.
Los Angeles, CA 90045
(215) 410-3977
Denny Mosier, marketing manager
Established 1980

COMPANY PROFILE

Personal financial management. Also buys business and professional management, systems. **Micros; Operating Systems:** Apple, IBM PC; Apple DOS 3.3, IBM PC-DOS 1.1 and 2.0. **Recent Titles:** *FCM/Form Letter, ULTRAFILE*. **Distribution Channels:** bookstores, catalogs, computer stores, consumer electronics stores, direct mail, software stores. No annual buying limit.

SUBMISSION GUIDELINES

Preferred Medium: floppy disk. Complete documentation required. **Average Company Response Time:** 12 weeks; rejected programs returned. **Payment:** negotiable royalty. **Distribution Rights:** exclusive.

Digital Marketing Corporation
2363 Boulevard Circle
Walnut Creek, CA 94595
(415) 947-1000 or (800) 826-2222
Eric J. Matson, marketing coordinator
Established 1979

COMPANY PROFILE

Project management, word processing, appointment scheduling. Also buys recreation, classroom education, business and professional management, systems. **Micros; Operating Systems:** CP/M, CP/M-86, MS-DOS, PC-DOS, UCSD. **Recent Titles:** *Notebook, Milestone, Datebook.* **Distribution Channels:** catalogs, computer stores, direct mail, discount stores, mass merchandisers, software stores. Buys 5 to 10 programs annually; buying outlook the same.

SUBMISSION GUIDELINES

Preferred Medium: floppy disk. Initial documentation required. **Average Company Response Time:** 8 weeks; rejected programs returned. **Payment:** nogotiable royalty paid monthly. **Distribution Rights:** exclusive. **Plugging In:** Firm is interested in programs that "are unique or offer better or easier ways to perform the tasks of an existing program; are easy to learn; provide valuable services to the user, such as saving time and/or money; are educating, entertaining, or challenging; make effective use of microcomputing technology." Author's guide available.

Dynacomp, Inc.
1427 Monroe Ave.
Rochester, NY 14618
(716) 442-8960
B. Rivers, director of software development
Established 1978

COMPANY PROFILE

Comprehensive personal financial management. Also buys recreation, classroom education, business and professional management, systems. **Micros; Operating Systems:** Apple, Atari, Canon, Commodore, IBM, NEC, Northstar, Osborne, SuperBrain, TRS-80; 8-bit CP/M. **Recent Titles:** *Personal Finance System, Microcomputer Stock Program, Basic Statistical Subroutines.* **Distribution Channels:** bookstores, catalogs, computer stores, consumer electronics stores, direct mail, software stores, video stores. Buys over 150 programs annually; buying outlook increasing.

SUBMISSION GUIDELINES

Preferred Medium: floppy disk. Complete documentation required. **Average Company Response Time:** 2 weeks; rejected programs returned. **Payment:** 10 to 20 percent royalty paid monthly. **Distribution Rights:** negotiable. **Plugging In:** Above all, Dynacomp asks intelligence. Game and simulation programs, for example, should not be considered trivial items but should provide many hours of intellectual stimulation.

Harper & Row Electronic and Technical
   Publishing
10 East 53d St.
New York, NY 10022
(212) 207-7000
Marjorie Singer and Laura Bachko, editors
Established 1982

COMPANY PROFILE

Word processing programs designed for ease of use. Also buys recreation and classroom education. **Micros; Operating Systems:** Apple II and IIe, IBM PC. **Recent Titles:** *The Write Stuff, Quiz Master.* **Distribution Channels:** bookstores, computer stores, software stores. Buys all its programs from outside (two to date); buying outlook increasing.

SUBMISSION GUIDELINES

Preferred Medium: floppy disk. Complete documentation required. **Average Company Response Time:** 4 to 6 weeks; rejected programs returned. **Payment:** Negotiable royalty paid biannually. **Distribution Rights:** exclusive.

Hoyle and Hoyle Software, Inc.
716 S. Elam Ave.
Greensboro, NC 27403
(919) 378-1050
Hughes B. Hoyle, III, director of software
   development and acquisitions
Established 1980

COMPANY PROFILE

Word processing. Also buys recreation, classroom education, business and professional management. **Micros; Operating Systems:** Apple, Heath, IBM PC, TRS-80. **Recent Titles:** *Report Writer, QUERY!, A Remarkable Experience.* **Distribution Channels:** catalogs, computer stores, consumer electronics stores, discount stores. Buys two to three programs annually; buying outlook increasing.

SUBMISSION GUIDELINES

Preferred Medium: floppy disk. Complete documentation required. **Average Company Response Time:** 4 weeks; rejected programs returned. **Payment:** 20 to 25 percent royalty paid quarterly. **Distribution Rights:** negotiable. **Plugging In:** Use assembly language only.

IJG, Inc.
1953 W. 11th Street
Upland, CA 91786
(714) 946-5805
Harve Pennington, president
Established 1976

COMPANY PROFILE

Word processing and support programs. Also buys business and professional management and systems. **Micros; Operating Systems:** Apple II, IIe, and II+, Atari, Commodore 64, IBM PC, Sharp, Timex, TRS-80. **Recent Titles:** *Electric Pencil PC, Pencil Tutor, Pencil Ace.* **Distribution Channels:** bookstores, computer stores, direct mail, software stores. Buys 20 programs annually; buying outlook increasing.

SUBMISSION GUIDELINES

Preferred Medium: floppy disk. Initial documentation required. **Average Company Response Time:** 2 to 3 weeks; rejected programs returned. **Payment:** 10 to 25 percent royalty paid monthly. **Distribution Rights:** exclusive. **Plugging In:** Company wants to see a "finished software product, not a work in progress." Also wants—at the least—a manual outline, although

manual will be finished in house. Is also eager to look at programs that support those already in the company line.

Masterworks Software, Inc.
25834 Narbonne Ave.
Lomita, CA 90274
(213) 539-7486
Thomas K. Moch, president
Established 1980

COMPANY PROFILE

Financial management. Also buys business and professional management. **Micros; Operating Systems:** Apple II, IBM PC. **Recent Title:** *Chequemate Plus.* **Distribution Channels:** computer stores, direct mail. No annual buying limit.

SUBMISSION GUIDELINES

Preferred Medium: floppy disk. Complete documentation required. **Average Company Response Time:** 2 weeks; rejected programs returned. **Payment:** 10 to 25 percent royalty paid quarterly. **Distribution Rights:** negotiable.

Micromatic Programming Company
Cedar Corners Station
P.O. Box 16735
Stamford, CT 06905
(203) 324-3009
Netta Stern, president
Established 1979

COMPANY PROFILE

Personal finance programs. **Micros; Operating Systems:** IBM PC, TRS-80 I, III, and IV. **Recent Titles:** *Tax/Saver, Tax/Forecaster, Pro Tax/Forecaster.* **Distribution Channels:** catalogs, direct mail, software stores. Has not yet bought outside programs; company is now actively soliciting.

SUBMISSION GUIDELINES

Preferred Medium: floppy disk. Complete documentation required. **Average Company Re-**

sponse Time: 6 to 8 weeks; rejected programs returned. **Payment:** negotiable royalty. **Distribution Rights:** exclusive.

MicroPRO International Corporation
33 San Pablo Ave.
San Rafael, CA 94901
(415) 499-1200
Does not actively solicit.

Mindware
15 Tech Circle
Natick, MA 01760
(617) 655-3388
Does not actively solicit.

Orbyte Software
P.O. Box 948
Waterbury, CT 06720
(203) 753-8308
Douglas Adams, director of software
    development and acquisitions
Established 1982

COMPANY PROFILE

Financial planning. Also buys recreation, classroom education, business and professional management. **Micros; Operating Systems:** Commodore 64 and VIC-20. **Recent Titles:** *Accounts Receivable, Accounts Payable, Payroll.* **Distribution Channels:** bookstores, computer stores, consumer electronics stores, department stores, mass merchandisers, software stores, toy stores, video stores. Buys 20 programs annually; buying outlook increasing.

SUBMISSION GUIDELINES

Preferred Media: floppy disk, cassette tape, paper printout. Complete documentation required. **Average Company Response Time:** 2 weeks; rejected programs returned with SASE. **Payment:** negotiable royalty or outright purchase. **Distribution Rights:** exclusive. **Plugging In:** Since most of Orbyte's programming is done in house, the company is seeking only "high-quality

programs." Orbyte's current major needs are "high-action" games, business and educational software.

Pacific TriMicro
901 East Summit Hill
Knoxville, TN 37915
(615) 522-4824
Barry L. Rice, vice president
Established 1982

COMPANY PROFILE

Home and personal financial management. Also buys recreation, business and professional management, systems. **Micros; Operating Systems:** Commodore 64, Timex Sinclair. **Recent Titles:** *EZ Tutor, The Trilogy Series, Tri Fourth.* **Distribution Channels:** computer stores, consumer electronics stores, department stores, software stores, video stores. Buys 6 to 12 programs annually; buying outlook the same.

SUBMISSION GUIDELINES

Preferred Medium: floppy disk. Complete documentation required. **Average Company Response Time:** 1 week; rejected programs not returned. **Payment:** 10 percent royalty paid quarterly or outright purchase. **Distribution Rights:** exclusive. **Plugging In:** Pacific Tri-Micro is looking for more business and educational software for the Commodore 64.

Panasonic, Consumer Electronics Group
One Panasonic Way
Secaucus, NJ 07094
(201) 348-7000
Does not actively solicit.

PBL Corporation
P.O. Box 559
Wayzata, MN 55341
(612) 471-7644
Richard S. Parker, director of software
    development and acquisitions
Established 1981

COMPANY PROFILE

Personal portfolio management. Also buys business and professional management. **Micros; Operating Systems:** Apple DOS, MS-DOS. **Recent Title:** *The Personal Investor.* **Distribution Channels:** computer stores, distributors, software stores. Buys three programs annually; buying outlook the same.

SUBMISSION GUIDELINES

Preferred Medium: floppy disk. Complete documentation required. **Average Company Response Time:** 8 weeks; rejected programs returned. **Payment:** negotiable royalty paid quarterly. **Distribution Rights:** exclusive.

PC Disk Magazine
One Park Ave., Dept. 732
New York, NY 10016
(212) 725-7947
Morris Effron, editor
Established 1983

COMPANY PROFILE

Disk-based magazine issued every 6 weeks featuring a variety of personal finance, household chore management, and word processing packages. Also buys recreation, classroom education, business and professional management, systems. **Micros; Operating Systems:** IBM PC and compatibles. **Recent Titles:** *DiskMap, Loan Analyzer, Perpetual Calendar, Hide and Sink.* **Distribution Channels:** bookstores, computer stores, direct mail, software stores. Buys over 100 programs annually; buying outlook increasing.

SUBMISSION GUIDELINES

Preferred Medium: floppy disk. Complete documentation required. **Average Company Response Time:** 4 weeks; rejected programs returned. **Payment:** negotiable royalty (per copy sold). **Distribution Rights:** nonexclusive. **Plugging In:** *PC Disk Magazine* showcases the "less-expensive programs, the small programs that don't generally reach the market." Author's guide available.

Powersoft, Inc.
P.O. Box 157
Pitman, NJ 08071
(609) 589-5500
Jim Powers, president
Established 1978

COMPANY PROFILE

Filing, checkbook, and other personal managers. Also buys recreation (primarily home education), classroom education, business and professional management, systems. **Micros; Operating Systems:** Apple, IBM PC. **Recent Titles:** *Spanish Vocabulary Drill, Supercheckbook III, Address File Generator.* **Distribution Channels:** computer stores, direct mail, software stores. Buys "60 percent" of the titles it sells; buying outlook increasing.

SUBMISSION GUIDELINES

Preferred Medium: floppy disk. Complete documentation required. **Average Company Response Time:** 3 to 4 weeks; rejected programs returned. **Payment:** usually 20 percent royalty (on gross receipts) paid quarterly. **Distribution Rights:** negotiable (majority of licenses are exclusive; nonexclusive license lowers royalty rate). **Plugging In:** "We would like to see software for small business customers, such as accounting packages. Don't make them too complex. We're fairly selective, but we'll look at anything, as long as the author has clearly defined the market for his product."

Practical Programs
1104 Aspen Dr.
Toms River, NJ 08753
(201) 349-6070
Gerry Wagner, director of software development
Established 1980

COMPANY PROFILE

Household helper programs, chore managers, and other applications that ease the stress of everyday living. Also buys business and professional management. **Micros; Operating Systems:** TRS-DOS, NEWDOS 80, DOSPLUS. **Recent Titles:** *Compucal* (calorie counter), *Computer*

Notepad, Electronic Scratchpad, Invoice Genera-tor. **Distribution Channels:** catalogs, computer stores, direct mail, software stores. Buys two to three programs annually; buying outlook increasing.

SUBMISSION GUIDELINES

Preferred Medium: floppy disk. Initial documentation required. **Average Company Response Time:** 3 weeks; rejected programs returned. **Payment:** 20 percent royalty paid quarterly. **Distribution Rights:** nonexclusive. **Plugging In:** Author's guide available.

The Quick Brown Fox Company
548 Broadway
New York, NY 10012
(212) 925-8290
June Spirer, president
Established 1980

COMPANY PROFILE

Word processing, home, and work chore managers. Also buys recreation (primarily home education), classroom education, business and professional management. **Micros; Operating Systems:** Commodore 64 and VIC-20. **Recent Titles:** *Quick Brown Fox Word Processing Program, Quick Finger.* **Distribution Channels:** bookstores, catalogs, computer stores, consumer electronics stores, department stores, direct mail, mass merchandisers, software stores, video stores. Has not yet bought outside programs; company is now actively soliciting.

SUBMISSION GUIDELINES

Preferred media: floppy disk, cassette tape. Initial documentation required. **Average Company Response Time:** 6 to 8 weeks; rejected programs returned. **Payment:** negotiable royalty or outright purchase. **Distribution Rights:** negotiable. **Plugging In:** "We actively encourage authors with bright ideas. We'll review your program even if it's only 60 percent or 70 percent finished; if it shows good commercial potential, we'll market it." Company's goal is to "develop a line of useful productivity software for the home user—spreadsheets, database managers, mailing

lists, etc." Also needed is how-to software ("How about 'how to repair your car' or similar practical tutorials?") and edutainment programs—games with learning values. Author's guide available.

Reader's Digest Services, Inc., Microcomputer
  Software Division
Pleasantville, NY 10570
(914) 241-5738
Ellen Smith, software development design
  manager
Established 1981

COMPANY PROFILE

Personal organization. Also buys recreation, classroom education, business and professional management. **Micros; Operating Systems:** Apple II, II+, and IIe, IBM PC, Commodore 64, TRS-80 III. **Recent Titles:** *ListMaker, Trickster Coyote, Problem Solving Strategies.* **Distribution Channels:** catalogs, software stores. Buys four programs annually; buying outlook increasing.

SUBMISSION GUIDELINES

Preferred Medium: floppy disk. Initial documentation required. **Average Company Response Time:** 10 weeks; rejected programs returned. **Payment:** 5 to 15 percent royalty paid quarterly, or outright purchase. **Distribution Rights:** exclusive. **Plugging In:** Reader's Digest is looking for "educational games and productivity programs for small businesses, homes and schools. We request that interested authors submit original, well-documented and debugged programs, with an accompanying flowchart for our internal evaluation and determination of marketability. Naturally, we encourage the best use of the microcomputer medium." Author's guide available.

Sams Software, Division of Howard W. Sams,
  Inc.
4300 W. 62d St.
Indianapolis, IN 46206
(317) 298-5707
Jim Hunter, director of software development
Established 1980

COMPANY PROFILE

Financial management, real estate analysis. Also buys recreation, systems. **Micros, Operating Systems:** Apple and compatibles, IBM and compatibles. **Recent Titles:** *Mind Tools, Financial Planning, Real Estate Analysis.* **Distribution Channels:** computer stores, direct mail, mass merchandisers, software stores. No annual buying limit.

SUBMISSION GUIDELINES

Preferred Medium: floppy disk. Initial documentation required. **Average Company Response Time:** 2 weeks; rejected programs returned. **Payment:** negotiable royalty (preferred) or outright purchase. **Distribution Rights:** exclusive. **Plugging In:** Author's guide available.

Scarborough Systems, Inc.
25 N. Broadway
Tarrytown, NY 10591
(914) 332-4545
J. Scott Barrus, manager of technical
  development
Established 1983

COMPANY PROFILE

Word processing, household chores, and personal finance. Also buys recreation, classroom education. **Micros; Operating Systems:** Apple, Atari, Commodore 64, IBM PC and PC jr. **Recent Titles:** *Songwriter, Picturewriter, Phi Beta Filer, Pattern Maker.* **Distribution Channels:** bookstores, catalogs, computer stores, consumer electronics stores, department stores, mass merchandisers, software stores, toy stores. No annual buying limit.

SUBMISSION GUIDELINES

Preferred Medium: floppy disk. Initial documentation required. **Average Company Response Time:** 4 to 6 weeks; rejected programs returned. **Payment:** negotiable royalty or outright purchase. **Distribution Rights:** negotiable. **Plugging In:** Scarborough Systems acquired Lightning Software (see Lightning Software, Inc., in Section One) in 1983.

Silicon Valley Systems, Inc.
1625 E. Camino Real #4
Belmont, CA 94002
(415) 593-4344
Suzanne K. Stitt, director of software
  development
Established 1980

COMPANY PROFILE

Word processing. Also buys recreation, classroom education, business and professional management, systems. **Micros; Operating Systems:** Atari, IBM PC; Apple DOS 3.3. **Recent Titles:** *Word Handler II, List Handler, E-Z Learner.* **Distribution Channels:** bookstores, catalogs, computer stores, direct mail, software stores, video stores. Buys 10 programs annually; buying outlook increasing.

SUBMISSION GUIDELINES

Preferred Medium: floppy disk. Initial documentation required. **Average Company Response Time:** 4 weeks; rejected programs returned. **Payment:** 10 to 20 percent royalty paid bi-monthly. **Distribution Rights:** exclusive. **Plugging In:** Author's guide available.

Software Publishing Corporation
1901 Landings Dr.
Mt. View, CA 94043
(415) 962-8910
Pete Sinclair, director of software development
Established 1980

COMPANY PROFILE

Personal organization and planning. also buys recreation, business and professional management. **Micros; Operating Systems:** Apple II and IIe, IBM PC and XT, TRS-80 III and IV. Recent titles: *PFS: File, PFS: Report, PFS: Graph.* **Distribution Channels:** bookstores, catalogs, computer stores, direct mail, mass merchandisers, software stores. Buys 20 programs annually; buying outlook increasing.

SUBMISSION GUIDELINES

Preferred Medium: floppy disk. Initial documentation required. **Average Company Response**

Time: 1 to 4 weeks; rejected programs returned. **Payment:** negotiable royalty. **Distribution Rights:** exclusive. **Plugging In:** Software Publishing is interested in "most kinds of software, with the exception of arcade games and indepth vertical market applications. Personal growth, professional tools, mentally challenging entertainment and educational packages, home management, children's software, personal finance, and hobby software are just some of the applications that we desire." Author's guide available.

T&F Software
10902 Riverside Dr.
North Hollywood, CA 91602
(213) 501-5845
Tracy Talco, cofounder
Established 1981

COMPANY PROFILE

Personal finance, word processing, and information management. Also buys recreation. **Micros; Operating Systems:** Commodore 64, IBM PC and PCjr. **Recent Titles:** *Check-Ease, Data Wiz, Speed Racer, Jet Star.* **Distribution Channels:** computer stores, department stores, discount stores, mass merchandisers, record stores, software stores, toy stores, video stores. Buys one program annually; buying outlook increasing.

SUBMISSION GUIDELINES

Preferred Medium: floppy disk. Complete documentation required. **Average Company Response Time:** 1 week; rejected programs returned. **Payment:** 10 to 15 percent royalty (on gross receipts) paid monthly. **Distribution Rights:** exclusive. **Plugging In:** Company is

particularly interested in home applications and home education. Such titles should have entertainment and play value. "We suggest the author try out anything he writes on other people to see if it has wide appeal before sending it on to us."

Texas Instruments, Inc., Consumer Relations
   Division
P.O. Box 53
Lubbock, TX 79408
(800) 858-4565
Company has discontinued the TI 99/4A home
   computer and is no longer actively soliciting.

———————

Woolf Software Systems, Inc.
6754 Eton Ave.
Canoga Park, CA 91303
(213) 703-8112
Att.: software development manager
Established 1977

COMPANY PROFILE

Personal finance and household chore management. **Micros; Operating Systems:** CP/M, CP/M-86. **Recent Titles:** *Move-It, Money Manager.* **Distribution Channels:** computer stores, software stores. Has no annual buying limit.

SUBMISSION GUIDELINES

Preferred Medium: floppy disk. Initial documentation required. **Average Company Response Time:** 6 to 8 weeks; rejected programs returned. **Payment:** Negotiable royalty or outright purchase. **Distribution Rights:** negotiable.

———————

CROSS-REFERENCES—PERSONAL PRODUCTIVITY

The following companies also buy personal productivity software. Their complete listings may be found under the major headings shown.

RECREATION

Addison-Wesley Publishing Company
Adventure International, Division of Scott Adams, Inc.
Artificial Intelligence Research Group
Artworx Software Company, Inc.
Atari, Inc.
Atari Program Exchange (APX)
Avant-Garde Creations, Inc.
Broderbund Software, Inc.
CBS Software
Cload Publications, Inc.
Coleco Industries, Inc.
Comm*Data Computer House, Inc.
Commodore, Computer Systems Division
CompuServe, Inc.
Cornsoft Group, Inc.
Creative Software
Databar Corporation
Datamost, Inc.
Datasoft, Inc.
Dilithium Press
Electronic Arts
Hayden Software Company
HESWARE
Instant Software, Inc., Division of Wayne Green, Inc.
Intelligent Statements (Screenplay)
International Publishing & Software, Inc.
JMG Software International
Koala Technologies
Lightning Software, Inc., subsidiary of Scarborough Systems
Microcomputers Corporation
MicroLab, Inc.
Muse Software, Inc.
Not-Polyoptics
Passport Designs, Inc.
Penguin Software
Prentice-Hall, Inc.
Quality Software
Rainbow Computing, Inc.
Ranco Software Games, Inc.
Rantom Software
RB Robot Corporation
Roklan Software

Royal Software/COMPUTER PALACE
Sentient Software, Inc.
Sierra On-Line, Inc.
Sim Computer Products, Inc.
Simon and Schuster, Electronic Publishing Group
Sir-tech Software, Inc.
Softsel Computer Products, Inc.
Softside Magazine
Softsync, Inc.
The Software Guild
Source Telecomputing Corporation
SpectraVideo, Inc.
Sterling Swift Publishing Company
Synapse Software
TG Products
THORN EMI Home Video
TMQ Software
Tom Mix Software
Tronix Publishing, Inc.
United Microware Industries, Inc.
Warner Software
Windcrest Software, Inc.
Window, Inc.

CLASSROOM EDUCATION

Electronic Courseware Systems, Inc.
Houghton Mifflin Company
McGraw-Hill Book Company
Science Research Associates, Inc.
T.H.E.S.I.S.
John Wiley & Sons

BUSINESS AND PROFESSIONAL MANAGEMENT

The Business Division, Division of Scott Adams, Inc.
Century Software Systems
CompuTech Group, Inc.
Designer Software
Eagle Software Publishing, Inc.
Epson America, Inc.
IBM External Submissions

Kensington Microware
Legend Industries, Ltd.
Level IV Products, Inc.
Manhattan Software
Mark of the Unicorn
Max Ule & Company
Peachtree Associates, Inc.
Peachtree Software, Inc.
Pioneer Software
Sensible Software, Inc.
Sunrise Software, Inc.
Systems Plus, Inc.
Tristar Data Systems
Western Properties Investment Company, Software Division
Westico, Inc.

SYSTEMS

Alpha Software Corporation
Apparat, Inc.
Cosmopolitan Electronics Corporation
Digital Research, Inc., Computer Products Division
InfoSoft Systems, Inc.
Micro Ap
Micro Works, Inc.
MicroSPARC, Inc.
The Software Toolworks
Southeastern Software
Southwestern Data Systems
Stoneware, Inc.
SuperSoft, Inc.

Classroom Education

Bertamax, Inc.
3647 Stone Way N.
Seattle, WA 98103
(206) 547-4056
Max Jerman, director of software development
and acquisitions
Established 1979

COMPANY PROFILE

Math and reading games primarily for ages 3 to 7. Also buys recreation (home education). **Micros; Operating Systems:** Apple, Atari, Commodore 64, TRS-80; Applesoft, MS-DOS, TRS-DOS. **Recent Titles:** *The Reader, Number Cruncher, Grand Prix Math.* **Distribution Channels:** catalogs, computer stores, educational dealers, mass merchandisers. Buys two to five programs annually; buying outlook the same.

SUBMISSION GUIDELINES

Preferred Medium: floppy disk. Complete documentation required. **Average Company Response Time:** 2 weeks; rejected programs returned. **Payment:** 5 to 10 percent royalty quarterly. **Distribution Rights:** exclusive.

Borg-Warner Educational Systems
600 W. University Dr.
Arlington Heights, IL 60004
(312) 394-1010
Randall L. Gull, director of curriculum
development
Established 1980

COMPANY PROFILE

K-12 skills packages, particularly language skills. **Micros; Operating Systems:** Apple II, TRS-80. **Recent Titles:** *Geometric Concepts, Sentence Structure, Critical Reading.* **Distribution Channel:** direct sales representative. No annual buying limit.

SUBMISSION GUIDELINES

Preferred Medium: floppy disk. Complete documentation to be arranged between author and company. **Average Company Response Time:** 4 weeks; rejected programs returned with SASE. **Payment:** outright purchase. **Distribution Rights:** exclusive.

BrainBank, Inc.
220 Fifth Ave.
New York, NY 10001
(212) 686-6565
Ruth K. Landa, president
Established 1981

COMPANY PROFILE

Tutorials, drill and practice aimed at students who have no computer experience. Also buys recreation. **Micros; Operating Systems:** Apple, Commodore PET. **Recent Titles:** *Word Functions, Classes of Nouns, The Skeletal System.* **Distribution Channels:** catalogs, direct mail, mass merchandisers, software stores. Buys 10 programs annually; buying outlook the same.

SUBMISSION GUIDELINES

Preferred Medium: floppy disk. Complete documentation required. **Average Company Response Time:** 8 weeks; rejected programs returned. **Payment:** negotiable royalty or outright purchase. **Distribution Rights:** negotiable. **Plugging In:** Company is particularly interested in software from classroom teachers or those with teaching experience.

Cavri Systems, Inc.
26 Trumbull St.
New Haven, CT 06511
(203) 562-4979
Marc Schwartz, director of software
   development and acquisitions
Established 1980

COMPANY PROFILE

Game-oriented language arts and instructional programs for K-12. **Micros; Operating System:** Apple. **Recent Titles:** *Wizard of Oz, Of Mice and Men.* **Distribution Channel:** Textbook publishers. Buys three programs annually; buying outlook increasing.

SUBMISSION GUIDELINES

Preferred Medium: floppy disk. Complete documentation to be arranged between author and company. **Average Company Response Time:** 4 weeks: rejected programs returned. **Payment:** outright purchase. **Distribution Rights:** exclusive. **Plugging In:** Cavri wants "game simulations with graphics, *not* drill and practice."

COMPress, Inc.
P.O. Box 102

Wentworth, NH 03282
(603) 764-5831
Tom Sears, general manager
Established 1978

COMPANY PROFILE

Science skills, games, drill and practice aimed at high school and up. **Micros; Operating Systems:** Apple II, II+, IIe, (and compatibles). **Recent Titles:** *Chemistry, Biology Series.* **Distribution Channels:** computer stores, direct mail, software stores. Buys 12 programs annually; buying outlook increasing.

SUBMISSION GUIDELINES

Preferred Medium: floppy disk. Complete documentation required. **Average Company Response Time:** "several weeks"; rejected programs returned. **Payment:** negotiable royalty paid biannually. **Distribution Rights:** exclusive. **Plugging In:** "We concentrate on the hard sciences and languages, such as English as a second language. We look at both hard drill and practices and games that teach."

Compu-Tations, Inc.
P.O. Box 502
Troy, MI 48099
(313) 689-5059
Charles D. James, director of software
   development and acquisitions
Established 1981

COMPANY PROFILE

Skill-building programs. **Micros; Operating Systems:** Apple II+ and IIe, Atari 800, IBM PC. **Recent Titles:** *Word Power, Special Skill Builders I.* **Distribution Channels:** bookstores, catalogs, computer stores, consumer electronics stores, department stores, direct mail, mass merchandisers, software stores. No annual buying limit.

SUBMISSION GUIDELINES

Preferred Medium: floppy disk. Complete documentation required. **Average Company Response Time:** 6 weeks; rejected programs returned. **Payment:** 15 to 25 percent royalty paid quarterly or outright purchase. **Distribution Rights:** exclusive.

Computer Curriculum Corporation
P.O. Box 10080
Palo Alto, CA 94303
(415) 494-8450
Does not actively solicit.

Cybertronics International
999 Mt. Kemble Ave.
Morristown, NJ 07960
(201) 766-7681
Hank Vigel, product manager
Established 1980

COMPANY PROFILE

Programming languages tutorials. Also buys recreation. **Micros; Operating Systems:** Apple II, IIe, and III, IBM PC. **Recent Titles:** *Karec the Robot, Cyber LOGO Turtle.* **Distribution Channels:** computer stores, direct mail, educational catalogs, software stores. Buys three to four programs annually; buying outlook increasing.

SUBMISSION GUIDELINES

Preferred Medium: floppy disk. Complete documentation required. **Average Company Response Time:** 2 to 8 weeks; rejected programs returned. **Payment:** negotiable royalty or outright purchase. **Distribution Rights:** exclusive. **Plugging In:** "A great deal of work is going on in converting. Our primary interest is educational software and games."

DesignWare, Inc.
185 Berry St., Suite 158
San Francisco, CA 94107
(415) 546-1866
Marcia Zier, editor
Established 1980

COMPANY PROFILE

K-12 software designed around familiar game scenarios. Also buys recreation (home education). **Micros; Operating Systems:** Apple, Atari,

Commodore 64, IBM PC and PCjr. **Recent Titles:** *Spellicopter, Math Maze, Spellagraph, CryptoCube.* **Distribution Channels:** computer stores, direct mail, software stores, third-party educational publishers. Has not yet bought outside programs; company is now actively soliciting.

SUBMISSION GUIDELINES

Preferred Medium: floppy disk. Complete documentation required. **Average Company Response Time:** 4 weeks; rejected programs returned. **Payment:** negotiable royalty (depending on level of program development). **Distribution Rights:** exclusive. **Plugging In:** Company prefers "fully developed programs, but will look at storyboards." Firm is particularly interested in programs that are "highly graphics-oriented." Author's guide available.

Developmental Learning Materials
One DLM Park
Allen, TX 75002
(800) 527-4747
Karen Piper, project editor, microcomputer
   software
Established 1982

COMPANY PROFILE

Special education, math, language arts skills development for preschool, elementary. Also buys recreation. **Micros; Operating Systems:** Apple II, II+, and IIe, Atari 800, Commodore 64, IBM PC, TI 99/4A. **Recent Title:** *Academic Skill Builders.* **Distribution Channels:** catalogs, computer stores, consumer electronics stores, sales representatives, software stores. Buys 10 to 12 programs annually; buying outlook the same.

SUBMISSION GUIDELINES

Preferred Medium; floppy disk. Complete documentation required. **Average Company Response Time:** 6 weeks; rejected programs returned on request. **Payment:** negotiable royalty. **Distribution Rights:** negotiable. **Plugging In:** "We will consider applications in all curricula. Programs should be drill and practice with an arcade format and an educational flavor."

Discovery Games
936 W. Highway 36
St. Paul, MN 55113
(612) 488-6843
David A. Wesely, partner

COMPANY PROFILE

Flight simulations, geography games. Also buys recreation. **Micros; Operating Systems:** Apple II, II+, and IIe, Atari home computers, Commodore 64, PET, CBM, and VIC-20, Osborne, TRS-80 I and III. **Recent Titles:** *Lafayette Escadrille, Chennault's Flying Tigers.* **Distribution Channels:** bookstores, computer stores, direct mail, software stores, toy stores. Buys two programs annually; buying outlook the same.

SUBMISSION GUIDELINES

Preferred Media: floppy disk, cassette tape, paper printout (choose medium appropriate to system). Initial documentation required. **Average Company Response Time:** 8 weeks; rejected programs returned. **Payment:** 2.5 to 7.5 percent royalty paid quarterly with advances on contract signing and program release. **Distribution Rights:** negotiable. **Plugging In:** Discovery is "primarily interested in historical simulations, not hand-eye reflex games."

Ed-Sci Development
1412 Riveroaks
Modesto, CA 95356
(209) 545-3656
Martin S. Cohen, director of software
   development and acquisitions
Established 1981

COMPANY PROFILE

Statistics. Also buys business and professional management. **Micros; Operating System:** Apple. **Recent Title:** *Ed-Sci Statistics.* **Distribution Channels:** computer stores, consumer electronics stores, direct mail, software stores. No annual buying limit.

SUBMISSION GUIDELINES

Preferred Medium: floppy disk. Complete documentation required. **Average Company Re-**

sponse Time: 8 weeks; rejected programs returned. **Payment:** negotiable royalty paid quarterly. **Distribution Rights:** negotiable.

Educational Activities, Inc.
1937 Grand Ave.
Baldwin, NY 11510
(516) 223-4666
Martin Batey, manager of microcomputer
   department
Established 1979

COMPANY PROFILE

Quizzes, games, drill and practice for science, reading, spelling, language arts, computer literacy, social studies, math, writing, and phonics; classroom management. **Micros; Operating Systems:** Apple II, Atari, Commodore 64 and PET, TRS-80 I, III, and IV. **Recent Titles:** *Comp-u-solve, Our Wild and Crazy World, Spelltronics.* **Distribution Channel:** direct to schools. No annual buying limit.

SUBMISSION GUIDELINES

Preferred Medium: floppy disk. Complete documentation required. **Average Company Response Time:** 4 weeks; rejected programs returned. **Payment:** negotiable royalty or outright purchase. **Distribution Rights:** exclusive. **Plugging In:** Author's guide available.

Educational Courseware
67A Willard St.
Hartford, CT 06105
(203) 247-6609
Victor C. King, director of software development
   and acquisitions
Established 1980

COMPANY PROFILE

Simulations, teacher management, lesson and test formatters. **Micros; Operating Systems:** Apple and compatibles. **Recent Titles:** *Testing Series, Astronomy I, Astronomy II.* **Distribution Channels:** bookstores, catalogs, computer stores, direct mail, software stores. No annual buying limit.

SUBMISSION GUIDELINES

Preferred Medium: floppy disk. Complete documentation required. **Average Company Response Time:** 2 weeks; rejected programs returned. **Payment:** 5 to 8 percent royalty (based on gross receipts) or outright purchase. **Distribution Rights:** exclusive. **Plugging In:** Company has two commandments: "Programs should be educational in nature and user friendly."

_____

Educational Software, Inc.
4565 Cherryvale Ave.
Soquel, CA 95073
(408) 476-4901
Robin A. Sherer, president
Established 1981

COMPANY PROFILE

Home education, computer tutorials. **Micros; Operating Systems:** Atari, Commodore 64 and VIC-20, IBM PC. **Recent Titles:** *Character Graphics Tutorial, Advanced Animation Tutorial, Children's Creative Learning Series.* **Distribution Channels:** bookstores, catalogs, computer stores, consumer electronics stores, department stores, direct mail, discount stores, mass merchandisers, software stores, toy stores. Buys six programs annually; buying outlook increasing.

SUBMISSION GUIDELINES

Preferred Medium: floppy disk. Complete documentation preferred. **Average Company Response Time:** ~2 weeks; rejected programs returned. **Payment:** 15 percent royalty paid quarterly. **Distribution Rights:** exclusive. **Plugging In:** Author's guide available.

_____

EduSoft
P.O. Box 2560
Berkeley, CA 94702
(800) 227-2778 or (415) 548-2304 (in Calif., Hawaii, Alaska)
Steven Rasmussen, editor
Established 1980

COMPANY PROFILE

K-12 drill and practice, games, teacher management. **Micros; Operating Systems:** Apple,

Atari, TRS-80. **Recent Titles:** *Worksheet Wizard, Estimation Skill Builder, Fast Facts.* **Distribution Channels:** bookstores, catalogs, computer stores, consumer electronics stores, direct mail, software stores, video stores. Buys four programs annually; buying outlook increasing.

SUBMISSION GUIDELINES

Preferred Medium: floppy disk. Complete documentation required. **Average Company Response Time:** 4 weeks; rejected programs returned. **Payment:** 10 to 15 percent royalty paid quarterly. **Distribution Rights:** exclusive.

_____

Edutek Corporation
415 Cambridge 14
Palo Alto, CA 94306
(415) 325-9965
Does not actively solicit.

_____

Edu-Ware Services, Inc. (an MSA Company)
P.O. Box 22222
28035 Dorothy Dr.
Agoura Hills, CA 91031
(213) 706-0661
Douglas J. Sietsema, director of acquisitions
Established 1979

COMPANY PROFILE

Instructional programs presented as tutorials, simulations, or "exemplary" games. Also buys recreation (adventure games and simulations). **Micros; Operating Systems:** Apple, Atari, Commodore 64, IBM PC; MS-DOS. **Recent Titles:** *Spelling Bee Games, Hands on BASIC Programming, Prisoner 2, Algebra Volume I.* **Distribution Channels:** bookstores, catalogs, computer stores, consumer electronics stores, mass merchandisers, software stores, toy stores, video stores, "direct" to Fortune 1000 companies. Buys 6 to 10 programs annually; buying outlook increasing.

SUBMISSION GUIDELINES

Preferred Medium: floppy disk. Complete documentation to be arranged between author and company. **Average Company Response Time:** 2 to 8 weeks: rejected programs returned. **Payment:** 8 to 10 percent royalty (with cash advance) paid quarterly or outright purchase. **Distribution Rights:** exclusive. **Plugging In:** "Our product's focus is in three lines: (1) the development of instructional software targeted to meet the needs of both consumers and instructional users; (2) intellectually challenging games in the adventure genre; (3) realistic simulations of social or physical phenomena. In education lines, both user and learner manuals or accompanying workbook materials should be presented at the time of submission." Author's guide available.

Electronic Courseware Systems, Inc.
309 Windsor Rd.
Champaign, IL 61820
(217) 359-7099
Sue Saeger, manager
Established 1981

COMPANY PROFILE

Skills development. Also buys recreation, personal productivity. **Micros; Operating Systems:** Apple, IBM. **Recent Titles:** *Elements of Mathematics, Elements of Verb Usage, Aural Skill Development.* **Distribution Channels:** catalogs, computer stores, direct mail, software stores. Buys 25 programs annually; buying outlook increasing.

SUBMISSION GUIDELINES

Preferred Medium:: floppy disk. Complete documentation required. **Average Company Response Time:** 3 weeks; rejected programs returned. **Payment:** negotiable royalty or outright purchase. **Distribution Rights:** exclusive.

Harcourt Brace Jovanovich Electronic Publishing
1250 Sixth Ave.
San Diego, CA 92101
(619) 699-6213
John Storojev, director of direct marketing
Established 1982

COMPANY PROFILE

Computer-assisted instruction for college achievement tests. **Micros; Operating Systems:** Apple, Atari, Commodore 64, IBM PC,

TRS-80. **Recent Titles:** *Computer Preparation for the SAT, Computer Preparation for the GRE, Computer Preparation for the ACT.* **Distribution Channels:** bookstores, computer stores, direct mail, software stores. Has not yet bought outside programs; company is now actively soliciting.

SUBMISSION GUIDELINES

Preferred Medium: floppy disk. Complete documentation required. **Average Company Response Time:** 2 to 4 weeks; rejected programs returned. **Payment:** 10 to 15 percent royalty paid biannually. **Distribution Rights:** exclusive. **Plugging In:** "We are looking for programs designed to aid study for standard education and professional tests."

Hartley Courseware
123 Bridge
Dimondale, MI 48821
(517) 646-6458
Jane Hartley, new product development manager
Established 1979

COMPANY PROFILE

Drill and practice, games, and tutorials for K-10 and various special education classes. **Micros; Operating Systems:** Apple, IBM PC (planning Commodore 64 and TRS-80). **Recent Titles:** *Black Americans, Women in History (Medalists Series), Analogies Tutorial, Memory Match.* **Distribution Channels:** computer stores, direct mail, school supply firms, software stores. Buys two to three programs annually; buying outlook increasing.

SUBMISSION GUIDELINES

Preferred Medium: floppy disk. Initial documentation required. **Average Company Response Time:** "at least 8 weeks"; rejected programs returned. **Payment:** Negotiable royalty or outright purchase. **Distribution Rights:** exclusive. **Plugging In:** "The more compatible your program is with Apple and assembly language, the better chance you have. We are looking primarily for language arts and math software and prefer to buy the program outright from the author."

Holt, Rinehart and Winston, Electronic
Publishing Division
School Marketing Department
383 Madison Ave.
New York, NY 10017
(212) 872-2000
Terry Gilbreth, director of electronic publishing
Established 1983

COMPANY PROFILE

Classroom management and record-keeping programs, interactive tutorials and drills in major subject areas. **Micros; Operating Systems:** Apple, Commodore 64 and PET, TRS-80. **Recent Titles:** *CLASS* (school management), *MathFinder* (K-6). **Distribution Channel:** company sales force direct to schools. Buys two programs annually; buying outlook increasing.

SUBMISSION GUIDELINES

Preferred Medium: floppy disk. Complete documentation required. **Average Company Response Time:** 4 weeks; rejected programs returned. **Payment:** 7 to 15 percent royalty paid biannually or outright purchase (if author completes a project assigned by the company). **Distribution Rights:** exclusive. **Plugging In:** "We need educational programs that relate to our textbooks on all major curricula."

Houghton Mifflin Company
One Beacon St.
Boston, MA 02108
(617) 725-5526
Clifton Rice, assistant to the president
Established 1832 (parent firm); 1982 (diskette-based software division)

COMPANY PROFILE

Drill and practice, games, and simulations for levels K-12. Also buys recreation, personal productivity, business and professional management. **Micros; Operating Systems:** Apple, IBM PC, TRS-80 III and IV. **Recent Titles:** *Mathematics Activities Courseware, Keystrokes, The Houghton Mifflin Microcourse.* **Distribution Channels:** bookstores, computer stores, direct mail, direct to schools (through in-house sales force),

software stores. Has not yet bought outside programs; company is now actively soliciting.

SUBMISSIONS GUIDELINES

Preferred Medium: floppy disk. Initial documentation required (firm will work with author on final draft). **Average Company Response Time:** 2 weeks; rejected programs returned. **Payment:** negotiable royalty or outright purchase. **Distribution Rights:** negotiable. **Plugging In:** Company requires author to fill out submission form detailing the type of software proposed and the program's target market. All programs must go through submission-form phase. Ideally, publisher seeks "useful educational (home and classroom) and productivity programs that differ in some way from those currently on the market." Author's guide available.

Innovative Programming Associates, Inc.
One Airport Pl.
Princeton, NJ 08540
(609) 924-7272
Lynne Kozicki, director of packaged software
division
Established 1980

COMPANY PROFILE

Computer literacy, scientific research software. Also buys recreation, business and professional management. **Micros; Operating Systems:** Apple DOS 3.3. **Recent Titles:** *Computer Literacy Modules I–IX, Lacat, Real Estate Maintenance.* **Distribution Channels:** catalogs, computer stores, direct mail, software stores. Buys 10 to 15 programs annually; buying outlook increasing.

SUBMISSION GUIDELINES

Preferred Medium: floppy disk. Complete documentation required. **Average Company Response Time:** 3 to 4 weeks; rejected programs returned. **Payment:** negotiable royalty or outright purchase. **Distribution Rights:** negotiable.

J&S Software
140 Reid Ave.

Port Washington, NY 11050
(516) 944-9304
Jay Grosmark, director software development/
   acquisitions
Established 1979

COMPANY PROFILE

Science skills, exercises, language arts games, teacher management. **Micros; Operating Systems:** Apple II and IIe, TRS-80. **Recent Titles:** *The Apple Grade Book, The Antonym Game, The Biology Programs.* **Distribution Channels:** catalogs, computer stores, direct mail, mail-order distributors, software stores. Buys 10 programs annually; buying outlook increasing.

SUBMISSION GUIDELINES

Preferred Medium: floppy disk. Initial documentation required. **Average Company Response Time:** 1 week; rejected programs returned. **Payment:** 10 to 25 percent royalty paid semiannually. **Distribution Rights:** exclusive. **Plugging In:** If firm feels a program has potential, "we will do all we can to help the designer."

Krell Software Corporation
1320 Stony Brook Rd.
Stony Brook, NY 11790
(516) 751-5139
Mark Friedland, director of new products
Established 1979

COMPANY PROFILE

Drill and practice for standard achievement tests, games, tutorials. Also buys recreation (home education and games). **Micros; Operating Systems:** Apple, Atari, Commodore 64, IBM PC, TRS-80. **Recent Titles:** *Krell's College Board SAT Preparation Series, The Best LOGO for Apple, Botticelli, Shelby Lyman Chess Tutorial Series.* **Distribution Channels:** computer stores, direct mail, software stores. Buys two programs annually; buying outlook increasing.

SUBMISSION GUIDELINES

Preferred Medium: floppy disk. Complete documentation required. **Average Company Re-**

sponse Time: 2 weeks or more; rejected programs returned. **Payment:** 5 to 25 percent royalty. **Distribution Rights:** exclusive. **Plugging In:** "The vast majority of the submissions we receive are refused because they do not fit in with our line. We are looking for technically oriented educational software."

Learning Well
200 S. Service Rd.
Roslyn Heights, NY 11577
(800) 645-6564 or (516) 621-1540
David Savitsky, director of software development
   and acquisitions
Established 1981

COMPANY PROFILE

Skill-building classroom games. Also buys recreation. **Micros; Operating Systems:** Apple II, Atari 800. **Recent Titles:** *Reading between the Lines, Space Math, Vocabulary Building.* **Distribution Channels:** bookstores, catalogs, computer stores, direct mail, mass merchandisers, software stores. No annual buying limit.

SUBMISSION GUIDELINES

Preferred Medium: floppy disk. Complete documentation required. **Average Company Response Time:** 2 to 4 weeks; rejected programs returned. **Payment:** negotiable royalty. **Distribution Rights:** negotiable. **Plugging In:** Company wants educational material in the truest sense of the word; programs should concentrate on directly improving a skill, such as spelling, and not approach such matters in a peripheral way. The firm also insists on a game format, favoring this over a rote exercise, the theory being that if children enjoy their work, they will learn more. Teachers should be able to modify any program easily for individual students' abilities.

LOGO Computer Systems
220 Fifth Ave., Suite 1604
New York, NY 10001
(212) 684-0710
Michael Tempel, manager of training and
   marketing
Established 1980

COMPANY PROFILE

Drill and practice, games, simulations using LOGO. **Micros; Operating Systems:** Apple, Atari, Coleco's ADAM, IBM PC. **Recent Titles:** *The Apple LOGO Sample Disk and Tool Kit, Sprite LOGO for the Apple II Family, French Edition of the Apple LOGO.* **Distribution Channels:** computer stores, department stores, mass merchandisers, original equipment manufacturers, software stores. Has not yet bought outside programs; company is now actively soliciting.

SUBMISSION GUIDELINES

Preferred Medium: floppy disk. Complete documentation required. **Average Company Response Time:** 2 to 4 weeks; rejected programs not returned unless specifically requested. **Payment:** negotiable royalty or outright purchase. **Distribution Rights:** negotiable. **Plugging In:** "We are looking for applications, in any area of traditional education, which utilize the LOGO language. We prefer self-documenting programs."

MCE, Inc.
157 South Kalamazoo Mall, Suite 250
Kalamazoo, MI 49007
(800) 421-4157 or (616) 345-8681 (in Mich., call collect)
Dr. Florence M. Taber, director of media development
Established 1980

COMPANY PROFILE

Math skills for grades 6 to 12, study and test-taking skills, consumer education. **Micros; Operating Systems:** Apple II and IIe. **Recent Titles:** *Job Survival Series, Analyzing An Ad, Problem Solving in Everyday Math Series.* **Distribution Channel:** catalogs. Has not yet bought outside programs; company is now actively soliciting.

SUBMISSION GUIDELINES

Preferred Media: floppy disk, paper printout. Initial documentation required. **Average Company Response Time:** 4 weeks; rejected programs "usually" returned. **Payment:** 5 to 10 percent royalty. **Distribution Rights:** "usually" exclusive but can be negotiable. **Plugging**

In: MCE's programs must meet educational and technological evaluation criteria for effective educational software. Some of the criteria set forth include: "Is the content consistent with the goals and objectives of the program? Are program goals provided which are usable for individualized educational plans? Are learners always the target of interaction with the computer—a personalized element?" Author's guide available.

McGraw-Hill Book Company
1221 Avenue of the Americas
New York, NY 10020
(212) 512-2000
Jerry Gleason, editor in chief, microcomputer unit
Established 1980

COMPANY PROFILE

On-the-job training and development programs; adult home study; school and home education programs in all major subjects. Also buys recreation, personal productivity, business and professional management, systems. **Micros; Operating Systems:** Apple, IBM, TRS-80, will consider Commodore, other selected popular computers. **Recent Title:** *McGraw-Hill Interactive Authoring System.* **Distribution Channels:** bookstores, catalogs, computer stores, consumer electronics stores, department stores, direct mail, mass merchandisers, software stores, video stores, company sales force direct to schools. Buys "as many good programs as flow in"; buying outlook increasing.

SUBMISSION GUIDELINES

Preferred Medium: floppy disk. Initial documentation required. **Average Company Response Time:** 6 to 8 weeks or longer; rejected programs returned. **Payment:** negotiable royalty; advance possible. **Distribution Rights:** negotiable. **Plugging In:** McGraw-Hill Book Co. contains 13 divisions; all publish books and software for professional, business, and educational audiences. After determining the appropriate division for the proposed product, authors should send a detailed query letter to that division's editorial director. If the product seems to cover a very broad range of users, then address the query to Jerry Gleason. "We'll review any program designed for home or school study or for the professional training effort. For example, a high school accounting package might suit our Gregg Division; a college-level economics program may fit the College Division. Keep in mind that a program can be fun as well as educational, but it shouldn't be a straight game."

Merry Bee Communications
815 Crest Dr.
Papillion, NE 68046
(402) 592-3479
Dr. Mary Berry, director of software
  development and acquisitions
Established 1982

COMPANY PROFILE

Language arts skills for ages 4 to 12, music skills for ages 6 and up, teacher management. **Micros; Operating Systems:** Apple II. **Recent Titles:** *ESL Easy Words, Nursery Time, Word Games.* **Distribution Channels:** catalogs, computer stores, direct mail, educational representatives, software stores. Buys five programs annually; buying outlook increasing.

SUBMISSION GUIDELINES

Preferred Medium: floppy disk. Initial documentation required. **Average Company Response Time:** 4 weeks; rejected programs returned with SASE. **Payment:** 7.5 to 12.5 percent royalty paid quarterly. **Distribution Rights:** exclusive.

Micro-Ed, Inc.
P.O. Box 444005
Minneapolis, MN 55344
(800) MICROED
George F. Esbensen, director of software
  acquisitions
Established 1978

COMPANY PROFILE

Skill games for math, science, language arts. Also buys recreation. **Micros; Operating Systems:** Apple, Atari, Commodore, TI, TRS-80 III and Color Computer. **Recent Titles:** *The Atom, Lawn of the Lost Rings, Guess That Word.* **Distri-**

bution Channels: bookstores, catalogs, computer stores, direct mail. Buys 50 to 100 programs annually; buying outlook increasing.

SUBMISSION GUIDELINES

Preferred Media: floppy disk, cassette tape. Complete documentation required. **Average Company Response Time:** 4 weeks; rejected programs returned. **Payment:** 20 percent royalty. **Distribution Rights:** negotiable.

Micro Power & Light Company
12820 Hillcrest Rd., Suite 219
Dallas, TX 75230
(214) 239-6620
Ed Frantz, president
Established 1979

COMPANY PROFILE

Math, science, English, and computer literacy puzzles, quizzes, drill and practice for K-12. Also buys recreation. **Micros; Operating Systems:** Apple II, IBM PC. **Recent Titles:** *The Electronic Tool, Space Array, Mind Warp.* **Distribution Channels:** catalogs, computer stores, consumer electronics stores, direct mail, video stores. Buys 12 programs annually; buying outlook increasing.

SUBMISSION GUIDELINES

Preferred Medium: floppy disk. Complete documentation to be arranged between author and company. **Average Company Response Time:** 3 to 4 weeks; rejected programs returned. **Payment:** 20 percent royalty paid quarterly or outright purchase. **Distribution Rights:** exclusive. **Plugging In:** Micro Power warns prospective authors to "include all documentation necessary to effectively use the program. Be sure the program has been tested thoroughly and that it can handle all common operator errors. The program should not require any uncommon hardware facilities nor proprietary routines."

Milliken Publishing Company
1110 Research Blvd.
St. Louis, MO 63132

(314) 991-4220
Bodie Marx, vice president
Established 1977

COMPANY PROFILE

Reading, math, and language arts skills games and exercises. Also buys recreation. **Micros; Operating Systems:** Apple II, Atari, Commodore 64 and VIC-20, IBM PC, TI 99/4A. **Recent Titles:** *The Spelling System, Cloze Plus, Grammar Problems for Practice.* **Distribution Channels:** audiovisual dealers, bookstores, catalogs, computer stores, consumer electronics stores, department stores, discount stores, mass merchandisers, school supply dealers, software stores, supermarkets, toy stores, video stores. Buys 10 programs annually; buying outlook increasing.

SUBMISSION GUIDELINES

Preferred Medium: floppy disk. Initial documentation required. **Average Company Response Time:** 2 weeks; rejected programs returned. **Payment:** 5 to 12.5 percent royalty paid quarterly plus development fee. **Distribution Rights:** exclusive. **Plugging In:** Milliken and its games division EduFun! says it has a simple goal. ''We want to turn our customers' computer systems into learning systems that benefit all teachers and students. Our software should be as easy to use as possible.''

Minnesota Educational Computing Consortium (MECC)
3490 Lexington Ave.
St. Paul, MN 55112
(612) 481-3500
Kent Kehrberg, director of courseware development
Established 1973

COMPANY PROFILE

Educational software geared for K-12 in major curriculum areas. **Micros; Operating Systems:** Apple, IBM PC and PCjr. **Recent Titles:** *Oh, Deer, the Friendly Computer, Writing a Character Sketch, Easy LOGO.* **Distribution Channels:** direct mail, sales and licensing to schools through educational product distributors. Buys 15 programs annually. Buying outlook increasing.

SUBMISSION GUIDELINES

Preferred Medium: floppy disk or fully detailed proposal. Initial documentation required. **Average Company Response Time:** 4 to 6 weeks; rejected programs returned. **Payment:** negotiable royalty or outright purchase. **Distribution Rights:** exclusive. **Plugging In:** Company seeks elementary school–level programs for such major curriculum areas as social studies, language arts, mathematics, and science. Secondary school programs are of secondary interest. Programs should use graphics to motivate learning.

Osborne/McGraw-Hill Book Company
630 Bancroft Way
Berkeley, CA 94710
(415) 726-0280
Att: editorial director of software
See McGraw-Hill Book Company in this section for full company profile and submission guidelines.

Radio Shack Education Division
1400 One Tandy Center
Fort Worth, TX 76102
(817) 390-3832
Bill D. Gattis, director
Established 1979

COMPANY PROFILE

Classroom materials and courseware development. **Micros; Operating Systems:** TRS-80. **Recent Titles:** *Color LOGO, Discover the Solar System, Color Chemistry.* **Distribution Channels:** catalogs, computer stores. No annual buying limit.

SUBMISSION GUIDELINES

Preferred Medium: floppy disk. Complete documentation required. **Average Company Response Time:** 12 weeks; rejected programs returned. **Payment:** outright purchase. **Distribution Rights:** exclusive. **Plugging In:** Company will accept copies of unsolicited software for evaluation *without* a release form *only* if the package is already being sold through another publisher or the author. Programs for the TRS-80 Color Computer are an immediate need.

Random House School Division
201 E. 50th St.
New York, NY 10022
(212) 572-2521
Eric Hawks, senior product manager
Established 1982

COMPANY PROFILE

Classroom management, drill and practice, computer literacy, and other tutorials for K-12, adult, basic, and vocational students. Also buys recreation (home education), systems. **Micros; Operating Systems:** TRS-80 III (48K disk 3.3 DOS), TRS-80 I and III (16K cassette), Apple II+ and IIe (Applesoft 48K disk 3.3 DOS), Atari 400 and 800 (48K), IBM PC (96K), Franklin ACE. **Recent Titles:** *Customware, Lessonwriter, Word Focus II—Prefixes and Suffixes, Math Mastery.* **Distribution Channels:** catalogs, direct mail, software stores, sales force. No annual buying limit.

SUBMISSION GUIDELINES

Preferred Medium: floppy disk. Initial documentation required. **Average Company Response Time:** 6 to 8 weeks; rejected programs returned. **Payment:** approximately 10 percent royalty paid yearly. **Distribution Rights:** negotiable (Random House copyright must be used).

REMsoft, Inc.
571 E. 185th St.
Euclid, OH 44119
(216) 531-1338
Raymond T. Furlong, president
Established 1979

COMPANY PROFILE

Classroom management and computer tutorials. Also buys business and professional management, systems. **Micros; Operating Systems:** TRS-80, company is also planning software for Apple, Atari, IBM PC, and NEC. **Recent Titles:** *REMassem, REMdisk, The Living TRS-80.* **Distribution Channels:** computer stores, direct mail, software stores. Buys two programs annually; buying outlook increasing.

SUBMISSION GUIDELINES

Preferred Medium: floppy disk. Initial documentation required; staff will polish and refine. **Average Company Response Time:** 2 weeks; rejected programs returned. **Payment:** 20 percent royalty (based on gross receipts) paid quarterly. **Distribution Rights:** exclusive. **Plugging In:** Company is particularly interested in utilities and educational programs geared to teaching and expanding the uses of the computer. Firm also writes custom programs for insurance and finance industries.

RockRoy, Inc.
7741 E. Gray Rd., Suite 6
Scottsdale, AZ 85260
(800) 528-2361 or (602) 998-1577
Paul Mason, president
Established 1981

COMPANY PROFILE

Simulations aimed at grades 3-12 and college level. Also buys recreation. **Micros; Operating Systems:** Apple, IBM PC. **Recent Titles:** *Conglomerates Collide, Max-Command.* **Distribution Channels:** bookstores, computer stores, direct mail, software stores. Has not yet bought outside programs; company is now actively soliciting.

SUBMISSION GUIDELINES

Preferred Medium: floppy disk. Complete documentation required. **Average Company Response Time:** 2 weeks; rejected programs returned. **Payment:** Up to 15 percent royalty paid quarterly. **Distribution Rights:** exclusive. **Plugging In:** "There are no 30-day wonders here. All submitted programs must be dynamic and create a situation that will stimulate learning. The software must appeal to all ages on an intellectual level and walk the fine line between education and entertainment."

Scholastic, Inc.
730 Broadway
New York, NY 10003

(212) 595-3000
Don Molner, director of microcomputer catalog
Established 1981

COMPANY PROFILE

Skills games for younger children, test simulations for older students. Also buys recreation. **Micros; Operating Systems:** Apple II and IIe, Atari, Commodore PET, IBM, TI, TRS-80. **Recent Titles:** *Bank Street Writer, Turtle Tracks, Microzine.* **Distribution Channels:** bookstores, catalogs, computer stores, department stores, direct mail, software stores. Buys 40 programs annually; buying outlook increasing.

SUBMISSION GUIDELINES

Preferred Medium: floppy disk. Complete documentation required. **Average Company Response Time:** 1 month; rejected programs returned. **Payment:** 5 to 15 percent royalty paid semiannually or outright purchase. **Distribution Rights:** negotiable. **Plugging In:** Scholastic chooses programs based on "ease of loading, required computer memory, and a host of academic criteria. Chosen programs are classified by grade level, subject area, and difficulty. We are especially interested in fun learning programs."

———————

Science Research Associates, Inc.
155 North Wacker Dr.
Chicago, IL 60606
(312) 984-7000
Att.: rights and permissions department
Established 1980

COMPANY PROFILE

Business and historical simulations, adult and children's tutorials, games, personal interest, and enrichment. Also buys recreation, personal productivity. **Micros, Operating Systems:** Apple, Atari, Commodore, IBM, Radio Shack, TI. **Recent Titles:** *Micros Made Easy, Using the IBM PC and DOS, Using the IBM PC and VisiCalc.* **Distribution Channels:** catalogs, company sales force direct to schools, computer stores, consumer electronics stores, direct mail, software stores. No annual buying limit.

SUBMISSION GUIDELINES

Preferred Medium: floppy disk. Complete documentation required. **Average Company Response Time:** 3 to 4 weeks; rejected programs not returned. **Payment:** negotiable royalty. **Distribution Rights:** negotiable. **Plugging In:** The SRA submission plan agreement must be on file prior to review of any material. SRA takes the following elements into account: use of color, sound, screen design, help screens and instructions, adequate error messages, consistency, speed, and supplementary publications. Author's guide available.

———————

Scott, Foresman and Company, Electronic
    Publishing Division
1900 East Lake Ave.
Glenview, IL 60025
(312) 729-3000
Dale LaFrenz, vice president
Established 1980

COMPANY PROFILE

Computer literacy tutorials, reading, language arts, and math skills programs, simulations and learning games for K-12. Also buys business and professional management (vertical applications). **Micros, Operating Systems:** Apple, Atari, Commodore PET, IBM PC, TI 99/4A, TRS-80. **Recent Titles:** *Reading Rainbows, Addition and Subtraction 3, PROBE: Beginning BASIC Programming Activities, Church Management System.* **Distribution Channels:** catalogs, company sales force direct to schools, direct mail. No annual buying limit.

SUBMISSION GUIDELINES

Preferred Media: floppy disk, cassette tape. Initial documentation required. **Average Company Response Time:** 6 to 8 weeks; rejected programs returned. **Payment:** negotiable royalty. **Distribution Rights:** negotiable. **Plugging In:** Author's guide available.

———————

Simtek, Business Games Division
P.O. Box 109
Cambridge, MA 02139-0109

(617) 232-5020
Judith Polk, director of software development
Established 1978

COMPANY PROFILE

Corporate training. **Micros; Operating Systems:** Apple, IBM PC; CP/M, MS-DOS. **Recent Titles:** *Busop, Electronic Industry Game, Pocket Calculator Boom.* **Distribution Channels:** catalogs, computer stores, direct mail, software stores. Buys five programs annually; buying outlook increasing.

SUBMISSION GUIDELINES

Preferred Medium: floppy disk. Initial documentation required. **Average Company Response Time:** 2 weeks; rejected programs not returned. **Payment:** 5 to 15 percent royalty or outright purchase. **Distribution Rights:** exclusive.

Southern Micro Systems for Educators
716 E. Davis St.
Burlington, NC 27215
(800) 334-5521 or (919) 226-7610 (North
   Carolina only)
Richard Swank, president
Established 1982

COMPANY PROFILE

Teacher management, administration, test evaluation and curriculum development aides for special education classes. **Micro; Operating Systems:** Apple, IBM PC, TRS-80 III. **Recent Titles:** *UNISTAR I Pre-IEP, WISC-R Computer Report, Accumulator II.* **Distribution Channels:** catalogs, direct-to-school sales, direct mail. Buys fewer than 10 programs annually; buying outlook the same.

SUBMISSION GUIDELINES

Preferred Medium: floppy disk. Initial documentation required. **Average Company Response Time:** 2 weeks; rejected programs returned. **Payment:** negotiable royalty. **Distribution Rights:** negotiable. **Plugging In:** Company is interested in acquiring programs for all classroom

education needs. Program author must have established education credentials, e.g., Ph.D. or university research background.

SouthWest EdPsych Services
P.O. Box 1870
Phoenix, AZ 85001
(602) 253-6528
Marley Watkins, president
Established 1981

COMPANY PROFILE

Language arts, reading, math skills games for younger children. Also buys recreation. **Micros; Operating Systems:** Apple II. **Recent Titles:** *The Reading Machine, Math Wars, The Vocabulary Machine.* **Distribution Channels:** catalogs, computer stores, direct mail, mass merchandisers, software stores. Buys four programs annually; buying outlook increasing.

SUBMISSION GUIDELINES

Preferred Medium: floppy disk. Initial documentation required. **Average Company Response Time:** 1 week; rejected programs returned. **Payment:** 10 to 20 percent royalty paid quarterly or outright purchase. **Distribution Rights:** exclusive.

Tara, Ltd.
P.O. Box 118
Selden, NY 11784
(516) 331-2537
Roger A. Schaefer, director of software
   development and acquisitions
Established 1981

COMPANY PROFILE

User-modifiable puzzles for all grade levels. **Micros; Operating Systems:** Apple, Atari, Commodore 64, and VIC-20, TI. **Recent Title:** *Puzzler.* **Distribution Channels:** catalogs, computer stores, direct mail, software stores. Buys two to four programs annually; buying outlook increasing.

SUBMISSION GUIDELINES

Preferred Media: floppy disk, paper printout. Initial documentation required. **Average Company Response Time:** 8 to 12 weeks; rejected programs returned. **Payment:** 25 to 55 percent royalty paid quarterly. **Distribution Rights:** negotiable.

Teach Yourself by Computer Software
2128 W. Jefferson Rd.
Pittsford, NY 14534
(716) 424-5453
Lois B. Bennet, director of marketing
Established 1978

COMPANY PROFILE

Study skills, earth science, meteorology. Also buys recreation. **Micros; Operating Systems:** Apple, Atari, TRS-80 I and III. **Recent Titles:** *Shore Features, Weather Fronts, The Authoring System.* **Distribution Channels:** bookstores, catalogs, computer stores, direct mail, software stores. Buys four programs annually; buying outlook increasing.

SUBMISSION GUIDELINES

Preferred Medium: floppy disk. Complete documentation required. **Average Company Response Time:** 4 weeks; rejected programs returned. **Payment:** 10 percent royalty paid monthly. **Distribution Rights:** exclusive. **Plugging In:** In reviewing educational software for publication, TYC looks for "graphics (color where appropriate), error handling, good reinforcement, material appropriate for grade level, user-teacher documentation; sound if appropriate; usability on minimum systems; flexibility of use for home and classroom." Author's guide available.

T.H.E.S.I.S.
P.O. Box 147
Garden City, MI 48135
(313) 595-4722
Linda Schreiber, director of software
   development and acquisitions
Established 1980

COMPANY PROFILE

English, math skills development for grades 1-6. Also buys recreation, personal productivity. **Micros; Operating Systems:** Apple II + and IIe, Atari, TI 99/4A. **Recent Titles:** *English Grammar, Weights and Measures, It's about Time.* **Distribution Channels:** catalogs, computer stores, direct mail, software stores, toy stores. Buys five programs annually; buying outlook increasing.

SUBMISSION GUIDELINES

Preferred Medium: floppy disk. Complete documentation to be arranged between company and author. **Average Company Response Time:** 4 to 6 weeks; rejected programs returned with SASE. **Payment:** 10 to 20 percent royalty paid quarterly. **Distribution Rights:** exclusive. **Plugging In:** All submitted programs "must utilize machine capabilities. Use of graphics is very important in educational material. The submission should also be easy to use and error-free." BASIC or assembly language only. Black-and-white programs not acceptable. Documentation should include loading procedure, features of the program, direction, system requirements. Programs should be protected against crashing if the wrong answer is entered. Company is currently expanding its product line to include home applications, adventures, arcade games, fantasy games, and family games. Author's guide available.

John Wiley & Sons, Inc.
605 Third Ave.
New York, NY 10158
(212) 850-6000
Gary Carlson, publisher of educational software
Established 1981

COMPANY PROFILE

Classroom management, CAI for college-level science. Also buys recreation, personal productivity, business and professional management. **Micros; Operating Systems:** Apple II and IIe, Commodore 64, Hewlett-Packard 85 and 86, IBM PC, TRS-80 (others as appropriate for specific programs). **Recent Titles:** *Gradisk, Calculus by Computer.* **Distribution Channels:** bookstores, catalogs, computer stores, direct mail, international subsidiaries, sales representatives, software stores. Buys 30 programs annually; buying outlook increasing.

SUBMISSION GUIDELINES

Preferred Medium: floppy disk. Complete documentation required. **Average Company Response Time:**   8 weeks; rejected programs returned. **Payment:**   10 to 20 percent royalty paid semiannually   (with   step-ups).   **Distribution**

Rights: "usually   nonexclusive."   **Plugging In:**   Company's professional software division publishes applications programs in business, science, engineering, and personal finance. Contact Dianne Littwin, publisher of professional software about noneducational programs. "We work intensively with authors and make both the software and documentation as useful and easy to use as possible." Author's guide available.

_____

CROSS-REFERENCES—CLASSROOM EDUCATION

The following companies also buy classroom education software. Their complete listings may be found under the major headings shown.

RECREATION

Addison-Wesley Publishing Company
Adventure International/Division of Scott Adams, Inc.
Alien Group
Artificial Intelligence Research Group
Artworx Software Company, Inc.
Atari, Inc.
Atari Program Exchange (APX)
Avalon Hill Microcomputer Games
Avant-Garde Creations, Inc.
Blue Chip Software
Boston Educational Computing
CBS Software
Chalk Board, Inc.
Cload Publications, Inc.
Comm*Data Computer House, Inc.
Commodore, Computer Systems Division
CompuServe, Inc.
Computer-Advanced Ideas, Inc.
Cornsoft Group, Inc.
Databar Corporation
Datasoft, Inc.
Dilithium Press
Don't Ask Computer Software, Inc.
Electronic Arts
Funtastic, Inc.
Gessler Educational Software, division of Gessler Publishing
Hayden Software Company
HESWARE
Inhome Software
Instant Software, Division of Wayne Green, Inc.
International Publishing & Software, Inc.

Koala Technologies
The Learning Company
Lightning Software, Inc., subsidiary of Scarborough Systems
Microcomputers Corporation
MicroLab, Inc.
Muse Software, Inc.
Passport Designs, Inc.
Penguin Software, Inc.
Piccadilly Software
Prentice-Hall, Inc.
Rainbow Computing, Inc.
Ranco Software Games, Inc.
Rantom Software
RB Robot Corporation
Reston Publishing Company, Inc.
Royal Software/COMPUTER PALACE
Sim Computer Products, Inc.
Simon and Schuster, Electronic Publishing Group
Sirius Software, Inc.
Sir-tech Software, Inc.
Softsel Computer Products, Inc.
Softside Magazine
Softsync, Inc.
The Software Guild
Source Telecomputing Corporation
Spectral Associates
SpectraVideo, Inc.
Sterling Swift Publishing Company
Strategic Simulations, Inc.
Synapse Software
Terrapin, Inc.
TG Products

TMQ Software
Tom Mix Software
United Microware Industries, Inc. (UMI)
Warlock Software, Division of Tylos, Inc.
Windcrest Software, Inc.
Window, Inc.
Wizard Video Games
Xerox Education Publications, Computer Software
  Division

PERSONAL PRODUCTIVITY

Alphanetics Software
Computer Software Associates, Inc.
Computerized Management Systems
Digital Marketing Corporation
Dynacomp, Inc.
Harper & Row Electronic and Technical Publish-
  ing Division
Hoyle and Hoyle Software, Inc.
PC Disk Magazine
Powersoft, Inc.
The Quick Brown Fox Company
Reader's Digest Services, Inc.
Scarborough Systems, Inc.
Silicon Valley Systems, Inc.

BUSINESS AND PROFESSIONAL MANAGEMENT

Alternative Software, Inc. (formerly Lens Master-
  son & Associates)
CMA Micro Computer
CompuTech Group, Inc.
Duosoft Corporation
Epson America, Inc.
IBM External Submissions
Level IV Products, Inc.
MMG Micro Software
Orbyte Software
Peachtree Software, Inc.
Pioneer Software
Resource Software International, Inc.
Sunrise Software, Inc.
Wadsworth Electronic Publishing Company, divi-
  sion of Wadsworth, Inc.

SYSTEMS

Alcor Systems
Apparat, Inc.
Cosmopolitan Electronics Corporation
Digital Research, Inc., Computer Products Division
The Software Toolworks

Business and Professional Management

Abacus Associates
6565 W. Loop South, Suite 220
Bellaire, TX 77401
Jim Ostrom, president
Established 1969

COMPANY PROFILE

Reporting systems, integrated software. **Micros; Operating Systems:** Apple, IBM PC, TRS-80. **Recent Titles:** *Viz-a-Con, Viz-a-Merge.* **Distribution Channel:** direct mail. Has not yet bought outside programs; company is now actively soliciting.

SUBMISSION GUIDELINES

Preferred Medium: floppy disk. Complete documentation required. **Average Company Response Time:** 2 to 4 weeks; rejected programs returned. **Payment:** 10 to 20 percent royalty paid monthly. **Distribution Rights:** exclusive. **Plugging In:** "Our products have a certain style, and we use certain techniques. Send us the program, and if we use it, we'll adapt it to our standards."

Advanced Logic Systems, Inc.
1195 E. Arques Ave.
Sunnyvale, CA 94086
(800) 538-8177
George Johnson, director of marketing
Established 1980

COMPANY PROFILE

Peripherals for the Apple. **Micros; Operating Systems:** Apple; CP/M. **Recent Titles:** *CP/M Card* (peripheral for application software). **Distribution Channels:** bookstores, computer stores, consumer electronics stores, software stores. Has not yet bought outside programs; company is now actively soliciting.

SUBMISSION GUIDELINES

Preferred Medium: floppy disk. Complete documentation required. **Average Company Response Time:** varies; rejected programs returned. **Payment:** negotiable royalty. **Distribution Rights:** exclusive. **Plugging In:** Company wants programs "that can be bundled with our peripherals to enhance their salability."

AlphaBit Communications, Inc.
13349 Michigan Ave.
Dearborn, MI 48126
(313) 581-2896
David Walsh, president
Established 1982

COMPANY PROFILE

Word processing programs to aid business productivity. Also buys systems. **Micros; Operating Systems:** TRS-80 I, III, and IV. **Recent Titles:** *Lazy Merge, Lazy Font.* **Distribution Channels:** catalogs, computer stores, direct mail, software stores. Buys two to three programs annually; buying outlook the same.

SUBMISSION GUIDELINES

Preferred Medium: floppy disk. Initial documentation required. **Average Company Response Time:** 3 weeks; rejected programs returned. **Payment:** 10 to 20 percent royalty paid monthly or outright purchase. **Distribution Rights:** negotiable, outright purchase preferred. **Plugging In:** AlphaBit's main program is the *Lazy Writer* word processing system. Main interest is in extension program for *Lazy Writer* or any program dealing with word processing.

Alternative Software, Inc. (formerly Lens
   Masterson & Associates)
1165 Barbara Dr.
Cherry Hill, NJ 08003
(609) 429-3838
Jay Lewis, sales manager and director of software
   development
Established 1981

COMPANY PROFILE

Office management. Also buys recreation, systems. **Micros; Operating Systems:** Cromenco, IBM PC and XT, NEC Northstar, TRS-80, Vector Graphic, Xerox. **Recent Titles:** *Mass Mailer, Micro Payroll, Micro Ledger.* **Distribution Channels:** computer stores, software stores. Buys eight programs annually; buying outlook increasing.

SUBMISSION GUIDELINES

Preferred Medium: floppy disk. Initial documentation required. **Average Company Response Time:** one to eight weeks; rejected programs returned with SASE. **Payment:** 30 to 50 percent royalty. **Distribution Rights:** exclusive (for 1 year with option to renew if sales goals are met). **Plugging In:** "We want software designed for specific industries such as exporting, law, and so forth. An 11-year-old recently sold us a game. If we accept, we let the author take the first crack at the documentation, then we modify it. In writing the users' manual, we assume the user is a complete novice."

Analytical Processes Corporation
635 Main St.
Montrose, CO 81401
(303) 249-1400
Mike Johnson, vice president of operations
Established 1980

COMPANY PROFILE

Accounting and vertical markets. **Micros; Operating Systems:** IBM PC, TRS-80 (except model I); CP/M, MS-DOS. **Recent Titles:** *Tax/Pack, Retail Inventory and Billing, Bulk Petroleum Distributing.* **Distribution Channel:** direct mail. Has not yet bought outside programs; company is now actively soliciting.

SUBMISSION GUIDELINES

Preferred Medium: floppy disk. Initial documentation required. **Average Company Response Time:** 2 to 4 weeks; rejected programs returned. **Payment:** negotiable royalty. **Distribution Rights:** exclusive. **Plugging In:** "We want source code that is written and well-documented, but if the program is good, we can write it. We want applications people can use—taxes, bookkeeping, real estate appraisal, etc."

Anderson-Bell
P.O. Box 191
Canon City, CO 81212

(303) 275-1661
Bruce Bell, managing partner
Established 1980

COMPANY PROFILE

Sophisticated software that will meet needs of Fortune 1000 companies. **Micros; Operating Systems:** Apple, DEC, IBM PC, Victor; Apple DOS, CP/M, MS-DOS. **Recent Titles:** *ABSTAT, ABTAB.* **Distribution Channels:** computer stores, direct mail, software stores. Has not yet bought outside programs; company is now actively soliciting.

SUBMISSIONS GUIDELINES

Preferred Medium: floppy disk. Initial documentation required. **Average Company Response Time:** 2 to 4 weeks; rejected programs returned. **Payment:** negotiable royalty or outright purchase. **Distribution Rights:** exclusive. **Plugging In:** Company is very flexible and will look at program during "any stage of development as long as it fits into our marketing policies and product lines."

Apple Computer, Inc.
20525 Mariani Ave.
Cupertino, CA 95014
(408) 996-1010
Does not actively solicit.

Ashton-Tate
10150 W. Jefferson Blvd.
Culver City, CA 90230
(213) 204-5570
John Houston, director of product acquisition
Established 1980

COMPANY PROFILE

Accounting, records management, and financial planning packages. **Micros; Operating Systems:** Apple, IBM PC, Victor 9000 and compatibles; CP/M 86, MS-DOS. **Recent Titles:** *D-Base II, Friday, Financial Planner, Bottom Line Strategist (BLS).* **Distribution Channels:** bookstores, computer stores, direct mail, software stores. Has not yet bought outside programs; company is now actively soliciting.

SUBMISSION GUIDELINES

Preferred Medium: floppy disk. Complete documentation required. **Average Company Response Time:** 1 week; rejected programs not returned. **Payment:** negotiable royalty or outright purchase. **Distribution Rights:** exclusive. **Plugging In:** Company seeks products that have a "wide market appeal, applicable to a broad range of businesses."

Aurora Systems, Inc.
2423 American La.
Madison, WI 53704
(608) 249-5875
Darryl Mataya, vice president
Established 1980

COMPANY PROFILE

Banking management. Also buys systems. **Micros; Operating Systems:** Apple, IBM PC, Victor; MS-DOS, P-System. **Recent Titles:** *Personal Banker, Credit Manager, Safe Deposit.* **Distribution Channel:** direct mail. Buys three to four programs annually; buying outlook increasing.

SUBMISSION GUIDELINES

Preferred Medium: floppy disk. Complete documentation required. **Average Company Response Time:** 2 to 4 weeks; rejected programs returned. **Payment:** negotiable royalty paid quarterly. **Distribution Rights:** exclusive. **Plugging In:** "We want to stay in the banking area. We see so much potential there and are really strong at it. General applications don't interest us."

Bridge Computer, Division of Sea Data
  Corporation
One Bridge St.
Newton, MA 02138
(617) 244-3203

Elaine Doll, general manager
Established 1981

COMPANY PROFILE

Science and engineering applications, general accounting, word processing. **Micros; Operating Systems:** CP/M-80, CP/M-86, MS-DOS. **Recent Titles:** *PlotPak, StringPak, EasyPak.* **Distribution Channel:** direct mail. Buys three to four programs annually; buying outlook increasing.

SUBMISSION GUIDELINES

Preferred Medium: floppy disk. Initial documentation required. **Average Company Response Time:** 2 weeks; rejected programs returned. **Payment:** negotiable royalty or outright purchase. **Distribution Rights:** negotiable. **Plugging In:** Firm seeks mathematics, plotting, statistical analysis for science and math applications as well as general office management software. Author's guide available.

The Business Division, Division of Scott Adams, Inc.
P.O. Box 3435
Longwood, FL 32750
(305) 862-6917
Paul Grupp, manager of product development
Established 1978

COMPANY PROFILE

Accounting, office management. Also buys personal productivity, systems. **Micros; Operating Systems:** Apple, Atari, IBM PC and compatibles, Osborne, Sanyo, TRS-80, Victor 9000. **Recent Titles:** *Integrated Accounting Package, Maxi Manager, Maxi Cras.* **Distribution Channels:** bookstores, catalogs, computer stores, consumer electronics stores, department stores, direct mail, discount stores, mass merchandisers, software stores, video stores. Buys eight programs annually; buying outlook increasing.

SUBMISSION GUIDELINES

Preferred Medium: floppy disk. Complete documentation required. **Average Company Response Time:** 2 to 4 weeks; rejected programs returned with SASE. **Payment:** negotiable roy-

alty paid monthly. **Distribution Rights:** exclusive. **Plugging In:** Author's guide available.

Century Software Systems
1875 Century Park E., Suite 1730
Los Angeles, CA 90067
(213) 879-5911
Richard Eng, vice president
Established 1981

COMPANY PROFILE

Financial management. Also buys personal productivity. **Micros; Operating Systems:** Altos, Apple III, IBM PC; CP/M, MS-DOS. **Recent Titles:** *Financial Decision, Lease vs. Buy Analysis, Econometrics.* **Distribution Channels:** computer stores, direct mail, software stores. Has not yet bought outside programs; company is now actively soliciting.

SUBMISSION GUIDELINES

Preferred Media: floppy disk, paper printout. Complete documentation required. **Average Company Response Time:** 1 to 2 weeks; rejected programs returned on request. **Payment:** minimum 10 percent royalty paid quarterly. **Distribution Rights:** exclusive. **Plugging In:** "We look at the end result—does the program serve its application? We've been seeing a lot of vertical management and general ledger for specific applications. These are the certain peculiarities in the industry we like addressed. We also seek analytical-type tools—the next step up. Graphics packages for business would be good for us too."

CMA Micro Computer
55722 Santa Fe
Yucca Valley, CA 92284
(619) 365-9718
Robert Bell, director of software development and acquisitions
Established 1976

COMPANY PROFILE

Word processing, office management, accounting. Also buys classroom education. **Micros; Op-**

erating Systems: Apple (including LISA), IBM PC and XT and compatibles, TRS-80, Wang PC; MS-DOS. **Recent Titles:** *Medical Office Management, Success Desk Accounting, Perfection.* **Distribution Channels:** bookstores, catalogs, computer stores, consumer electronics stores, department stores, software stores, video stores. Buys 35 programs annually; buying outlook increasing.

SUBMISSION GUIDELINES

Preferred Medium: floppy disk. Complete documentation required. **Average Company Response Time:** 4 weeks; rejected programs returned. **Payment:** 15 to 30 percent royalty paid quarterly or outright purchase. **Distribution Rights:** negotiable. **Plugging In:** Author's guide available.

CompuTech Group, Inc.
Main Line Industrial Park
Lee Blvd.
Frazer, PA 19355
(215) 644-3344
Peter Drinkwater, director of sales and marketing
Established 1980

COMPANY PROFILE

Accounting. Also buys personal productivity, classroom education, systems. **Micros; Operating Systems:** IBM PC; MS-DOS. **Recent Titles:** *Solomon I, Solomon II, Solomon III.* **Distribution Channels:** computer stores, software stores. Buys three programs annually; buying outlook increasing.

SUBMISSION GUIDELINES

Preferred Medium: floppy disk. Complete documentation "usually required." **Average Company Response Time:** 2 to 4 weeks; rejected programs returned. **Payment:** negotiable royalty. **Distribution Rights:** exclusive. **Plugging In:** "We need mostly IBM PC–type programs for small business applications. We're eager to consider nonaccounting packages."

Comshare Target Software
1935 Cliff Valley Way, Suite 200
Atlanta, GA 30329
(404) 634-9535
Does not actively solicit.

Context Management Systems
23868 Hawthorne Blvd.
Torrance, CA 90505
(213) 378-8277
Jim Peterson, vice president of research & development
Established 1980

COMPANY PROFILE

Integrated business programs. **Micros; Operating Systems:** Hewlett-Packard. **Recent Title:** *The Context MBA.* **Distribution Channels:** computer stores, direct mail, hardware manufacturers, software stores. Buys one program annually; buying outlook increasing.

SUBMISSION GUIDELINES

Preferred Medium: floppy disk. Complete documentation to be arranged between author and company. **Average Company Response Time:** 2 to 4 weeks; rejected programs returned. **Payment:** outright purchase. **Distribution Rights:** exclusive. **Plugging In:** "We need additions or enhancements to existing programs."

Cybernetics
8041 Newman Ave., Suite 208
Huntington Beach, CA 92647
(714) 848-1922
Joe Sheldon, president
Established 1974

COMPANY PROFILE

Sales management and accounting. **Micros; Operating Systems:** Apple, IBM PC, TRS-80 II and above; CP/M, CP/M-86, MS-DOS, PC-DOS. **Recent Titles:** *CRT!, Accounts Receivable, Accounts Payable.* **Distribution Channel:** direct mail. Buys one to three programs annually; buying outlook increasing.

SUBMISSION GUIDELINES

Preferred Medium: floppy disk. Complete documentation required. **Average Company Response Time:** 12 weeks; rejected programs returned. **Payment:** "usually 25 percent royalty" paid quarterly. **Distribution Rights:** exclusive. **Plugging In:** "We're searching for vertical marketing packages in COBOL."

Designer Software
3400 Montrose Blvd., Suite 718
Houston, TX 77006
(713) 520-8221
Att: director of software development
Established 1981

COMPANY PROFILE

Word processing packages. Also buys personal productivity, systems. **Micros; Operating Systems:** CP/M, MS-DOS, TURBO-DOS, MP/M. **Recent Title:** *Palantine Word Processor*. **Distribution Channels:** computer stores, software stores. Buys one program annually; buying outlook increasing.

SUBMISSION GUIDELINES

Preferred Medium: floppy disk. Initial documentation required. **Average Company Response Time:** 12 to 24 weeks; rejected programs returned. **Payment:** 10 to 20 percent royalty paid quarterly or outright purchase. **Distribution Rights:** negotiable.

Douthett Enterprises, Inc.
200 W. Douglas
Wichita, KS 67202
(316) 262-1040
Does not actively solicit.

Duosoft Corporation
1803 Woodfield Dr.
Savoy, IL 61874
(217) 356-2818
Clifford H. Emerick, director of marketing
Established 1981

COMPANY PROFILE

Help for small business, particularly planning and management. Also buys classroom education (college-level and employee training). **Micros; Operating Systems:** MS-DOS, PC-DOS, Microtutor. **Recent Titles:** *Business Planner, Business Planner Demo, Participative Management Skills*. **Distribution Channels:** bookstores, computer stores, direct mail, software stores. Buys six programs annually; buying outlook increasing.

SUBMISSION GUIDELINES

Preferred Medium: floppy disk. Complete documentation required. **Average Company Response Time:** 1 week; rejected programs returned. **Payment:** negotiable royalty paid quarterly or outright purchase. **Distribution Rights:** negotiable. **Plugging In:** Author's guide available.

Eagle Software Publishing, Inc.
993 Old Eagle School Rd., Suite 409
Wayne, PA 19087
(215) 964-8660
Joseph A. Mascio, vice president of development
   and manufacturing
Established 1981

COMPANY PROFILE

Financial programs. Also buys personal productivity, recreation. **Micros; Operating Systems:** Apple, Atari, Commodore 64, DEC, Professional, Wang (25 in all); CP/M. **Recent Titles:** *Money Decisions*, vols. I & II, *Tax Decisions, Lifestyle Analyzer*. **Distribution Channels:** bookstores, catalogs, computer stores, department stores, direct mail, mass merchandisers, software stores. Buys three to four programs annually; buying outlook increasing.

SUBMISSION GUIDELINES

Preferred Medium: floppy disk. Complete documentation required. **Average Company Response Time:** 4 to 6 weeks; rejected programs returned. **Payment:** 5 to 20 percent royalty paid quarterly. **Distribution Rights:** exclusive. **Plugging In:** Company wants "unique additions to personal enrichment and professional applications software lines." Will consider program even if it addresses a familiar need (such as household finance, stock market analysis) as long as the approach is "superior." Author's guide available.

The Einstein Corporation
11340 W. Olympic Blvd.
Los Angeles, CA 90064
(213) 477-6733
Chaim Levin, president
Established 1982

COMPANY PROFILE

"Very user friendly" word processing, spelling checker, and letter-writing packages. Also buys systems. **Micros; Operating Systems:** Apple, Atari, Commodore 64, IBM PC. **Recent Titles:** *Einstein Writer, Einstein Letter Series, Einstein Memory Trainer, Einstein Speller.* **Distribution Channels:** computer stores, department stores, mass merchandisers, software stores. Buys one program annually; buying outlook increasing.

SUBMISSION GUIDELINES

Preferred Medium: floppy disk. Complete documentation required. **Average Company Response Time:** 3 weeks; rejected programs returned. **Payment:** negotiable royalty paid quarterly or outright purchase. **Distribution Rights:** exclusive.

Epson America, Inc.
3415 Kashiwa St.
Torrance, CA 90505
(213) 539-9140
Steve Irving, manager of software development
Established 1983

COMPANY PROFILE

Integrated software (finance, database managers, word processing, etc.) and stand-alone applications for business users. Also buys recreation, personal productivity, classroom education, systems. **Micros; Operating Systems:** Epson QX-10 and HX-20 (both CP/M based). **Recent Ti-**

tle: *VALDOCS* (integrated). **Distribution Channels:** catalogs, company sales force direct to corporate accounts, computer stores, consumer electronics stores, department stores, mass merchandisers, and value-added resellers. Has not yet bought outside programs; company is now actively soliciting.

SUBMISSION GUIDELINES

Preferred Media: floppy disk, cassette tape. Initial documentation required. **Average Company Response Time:** 6 to 8 weeks. Rejected programs returned. **Payment:** negotiable royalty or outright purchase. **Distribution Rights:** negotiable. **Plugging In:** "VALDOCS is probably the only integrated program we will market, but we are looking for all applications for the HX-20, especially business programs, also vertical programs, such as insurance or real estate packages, for the QX-10."

Execuware, Inc.
4018 Country Club Road
Winston-Salem, NC 27104
(919) 760-3576
Michael Rahman, president

COMPANY PROFILE

Records management, financial analysis. **Micros; Operating Systems:** IBM PC. **Recent Titles:** *Financial Analysis Package, Real Estate Analysis Package, Know Your Client.* **Distribution Channels:** computer stores, direct mail, software stores. Buys three programs annually; buying outlook the same.

SUBMISSION GUIDELINES

Preferred Medium: floppy disk. Initial documentation required. **Average Company Response Time:** 1 month; rejected programs returned. **Payment:** negotiable royalty or outright purchase. **Distribution rights:** exclusive.

GMS Systems, Inc.
12 W. 37th St.
New York, NY 10018
(212) 947-3590
Les Yeamons, vice president of product
  development
Established 1973

COMPANY PROFILE

Database management and graphics programs for business applications. **Micros; Operating Systems:** IBM PC and XT. **Recent Title:** *Power-Base.* **Distribution Channels:** computer stores, software stores. Has not yet bought outside programs; company is now actively soliciting.

SUBMISSION GUIDELINES

Preferred Medium: floppy disk. Complete documentation required. **Average Company Response Time:** 4 weeks; rejected programs returned. **Payment:** negotiable royalty or outright purchase. **Distribution Rights:** exclusive.

Heath/Zenith Data Systems Corporation
1900 N. Austin Ave.
Chicago, IL 60634
(312) 745-2587
Mickey Kosanovich, manager of software
  acquisition
Established 1977

COMPANY PROFILE

Word processing, accounting, and graphics for firm's own hardware. **Micros; Operating Systems:** Heathkit (unassembled), Zenith (assembled). **Recent Titles:** *Lotus 1-2-3, Wordstar, Condor.* **Distribution Channels:** computer stores, direct mail. Buys 40 to 50 programs annually; buying outlook increasing.

SUBMISSION GUIDELINES

Preferred Medium: floppy disk. Complete documentation required. **Average Company Response Time:** 12 weeks; rejected programs returned. **Payment:** Negotiable royalty paid quarterly. **Distribution Rights:** nonexclusive.

Hewlett-Packard, Personal Computer Division
1010 Northeast Circle Blvd.
Corvallis, OR 97330
(503) 757-2000
Att.: HP Plus administrator
Established 1982

COMPANY PROFILE

Vertical packages, communications programs for engineering and other professionals and small-business users. Also evaluates recreation. **Micros; Operating Systems:** Hewlett-Packard series 80. **Recent Titles:** *Math, Text Formatter, Surveying, Data Communications.* **Distribution Channels:** catalogs, computer stores, consumer electronics stores, department stores, direct mail, software stores. Under the HP Plus program, rather than being acquired, finished packages that company evaluates and approves are simply listed in Hewlett-Packard catalog and/or distributed through its sales force.

SUBMISSION GUIDELINES

Preferred Medium: floppy disk. Complete documentation required. **Average Company Response Time:** varies; rejected programs returned. **Payment:** not applicable. **Distribution Rights:** nonexclusive. **Plugging In:** "HP Plus is designed to promote independent software development for HP personal computing products. We assist you in making your software available to both existing and prospective HP series 80 owners through our dealer network." Based on its current marketing strategy, HP has identified the following high-priority applications areas: vertical financial programs, electronic mail, real estate, time management, statistics, engineering (electrical, civil, chemical, mechanical).

Human Systems Dynamics
9010 Reseda Blvd., Suite 222
Northridge, CA 91324
(213) 993-8536
Dr. Virginia Lawrence, director of software
  development and acquisitions
Established 1981

COMPANY PROFILE

Statistical analysis. **Micros; Operating Systems:** Apple, IBM PC, Osborne. **Recent Ti-**

tles: *Regress, Stats Plus, Anova II.* **Distribution Channels:** computer stores, direct mail, software stores. Buys three programs annually; buying outlook increasing.

SUBMISSION GUIDELINES

Preferred Medium: floppy disk. Complete documentation required. **Average Company Response Time:** 4 weeks; rejected programs returned. **Payment:** 10 to 20 percent royalty paid monthly. **Distribution Rights:** exclusive. **Plugging In:** Company reviews only copyrighted material.

IBM External Submissions
Dept. 765 PC
Armonk, NY 10504
A. D. Hearn, manager of software submissions
Established 1981

COMPANY PROFILE

Financial management, database management, word processing for large and small businesses. Also buys recreation, personal productivity, classroom education, systems. **Micros; Operating Systems:** IBM PC, XT, and PCjr. **Recent Titles:** *Word Proof, Personal Editor, Private Tutor.* **Distribution Channels:** company's direct sales force, computer stores, IBM product center stores, software stores. No annual buying limit.

SUBMISSION GUIDELINES

Preferred Medium: floppy disk. Complete documentation preferred. **Average Company Response Time:** 12 to 24 weeks; rejected programs not returned. **Payment:** negotiable royalty paid quarterly. **Distribution Rights:** negotiable. **Plugging In:** IBM needs "quality software and documentation that will be easy to use; offer a better way to accomplish a task; be entertaining or challenging; provide something special and unique to the user of the software; use the IBM computers in new, useful, and interesting ways; or improve the computer's performance or function. Your submission may be in the areas of home, personal finance, education, recreation, business, professional, scientific medical, technical, or software development. However, sub-

missions need not be limited to these areas." Author's guide available.

IMSI Software Publishers (International Microcomputer Software Inc.)
635 Fifth Ave.
San Rafael, CA 94901
(415) 454-7101
John Deane, product acquisitions and analysis
Established 1982

COMPANY PROFILE

Business graphics, accounting, stock market analysis. **Micros; Operating Systems:** CP/M, CP/M-86, MP/M, MP/M-86, MS-DOS (for 8- and 16-bit machines). **Recent Titles:** *4-Point Graphics, Bisybase, Investment Manager, Checkbase, Job Estimator.* **Distribution Channels:** bookstores, computer stores, department stores, mass merchandisers, original equipment manufacturers, software stores, system houses. Buys all its programs from outside (31 to date); buying outlook increasing.

SUBMISSION GUIDELINES

Preferred Medium: floppy disk. Initial documentation required ("as much as possible"). **Average Company Response Time:** 4 weeks; rejected programs not returned. **Payment:** negotiable royalty (up to 20 percent for fully finished programs) paid quarterly. **Distribution Rights:** exclusive. **Plugging In:** Company seeks "business programs with broad market potential. We do not want a word processor to compete with *Word Star.* We'd rather see innovative programs that address an as yet untouched business area." Company keeps all programs (both accepted and rejected) in its personal database for possible future marketing through hardware manufacturers.

Information Unlimited Software, Inc.
2401 Marinship Way
Sausalito, CA 94965
(415) 331-6700
Kevin Ellis, product marketing manager
Established 1977

COMPANY PROFILE

Word processing and general accounting programs. **Micros; Operating Systems:** MS-DOS, PC-DOS 1.1 and 2.0. **Recent Titles:** *Easywriter II, Easyplanner, Easyspeller, EasyBusiness Systems*. **Distribution Channels:** bookstores, catalogs, computer stores, consumer electronics stores, direct mail, mass merchandisers, software stores, system houses. No annual buying limit.

SUBMISSION GUIDELINES

Preferred Medium: floppy disk. Initial documentation required. **Average Company Response Time:** 4 weeks; rejected programs returned. **Payment:** Negotiable royalty paid quarterly or outright purchase. **Distribution Rights:** exclusive. **Plugging In:** Author's guide available.

Kensington Microware
919 3rd Ave.
New York, NY 10022
(212) 486-7707
Philip Damiano, director of software
   development and acquisitions
Established 1981

COMPANY PROFILE

Word processing. Also buys personal productivity. **Micros; Operating Systems:** Apple, DEC, IBM, Tandy, Victory, Wang. **Recent Titles:** *Format II Word Processing*. **Distribution Channels:** bookstores, computer stores, department stores, discount stores, mass merchandisers, software stores. Buys six programs annually; buying outlook increasing.

SUBMISSION GUIDELINES

Preferred Medium: floppy disk. Initial documentation required. **Average Company Response Time:** 8 weeks; rejected programs returned. **Payment:** 5 to 15 percent royalty paid quarterly or outright purchase (outright purchase preferred). **Distribution Rights:** exclusive. **Plugging In:** Kensington specializes in word processing for communications, but the company will consider any idea that has mass market applications.

Key Software, Inc.
2350 E. Devon, Suite 138
Des Plaines, IL 60018
(312) 298-3610
Robert Brownworth, vice president of marketing
Established 1982

COMPANY PROFILE

Database management software for business applications. **Micros; Operating Systems:** IBM PC and compatibles. **Recent Titles:** *ResQ*. **Distribution Channels:** computer stores, direct mail, software stores, Has not yet bought outside programs; company is now actively soliciting.

SUBMISSION GUIDELINES

Preferred Medium: floppy disk. Complete documentation required. **Average Company Response Time:** 4 weeks; rejected programs returned. **Payment:** negotiable royalty. **Distribution Rights:** exclusive.

Legend Industries, Ltd.
2220 Scott Lake Rd.
Pontiac, MI 48054
(313) 674-0953
Steven Freeman, director of software
   development and acquisitions
Established 1981

COMPANY PROFILE

Office management applications. Also buys personal productivity, systems. **Micros; Operating Systems:** Apple and compatibles. **Recent Titles:** *Legend Mailer*. **Distribution Channel:** computer stores. Buys two to five programs annually; buying outlook increasing.

SUBMISSION GUIDELINES

Preferred Medium: floppy disk. Complete documentation to be arranged between author and company. **Average Company Response Time:** 2 weeks; rejected programs returned. **Payment:** negotiable. **Distribution Rights:** negotiable.

Level IV Products, Inc.
32429 Schoolcraft
Livonia, MI 48150
(313) 525-6200
Nancy Longwell, vice president and general
 manager
Established 1977

COMPANY PROFILE

Records management and accounting. Also buys classroom education, personal productivity. **Micros; Operating Systems:** TRS-80. **Recent Titles:** *Mail List, Easy Account, Color Book.* **Distribution Channels:** computer stores, direct mail, software stores. No annual buying limit.

SUBMISSION GUIDELINES

Preferred Medium: floppy disk. Complete documentation required. **Average Company Response Time:** 3 weeks; rejected programs returned. **Payment:** maximum 20 percent royalty paid monthly. **Distribution Rights:** exclusive. **Plugging In:** Company is eagerly seeking programs that address such vertical markets as church management, insurance, photo labs, and other turnkey programs.

Lifeboat Associates
1651 Third Ave.
New York, NY 10028
(212) 860-0300
Carol Abrams, operations coordinator
Established 1977

COMPANY PROFILE

Financial planning, records management, and other business-oriented packages geared to vertical markets. Also buys systems. **Micros; Operating Systems:** all major 8- and 16-bit machines (175 in total). **Recent Titles:** *Lattice "C" Compiler, Float 87, Proman, P Link 86.* **Distribution Channels:** bookstores, catalogs, computer stores, direct mail, software stores. Company has over 3000 accounts and international distribution. Buys over 100 programs annually; buying outlook increasing.

SUBMISSION GUIDELINES

Preferred Medium: floppy disk. Complete documentation required. **Average Company Response Time:** 4 to 6 weeks; rejected programs returned. **Payment:** negotiable royalty. **Distribution Rights:** negotiable. **Plugging In:** Company will not look at program unless it is copyrighted and fully operational. To stand out from the crowd (the firm receives as many as 30 submissions a week), offer programs geared to vertical markets that can run on IBM PC, CP/M, and 8- or 16-bit mainframes. Author's guide available.

Lotus Development Corporation
55 Wheeler St.
Cambridge, MA 02138
(617) 492-7171
Does not actively solicit.

Manhattan Software
P.O. Box 1063
Woodland Hills, CA 91365
(213) 453-6943
Charles Leedham, director of software
 development and acquisitions
Established 1979

COMPANY PROFILE

Business management. Also buys recreation, personal productivity. **Micros; Operating Systems:** Apple II, IBM PC, TRS-80. **Recent Titles:** *The Amway Business Manager, Cribbage Master II, Casino Blackjack Counter/Tutor.* **Distribution Channels:** direct mail, software stores. Buys five to six programs annually; buying outlook increasing.

SUBMISSION GUIDELINES

Preferred Medium: floppy disk. Complete documentation required. **Average Company Response Time:** 2 weeks; rejected programs returned. **Payment:** 10 to 20 percent royalty paid quarterly. **Distribution Rights:** exclusive.

Mark of the Unicorn
222 Third St.
Cambridge, MA 02142
(617) 576-2760
Robert Nathaniel, director of software acquisition
Established 1978

COMPANY PROFILE

Word processing, screen-oriented text editing and text formatter for professional use. Also buys personal productivity, systems. **Micros; Operating Systems:** Apple, Cromemco, Dynabyte, Heath/Zenith, IBM PC, Vector Graphics, SuperBrain, TRS-80; CP/M, CP/M-86, MS-DOS, PC-DOS, Venix. **Distribution Channels:** catalogs, computer stores, consumer electronics stores, direct mail, software stores. Buys fewer than 10 programs annually; buying outlook the same.

SUBMISSION GUIDELINES

Preferred Medium: floppy disk. Initial documentation required. **Average Company Response Time:** 6 to 8 weeks; rejected programs returned. **Payment:** negotiable royalty or outright purchase. **Distribution Rights:** negotiable.

Max Ule & Company
6 E. 42d St.
New York, NY 10017
(212) 687-0705
Max Ule, president
Established 1977

COMPANY PROFILE

Portfolio management. Also buys personal productivity. **Micros; Operating Systems:** Apple II, II+, and IIe, IBM PC, Northstar Horizon, Televideo 802 and 802H, TRS-80 I, II, III, IV, XII, and XVI. **Recent Title:** Tickertec. **Distribution Channel:** direct mail. No annual buying limit.

SUBMISSION GUIDELINES

Preferred Medium: floppy disk. Complete documentation required. **Average Company Response Time:** 1 week; rejected programs returned on request. **Payment:** outright purchase. **Distribution Rights:** exclusive.

MC ↑ 2 Programs
9655 S. Dixie Highway, No. 305
Miami, FL 33143
(305) 666-1300
Robert McClintock, president
Established 1977

COMPANY PROFILE

Simulations and economic analysis for engineering applications. **Micros; Operating Systems:** CP/M, MS-DOS, TRS-DOS, Xenix. **Recent Titles:** Energy Estimation, Structural Finite Element Analysis. **Distribution Channel:** direct mail. Buys four to six programs annually; buying outlook increasing.

SUBMISSION GUIDELINES

Preferred Medium: floppy disk. Complete documentation required. **Average Company Response Time:** 2 weeks; rejected programs returned. **Payment:** negotiable royalty paid quarterly. **Distribution Rights:** exclusive.

MicroRIM, Inc.
1750 112th Ave. N.E.
Bellevue, WA 98004
(206) 453-6017
Cyndi Willoughby, product manager
Established 1982

COMPANY PROFILE

Database managers for small-business use. Also buys systems. **Micros; Operating Systems:** DEC Rainbow, HP-150, IBM PC and compatibles, Professional; CP/M, C-TOS, MS-DOS. **Recent Titles:** MicroRIM, R:Base 4000, The Program Interface. **Distribution Channels:** Computer stores, department stores, direct mail, software stores. Has not yet bought outside programs; company is now actively soliciting.

SUBMISSION GUIDELINES

Preferred Medium: floppy disk. Complete documentation required. **Average Company Response Time:** 4 weeks; rejected programs returned. **Payment:** negotiable royalty. **Distribution Rights:** negotiable. **Plugging In:** ''We are interested in applications for small business that utilize our current packages."

Microsoft Corporation
10700 Northrup Way
Bellevue, WA 98004
(206) 828-8080
Alan Boyd, manager of product acquisition
Established 1975

COMPANY PROFILE

Word processing and spreadsheets. Also buys systems. **Micros; Operating Systems:** IBM PC and compatibles; MS-DOS. **Recent Titles:** *Multiplan Spreadsheet, Microsoft Word, Microsoft BASIC.* **Distribution Channels:** computer stores, software stores. Has bought one program (out of 20,000 submissions); buying outlook decreasing.

SUBMISSION GUIDELINES

Preferred Medium: floppy disk. Complete documentation required. **Average Company Response Time:** varies; rejected programs not returned. **Payment:** negotiable royalty or outright purchase. **Distribution Rights:** exclusive. **Plugging In:** "We will only look at finished products." Prefers to see work from accomplished professionals.

MMG Micro Software
P.O. Box 131
Marlboro, NJ 07746
(201) 431-3472
Mark Chasin, direction of software development
Established 1981

COMPANY PROFILE

Complete business packages. Also buys recreation, classroom education, systems. **Micros; Operating Systems:** Apple, Atari, Commodore 64, IBM PC. **Recent Titles:** *MMG Data Manager, MMG General Ledger, MMG Accounts Receivable.* **Distribution Channels:** bookstores, catalogs, computer stores, consumer electronics stores, department stores, direct mail, discount stores, mass merchandisers, software stores, toy stores, video stores. Buys 15 programs annually; buying outlook increasing.

SUBMISSION GUIDELINES

Preferred Medium: floppy disk. Initial documentation required. **Average Company Response Time:** 2 to 4 weeks; rejected programs returned. **Payment:** 20 percent royalty paid quarterly. **Distribution Rights:** exclusive.

NEC Home Electronics USA, Personal Computer
  Division
1401 Estes Ave.
Elk Grove Village, IL 60007
Roy Giampoli, software manager
Established 1981

COMPANY PROFILE

Word processing and database management for portable and desktop models. Also buys recreation (primarily home education) for its home computer. **Micros; Operating Systems:** NEC Trek PC-6000, PC-8800, PC-8200. **Recent Titles:** *Electric Pencil, File Manager, Colorcalc.* **Distribution Channels:** computer stores, "some" department stores for home computers, software stores. Buys 30-plus programs annually; buying outlook the same (depending on market acceptance of PC-6000).

SUBMISSION GUIDELINES

Preferred Medium: floppy disk. Complete documentation required. **Average Company Response Time:** from 1 week to 6 months; rejected programs returned. **Payment:** 10 percent royalty paid quarterly. **Distribution Rights:** exclusive. **Plugging In:** "For our home computer (NEC Trek) we're especially interested in entertainment programs with educational value."

Omni Software Systems, Inc.
146 N. Broad St.
Griffith, IN 46319
(219) 924-3522
Joe T. Alonso, director of software development
  and acquisitions.
Established 1979

COMPANY PROFILE

Accounting and business software. Also buys systems. **Micros; Operating Systems:** IBM PC, Northstar Advantage and Horizon. **Recent Titles:** *The Stock Manager, After-the-Fact Payroll, Client Information System.* **Distribution Channels:** catalogs, computer stores, direct mail. Buys 12 program annually; buying outlook increasing.

SUBMISSION GUIDELINES

Preferred Medium: floppy disk. Complete documentation required. **Average Company Response Time:** 2 to 3 weeks; rejected programs returned. **Payment:** 25 to 50 percent royalty paid quarterly. **Distribution Rights:** exclusive. **Plugging In:** Firm "appreciates" familiarity with Northstar systems and prior experience.

Peachtree Associates, Inc.
P.O. Box 1312
Decatur, GA 30031
(404) 373-3000
Edward Jacobson, president
Established 1983

COMPANY PROFILE

Energy control systems. Also buys recreation, personal productivity. **Micros; Operating Systems:** CP/M. **Recent Title:** *ENERGY-$AVE.* **Distribution Channels:** catalogs, computer stores, direct mail, software stores. Buys two to five programs annually; buying outlook increasing.

SUBMISSION GUIDELINES

Preferred Medium: floppy disk. Initial documentation required. **Average Company Response Time:** 3 weeks; rejected programs returned. **Payment:** 20 percent royalty paid quarterly. **Distribution Rights:** negotiable. **Plugging In:** Firm's major areas are energy and engineering, but the company will consider any technical applications. Also, in the near future, firm will look into business software for the manufacturer.

Peachtree Software, Inc.
3445 Peachtree Rd. N.E.

Atlanta, GA 30326
(404) 239-3000
Charles F. Tucker, assistant to president
Established 1977

COMPANY PROFILE

Office, project management, accounting. Also buys personal productivity, classroom education. **Micros; Operating Systems:** CP/M, MS-DOS, PC-DOS. **Recent Titles:** *List Manager, Project Management, PeachCalc.* **Distribution Channels:** bookstores, catalogs, computer stores, direct mail, original equipment manufacturers, software stores. No annual buying limit.

SUBMISSION GUIDELINES

Preferred Medium: floppy disk. Complete documentation required. **Average Company Response Time:** 4 weeks; rejected programs returned. **Payment:** negotiable royalty or outright purchase. **Distribution Rights:** exclusive. **Plugging In:** Programs should be simple and user-friendly.

Phase One Systems, Inc.
7700 Edgewater Dr., Suite 830
Oakland, CA 94621
(415) 562-8085
Joel Laffitte, sales representative
Established 1978

COMPANY PROFILE

Database managers, spreadsheets, word processors for horizontal markets. Also buys systems. **Micros; Operating System:** Oasis. **Recent Titles:** *MasterPlan, Data Base Manager, Oasis Operating System, BiSynz.* **Distribution Channel:** direct mail (to consultants). Buys three programs annually; buying outlook increasing.

SUBMISSION GUIDELINES

Preferred Medium: floppy disk. Complete documentation required. **Average Company Response Time:** 4 to 6 weeks; rejected programs not returned. **Payment:** negotiable royalty. **Distribution Rights:** exclusive. **Plugging In:**

Program must run on company's Oasis operating system for either 8- or 16-bit mainframes.

Pioneer Software
1746 N.W. 55th Ave., No. 204
Lauderhill, FL 33313
(305) 739-2071
Jerry Goodwin, director of software development
  and acquisition
Established 1980

COMPANY PROFILE

Office word processing, records management, graphics. Also buys recreation, personal productivity, classroom education. **Micros; Operating Systems:** TRS-80 I, III, and IV. **Recent Titles:** *Scriptr, Crayon, Crayon Deluxe, Music Magic.* **Distribution Channels:** catalogs, mail order. Has not yet bought outside programs; company is now actively soliciting.

SUBMISSION GUIDELINES

Preferred Medium: floppy disk. Complete documentation required. **Average Company Response Time:** 12 weeks; rejected programs returned. **Payment:** 20 percent royalty paid quarterly. **Distribution Rights:** nonexclusive.

Professional Software
51 Fremont St.
Needham, MA 02194
(617) 444-5224
Harold Dickerman, product manager
Established 1980

COMPANY PROFILE

Easy-to-use word processing. **Micros; Operating Systems:** Commodore 64, IBM PC, TI Professional. **Recent Titles:** *WordPro, InfoPro, WordPlus PC, SpellWright.* **Distribution Channels:** computer stores, direct mail, software stores. Buys one program annually; buying outlook increasing.

SUBMISSION GUIDELINES

Preferred Medium: floppy disk. Complete documentation required. **Average Company Re-**sponse Time: 4 weeks; rejected programs returned on request. **Payment:** negotiable royalty paid quarterly. **Distribution Rights:** exclusive.

Remote Computing, division of Hale Systems
1044 Northern Blvd.
Roslyn, NY 11576
(516) 484-4545
Lenore Salzbrunn, software acquisitions
Established 1983 (parent firm, 1966)

COMPANY PROFILE

Financial and investment analysis and management. **Micros; Operating Systems:** Apple and compatibles, IBM PC. **Recent Titles:** *Pear Systems Technical Analysis, Pear Systems Portfolio Management System.* **Distribution Channels:** computer stores, direct mail. Has not yet bought outside programs; company now actively soliciting.

SUBMISSION GUIDELINES

Preferred Medium: floppy disk. Initial documentation required. **Average Company Response Time:** 6 to 8 weeks. **Payment:** negotiable royalty or outright purchase. **Distribution Rights:** negotiable. **Plugging In:** Company is known for its financial and investment services software aimed at money managers, traders, investors, and stockbrokers.

Resource Software International, Inc.
330 New Brunswick Ave.
Fords, NJ 08863
(201) 738-8500
Peter Morley, sales manager
Established 1977

COMPANY PROFILE

Accounting, project management, and cost control for a variety of industries. Also buys recreation, classroom education. **Micros; Operating Systems:** APF Imagination, Apple II, IBM PC, Kaypro II, TRS-80, Xerox 820; CP/M, mBASIC. **Recent Titles:** *General Ledger, Broker Sales, Funzeez.* **Distribution Channels:** computer stores, consumer electronics stores, direct mail, software stores. Buys three programs annually; buying outlook increasing.

SUBMISSION GUIDELINES

Preferred Media: floppy disk, cassette tape. Initial documentation required. **Average Company Response Time:** 1 week; rejected programs returned. **Payment:** 50 percent royalty (gross sales) paid annually or outright purchase. **Distribution Rights:** exclusive. **Plugging In:** Resource's selection criteria are based on "buying particular applications for specific industries. The main characteristic or requirement is that it (the program) 'stand alone.' That is, it must not be dependent on some program nor may eventually output depend on another program not included in your offer." For the company to evaluate your offer, the following should be submitted promptly: a description of the basic functions performed in the application program set; number of individual programs; application (system) flow chart; minimum computer componentry on which system will operate (layout chart preferred); operating system used; programming language used; asking price for all source programs; number of current users. Author's guide available.

Sensible Software, Inc.
6619 Perham Dr.
West Bloomfield, MI 48033
(313) 399-8877
Roger Tuttleman, director of software
    development
Established 1978

COMPANY PROFILE

Word processing, records management, and graphics. Also buys personal productivity, recreation. **Micros; Operating Systems:** Apple, Atari, Commodore 64, IBM PC and PCjr. **Recent Titles:** *Bookends Graphics Department, Sensible Speller IV, Quadrants.* **Distribution Channels:** bookstores, computer stores, consumer electronics stores, department stores, direct mail, mass merchandisers, software stores. Buys five programs annually; buying outlook increasing.

SUBMISSION GUIDELINES

Preferred Medium: floppy disk. Initial documentation required. **Average Company Response Time:** 2 to 4 weeks; rejected programs returned. **Payment:** negotiable royalty. **Distribution Rights:** exclusive. **Plugging In:** Company prefers "unfinished packages because they are easier to refine to company standards." Author's guide available.

Software Arts, Inc.
27 Mica La.
Wellesley, MA 02180
(617) 237-4000
Does not actively solicit.

S.S.R. Corporation
1600 Lyell Ave.
Rochester, NY 14606
(716) 254-3200
Robert Bundy, director of software development
Established 1969

COMPANY PROFILE

Office inventory management. **Micros; Operating Systems:** Apple II, IIe, and III, DEC Rainbow, IBM PC and XT and compatibles, Victor 9000, Wang, Zenith 100; CP/M-86, MS-DOS. **Recent Titles:** *Infotory, Omnifile.* **Distribution Channels:** computer stores, software stores. No annual buying limit.

SUBMISSION GUIDELINES

Preferred Media: floppy disk, hard disk. Complete documentation required; company edits. **Average Company Response Time:** 8 weeks; rejected programs returned. **Payment:** negotiable royalty. **Distribution Rights:** negotiable. **Plugging In:** Author's guide available.

Sunrise Software, Inc.
P.O. Box 461
Owatonna, MN 55060
(507) 451-0860

G. Peter Czok, president
Established 1981

COMPANY PROFILE

Spreadsheets, business graphics, and records management designed for use with handheld computers. Also buys recreation, personal productivity, classroom education. **Micros; Operating Systems:** Handheld computers from Casio, Hewlett-Packard, Panasonic, Radio Shack, Sharp. **Recent Titles:** *MatrixCalc, Yardstick, Puzzles, Math Frame.* **Distribution Channels:** bookstores, catalogs, computer stores, consumer electronics stores, department stores, mass merchandisers, office supply stores, original equipment manufacturers, software stores. Buys four programs annually; buying outlook increasing.

SUBMISSION GUIDELINES

Preferred Medium: cassette tape. Initial documentation required. **Average Company Response Time:** 1 week; rejected programs returned. **Payment:** 10 percent royalty paid quarterly or monthly. **Distribution Rights:** negotiable. **Plugging In:** "We are looking for applications that are highly advantageous when portable. General ledgers are out. Programs that evaluate sales goals and productivity within a small memory are in. All programs should have password protection."

Systems Plus, Inc.
1120 San Antonio Rd.
Palo Alto, CA 94303
(415) 969-7047
Richard W. Mehrlich, director of software
    development
Established 1980

COMPANY PROFILE

Office, medical, accounting management. Also buys personal productivity. **Micros; Operating Systems:** Apple, IBM; CP/M, CP/M-86, MP/M, MP/M-86, MS-DOS. **Recent Titles:** *Medical Manager, Client Manager, The Landlord.* **Distribution Channels:** computer stores, software stores. Buys five programs annually; buying outlook increasing.

SUBMISSION GUIDELINES

Preferred Medium: floppy disk. Complete documentation required. **Average Company Response Time:** 6 weeks; rejected programs returned on request. **Payment:** negotiable royalty or outright purchase. **Distribution Rights:** exclusive.

TCS Software
3209 Fondren Rd.
Houston, TX 77063
(713) 977-7505
Linda L. Duttenhaver, marketing manager
Established 1975

COMPANY PROFILE

Word processing, accounting, and records management featuring QUICK database manager. **Micros; Operating Systems:** IBM PC and compatibles, TI, Vector Graphics (approximately 30 micros total); CP/M, MS-DOS. **Recent Titles:** *TCS Total Materials, TCS Q*WORD, TCS Total Sales, Client Ledger Systems.* **Distribution Channels:** computer stores, software stores, system houses and consultants. Buys one program annually; buying outlook increasing.

SUBMISSION GUIDELINES

Preferred Medium: floppy disk. Complete documentation required (in *WordStar* format). **Average Company Response Time:** 4 to 8 weeks; rejected programs returned. **Payment:** negotiable royalty. **Distribution Rights:** exclusive. **Plugging In:** Company needs vertical market applications incorporating its database management system.

Tristar Data Systems
2 Keystone Ave.
Cherry Hill, NJ 08003
(609) 424-4700
Pete Morley, director of software development
    and acquisitions
Established 1970

COMPANY PROFILE

Office, records management. Also buys personal productivity, systems. **Micros; Operating Systems:** CP/M, CP/M-86, MS-DOS. **Recent Titles:** *Librarian, The Manager.* **Distribution Channels:** computer stores, direct mail, software stores. Buys 15 programs annually; buying outlook increasing.

SUBMISSION GUIDELINES

Preferred Medium: floppy disk. Complete documentation required. **Average Company Response Time:** 4 weeks; rejected programs returned. **Payment:** negotiable royalty or outright purchase. **Distribution Rights:** negotiable. **Plugging In:** Tristar says business software accounts form the brunt of its business. "Our goal is to help the businessman."

VisiCorp
2895 Zanker Rd.
San Jose, CA 95134
(408) 946-9000
Horace Enea, director of research & development
Established 1978

COMPANY PROFILE

Family of business tools, including spreadsheet, graphing, indexing, and integrated packages. **Micros; Operating Systems:** Apple, DEC, IBM, TI, Sony; CP/M. **Recent Titles:** *VisiOn, VisiPlot/ VisiTrend, Advanced VisiCalc.* **Distribution Channels:** bookstores, computer stores, consumer electronics stores, department stores, software stores. No annual buying limit.

SUBMISSION GUIDELINES

Preferred Medium: floppy disk. Initial documentation required. **Average Company Response Time:** 6 to 8 weeks; rejected programs returned. **Payment:** negotiable royalty or outright purchase. **Distribution Rights:** exclusive.

Wadsworth Electronic Publishing Company,
    division of Wadsworth, Inc.
20 Park Plaza

Boston, MA 02116
(617) 423-0420
Rick Dunfey, executive software director
Established 1981

COMPANY PROFILE

Statistics, accounting, records management, business graphics, and forecasting. Also buys classroom education (through separate division). **Micros; Operating Systems:** Apple, IBM PC. **Recent Titles:** *StatPro, LP.* **Distribution Channels:** computer stores, direct mail, software stores. No annual buying limit (all programs written outside).

SUBMISSION GUIDELINES

Preferred Medium: floppy disk. Complete documentation required. **Average Company Response Time:** 2 weeks; rejected programs returned. **Payment:** negotiable royalty. **Distribution Rights:** exclusive. **Plugging In:** Company buys educational software out of its west coast office at 6 Davis Dr., Belmont, CA 94002, (415) 594-1900, attention Bob Evans, technical editor. Author's guide available.

Western Properties Investment Company,
    Software Division
P.O. Box 9602
Marina Del Rey, CA 90295
(213) 823-4444
Joel Binder, president
Established 1982

COMPANY PROFILE

Entrepreneurial and small-business financial and word processing software. Also buys personal productivity, systems. **Micros; Operating Systems:** TI 99/4A, selected others. **Recent Titles:** *Income and Expense Spreadsheet IV* (spreadsheet), *Income and Expense DP VI* (spreadsheet), *File Book IIIP* (database manager), *Printer Book* (word processor). **Distribution Channels:** catalogs, department stores, direct mail. Has not yet bought outside programs; company is now actively soliciting.

SUBMISSION GUIDELINES

Preferred Medium: cassette tape. Initial documentation required. **Average Company Response Time:** varies; rejected programs returned. **Payment:** negotiable royalty or outright purchase. **Distribution Rights:** negotiable. **Plugging In:** Company fits a specialized niche by providing TI small-business users with programs that run with TI's Extended BASIC module on cassette but without extra peripherals and memory, "thus saving users $500 to $600. The submission must be on cassette; must load on tape, but be capable of input/output through either disk or cassette; and must be usable with TI Extended BASIC and not require memory expansion. Write for our catalog to determine if your idea has already been produced before sending query letter."

Westico, Inc.
25 Van Zant St.
Norwalk, CT 06855
(203) 853-6880

Phillip Woellhof, vice president
Established 1980

COMPANY PROFILE

Accounting, telecommunications, planning and analysis, word processing. Also buys personal productivity, systems. **Micros; Operating Systems:** CP/M-80, CP/M-86, IBM PC-DOS, MS-DOS. **Recent Titles:** *Fixed Asset Accounting, Billkeeper, Supercalc.* **Distribution Channels:** catalogs, computer stores, direct mail, software stores. Buys 30 programs annually; buying outlook increasing.

SUBMISSION GUIDELINES

Preferred Medium: floppy disk. Complete documentation required. **Average Company Response Time:** 4 weeks; rejected programs not returned. **Payment:** negotiable royalty paid monthly. **Distribution Rights:** negotiable.

CROSS-REFERENCES—BUSINESS AND PROFESSIONAL MANAGEMENT

The following companies also buy business and professional management software. Their complete listings may be found under the major headings shown.

RECREATION

Adventure International, division of Scott Adams, Inc.
Atari, Inc.
Atari Program Exchange (APX)
Avant-Garde Creations, Inc.
Broderbund Software, Inc.
CBS Software
Comm*Data Computer House, Inc.
CompuServe, Inc.
Databar Corporation
Datasoft, Inc.
Dilithium Press
Hayden Software Company
Insoft, Inc.
Instant Software, Inc., division of Wayne Green, Inc.
International Publishing & Software, Inc.
JMG Software International

Microcomputers Corporation
MicroLab, Inc.
Muse Software, Inc.
Not-Polyoptics
Odesta
Passport Designs, Inc.
Penguin Software, Inc.
Phoenix Software, Inc.
Piccadilly Software
Prentice-Hall, Inc.
Rainbow Computing, Inc.
Ranco Software Games, Inc.
Rantom Software
RB Robot Corporation
Roklan Software
Royal Software/COMPUTER PALACE
Sentient Software, Inc.
Sierra On-Line, Inc.
Sir-tech Software, Inc.

Softsel Computer Products, Inc.
Softside Magazine
Softsync, Inc.
The Software Guild
Source Telecomputing Corporation
Spectral Associates
United Microware Industries, Inc.
Windcrest Software, Inc.

PERSONAL PRODUCTIVITY

Acorn Software, a division of Banbury Books
Alphanetics Software
Arlington Software + Systems
Artsci
Best Programs
Computerized Management Systems
Computer Software Associates, Inc.
Continental Software
Digital Marketing Corporation
Dynacomp, Inc.
Hoyle and Hoyle Software, Inc.
IJG, Inc.
Masterworks Software, Inc.
Orbyte Software
Pacific TriMicro
PBL Corporation
PC Disk Magazine
Powersoft, Inc.
Practical Programs
The Quick Brown Fox Company
Reader's Digest Services, Inc.

Silicon Valley Systems, Inc.
Software Publishing Corporation

CLASSROOM EDUCATION

Ed-Sci Development
Houghton Mifflin Company
Innovative Programming Associates, Inc.
McGraw-Hill Book Company
REMsoft, Inc.
Scott Foresman and Company, Electronic Publishing Division
John Wiley & Sons, Inc.

SYSTEMS

Alcor Systems
Alpha Software Corporation
Apparat, Inc.
Communications Research Group
Cosmopolitan Electronics Corporation
Digital Research, Inc., Computer Products Division
Fox & Geller, Inc.
Micro Ap
The Micro Works, Inc.
MicroSPARC, Inc.
Omega MicroWare Software Products
Optimized Systems Software, Inc.
The Software Toolworks
Southeastern Software
SuperSoft, Inc.

Systems

Alcor Systems
800 W. Garland Ave., No. 204
Garland, TX 75040
John Jennings, director of software development
and acquisitions
Established 1980

COMPANY PROFILE

Languages. Also buys classroom education, business and professional management. **Micros; Operating Systems:** CP/M, LDOS, NEWDOS, TRS-DOS. **Recent Titles:** *Alcor Pascal Language System, TRS-80 Pascal.* **Distribution Channels:** computer stores, direct mail, software stores. No annual buying limit.

SUBMISSION GUIDELINES

Preferred Medium: floppy disk. Complete documentation required. **Average Company Response Time:** 2 weeks; rejected programs returned. **Payment:** negotiable royalty or outright purchase. **Distribution Rights:** exclusive and nonexclusive.

Alpha Software Corporation
12 New England Executive Park

Burlington, MA 01803
(617) 229-2924
George Lechter, director of software
development and acquisitions
Established 1982

COMPANY PROFILE

Database management. Also buys recreation, personal productivity, business and professional management. **Micros; Operating Systems:** MS-DOS. **Recent Titles:** *Data Base Manager II, Executive Package.* **Distribution Channels:** bookstores, catalogs, computer stores, consumer electronics stores, department stores, discount stores, mass merchandisers. Buys five programs annually; buying outlook increasing.

SUBMISSION GUIDELINES

Preferred Medium: floppy disk. Initial documentation required. **Average Company Response Time:** 1 week; rejected programs returned. **Payment:** usually 10 percent royalty paid quarterly. **Distribution Rights:** exclusive.

Apparat, Inc.
4401 S. Tamarac Pkwy.

Denver, CO 80237
(303) 741-1778
Ed Abrams, director of marketing
Established 1978

COMPANY PROFILE

Operating systems. Also buys recreation, personal productivity, classroom education, business and professional management. **Micros; Operating Systems:** IBM PC, TRS-80. **Recent Titles:** *NEWDOS 80.* **Distribution Channel:** direct mail. Buys two to three programs annually; buying outlook increasing.

SUBMISSION GUIDELINES

Preferred Medium: floppy disk. Complete documentation required. **Average Company Response Time:** varies; rejected programs returned. **Payment:** negotiable royalty. **Distribution Rights:** exclusive. **Plugging In:** "We're looking for anything that will sell."

Aton International
260 Brooklyn Ave.
San Jose, CA 95128
(408) 554-9922
Chuck Wilde, president
Established 1981

COMPANY PROFILE

Videotext editors and programming languages. **Micros; Operating Systems:** TRS-80. **Recent Titles:** *Omniwriter Videotext Editor, BASIC Surrogate, VisiCalc Surrogate.* **Distribution Channels:** computer stores, direct mail, software stores. Buys four programs annually; buying outlook the same.

SUBMISSION GUIDELINES

Preferred Medium: floppy disk. Complete documentation required. **Average Company Response Time:** 1 to 3 weeks; rejected programs returned. **Payments:** 25 to 30 percent royalty paid monthly or outright purchase. **Distribution Rights:** exclusive. **Plugging In:** "We're looking for data communications."

Aurora Software
37 S. Mitchell
Arlington Heights, IL 60005
(312) 259-3150
Owen West, president
Established 1979

COMPANY PROFILE

Programming languages. Also buys recreation. **Micros; Operating Systems:** Ohio Scientific Personal Computers. **Recent Titles:** *S-Forth, Adventure, The Wizard's City.* **Distribution Channel:** direct mail. No annual buying limit.

SUBMISSION GUIDELINES

Preferred Media: floppy disk, cassette tape. Complete documentation required. **Average Company Response Time:** 4 to 8 weeks; rejected programs returned with SASE. **Payment:** 25 percent royalty paid semiannually. **Distribution Rights:** nonexclusive. **Plugging In:** "Make certain your program does not duplicate an idea we have already developed."

Beagle Brothers Micro Software
4315 Sierra Vista
San Diego, CA 92103
(619) 296-6400
Bert Kersey, president
Established 1980

COMPANY PROFILE

Utilities. **Micros; Operating Systems:** Apple. **Recent Titles:** *Utility City, DOS Boss, Apple Mechanics.* **Distribution Channel:** direct mail. Buys three programs annually; buying outlook increasing.

SUBMISSION GUIDELINES

Preferred Medium: floppy disk. Complete documentation required. **Average Company Response Time:** 2 to 3 weeks; rejected programs returned with SASE. **Payment:** 20 percent royalty (based on gross receipts) paid monthly. **Distribution Rights:** negotiable.

Central Point Software
P.O. Box 19730, no. 203
Portland, OR 97219
(503) 244-5782
Linda Swanson, software development and
acquisitions director
Established 1981

COMPANY PROFILE

Utilities and software tools. **Micros; Operating Systems:** Apple II and IIe, IBM PC. **Recent Titles:** *Copy II Plus, Copy II PC, The Filer.* **Distribution Channels:** bookstores, catalogs, computer stores, consumer electronics stores, department stores, direct mail, discount stores, mass merchandisers, software stores. Buys two programs annually; buying outlook the same.

SUBMISSION GUIDELINES

Preferred Medium: floppy disk. Complete documentation required. **Average Company Response Time:** 1 or 2 weeks "for good prospects," up to 8 weeks for others; rejected programs returned on request. **Payment:** negotiable royalty paid quarterly or outright purchase. **Distribution Rights:** exclusive. **Plugging In:** Central Point actively promotes the software it accepts. Therefore, programs with a "very broad appeal and a desirable unique quality that would place them above the rest" will get most serious consideration.

Communications Research Group
8939 Jefferson Hwy.
Baton Rouge, LA 70809
(504) 923-0888
Polly Henderson, director of software
development and acquisitions
Established 1980

COMPANY PROFILE

Computer-to-computer communications. Also buys business and professional management. **Micros; Operating Systems:** Apple, Data General, DEC, IBM PC; CP/M, UNIX. **Recent Title:** *BLAST* (*blocked asynchronous transmission*). **Distribution Channels:** computer stores, direct mail, mass merchandisers, original equip-

ment manufacturers, software stores. No annual buying limit.

SUBMISSION GUIDELINES

Preferred Media: floppy disk or cassette tape. Initial documentation required. **Average Company Response Time:** 1 week; rejected programs returned. **Payment:** 20 percent royalty paid quarterly and percentage of profit. **Distribution Rights:** exclusive. **Plugging In:** Communications Research distributes communications software worldwide to professional, industrial, government, and scientific markets.

Computer Applications Unlimited, division of
CAU, Inc.
Box 214
Rye, NY 10580
(914) 937-6286
David Willen, director of software development
and acquisitions
Established 1980

COMPANY PROFILE

Utilities (editors and assemblers). **Micros; Operating Systems:** IBM PC, TRS-80. **Recent Titles:** *M-ZAL, XBE.* **Distribution Channels:** bookstores, catalogs, computer stores, consumer electronics stores, direct mail, discount stores, mass merchandisers, software stores. No annual buying limit.

SUBMISSION GUIDELINES

Preferred Medium: floppy disk. Complete documentation required. **Average Company Response Time:** 26 weeks; rejected programs returned. **Payment:** 10 to 15 percent royalty paid quarterly or outright purchase. **Distribution Rights:** negotiable.

Cosmopolitan Electronics Corporation
P.O. Box 234
Plymouth, MI 48170
(313) 668-6600 or (800) 392-3785
Vernon B. Hester, president
Established 1981

COMPANY PROFILE

Programming languages, utilities, editors, assemblers. Also buys personal productivity, classroom education, business and professional management. **Micros; Operating Systems:** TRS-80 I, III, and Z80 systems. **Recent Titles:** *E BASIC, BOSS (Best Of the Single Steppers), ZEUS.* **Distribution Channels:** computer stores, direct mail, software stores. Buys one program annually; buying outlook increasing.

SUBMISSION GUIDELINES

Preferred Medium: floppy disk. Complete documentation required. **Average Company Response Time:** 2 weeks; rejected programs returned on request. **Payment:** negotiable royalty paid monthly. **Distribution Rights:** negotiable. **Plugging In:** "We want inventory, accounts payable and receivable—no games."

Data-RX, Inc.
686 Lighthouse Ave.
Monterey, CA 93940
(408) 375-2775
Dale Lum, director of software development
Established 1979

COMPANY PROFILE

Utilities. **Micros; Operating Systems:** CP/M, TURBO-DOS. **Recent Title:** *The Control Center.* **Distribution Channels:** computer stores, consumer electronics stores, software stores. Buys up to 12 programs annually; buying outlook increasing.

SUBMISSION GUIDELINES

Preferred Medium: floppy disk. Initial documentation required. **Average Company Response Time:** 4 weeks; rejected programs returned. **Payment:** 10 percent royalty (on retail sales) paid quarterly. **Distribution Rights:** negotiable.

Digital Research, Inc., Consumer Products
Division
160 Central Ave.
Pacific Grove, CA 93950

(408) 649-5500
Kenneth Harkness, general manager
Established 1976, consumer division, 1983

COMPANY PROFILE

Programming languages, easy-to-use utilities. Also buys recreation, classroom education, personal productivity, business and professional management. **Micros; Operating Systems:** CP/M, MP/M-86, concurrent CP/M. **Recent Titles:** *Personal BASIC, Despool, Tex, Dr. Plot, Dr. Logo.* **Distribution Channels:** bookstores, computer stores, consumer electronics stores, department stores, mass merchandisers, original equipment manufacturers, software stores, video stores. Has not yet bought outside programs; company is now actively soliciting.

SUBMISSION GUIDELINES

Preferred Medium: floppy disk. Initial documentation required. **Average Company Response Time:** 6 to 8 weeks; rejected programs returned. **Payment:** negotiable royalty. **Distribution Rights:** exclusive. **Plugging In:** "The Consumer Products Division will concentrate on broad-use, mass-market software products. The company will build the division around a strategic consumer software marketing program incorporating in-house and independent software developers."

Fox & Geller, Inc.
604 Market St.
Elmwood Park, NY 07407
(201) 794-8883
Jeff Fox and Jake Geller, cofounders
Established 1981

COMPANY PROFILE

Control systems for business-oriented programs. Also buys business and professional management. **Micros; Operating Systems:** CP/M 2.2 or higher for 8-bit machines, PC-DOS and MS-DOS for 16-bit mainframes. **Recent Titles:** *Quick Code, OZ, dUTIL, Grafox.* **Distribution Channels:** computer stores, consultants, direct mail, software stores. Has not yet bought outside programs; company is now actively soliciting.

SUBMISSION GUIDELINES

Preferred Medium: floppy disk. Complete documentation required. **Average Company Response Time:** 4 weeks; rejected programs returned. **Payment:** negotiable royalty or outright purchase. **Distribution Rights:** negotiable. **Plugging In:** Company is attempting to move away from its dependence on programs that work with dBase II, wants programs that operate with other major database management packages.

Frobco, division of Tri-Comp Polytechnical, Inc.
P.O. Box 8378
Santa Cruz, CA 95061
(408) 429-1551
Candace L. Brown, director of software
  development
Established 1980

COMPANY PROFILE

Programmers' development systems. **Micros; Operating Systems:** Atari 2600 and 5200, Coleco's ADAM; Z80. **Recent Titles:** *FROB-26 Development System, FROB-52 Development System, FROB Coleco Development System.* **Distribution Channels:** direct mail, trade shows. Has not yet bought outside programs; company is now actively soliciting.

SUBMISSION GUIDELINES

Preferred Medium: floppy disk. Complete documentation required. **Average Company Response Time:** 2 to 4 weeks; rejected programs returned. **Payment:** negotiable royalty paid quarterly or outright purchase. **Distribution Rights:** exclusive. **Plugging In:** Firm needs software that assists programmers in the design of cartridge prototypes as well as graphics tools, sound editors, file management, microprocessor emulators and debuggers for any cartridge game console or home computer.

InfoSoft Systems, Inc.
P.O. Box 640,
80 Washington St.

Norwalk, CT 06856
(203) 866-8833
Jerrold H. Koret, president
Established 1979

COMPANY PROFILE

Structured assemblers, debugging tools. Also buys recreation, personal productivity. **Micros; Operating Systems:** I/OS and "derivatives that are CP/M-compatible," "most" Z80- , 8080- , and 8085-based mainframes. **Recent Titles:** *I/SAL, DEB/ZDEB, MailMerge.* **Distribution Channels:** mass merchandisers, original equipment manufacturers. Has not yet bought outside programs; company is now actively soliciting.

SUBMISSION GUIDELINES

Preferred Media: floppy disk, paper printout. Complete documentation required. **Average Company Response Time:** varies; rejected programs returned. **Payment:** negotiable. **Distribution Rights:** negotiable. **Plugging In:** Mainly a systems publisher, firm is expanding "in a big way" into recreation and personal productivity. The company will consider any ideas relating to those applications.

Micro Ap
7033 Village Pkwy.
Dublin, CA 94568
(415) 828-6697
Robert B. Goodman, president
Established 1977

COMPANY PROFILE

Database management. Also buys personal productivity, business and professional management. **Micros; Operating Systems:** CP/M, CP/M-86, DOS, MP/M-86. **Recent Title:** *Selector.* **Distribution Channels:** bookstores, computer stores, direct mail, discount stores, software stores. No annual buying limit.

SUBMISSION GUIDELINES

Preferred Medium: floppy disk. Complete documentation required. **Average Company**

Response Time: 1 week; rejected programs not returned. **Payment:** outright purchase. **Distribution Rights:** negotiable.

The Micro Works, Inc.
P.O. Box 1110
Del Mar, CA 92014
(619) 942-2400
Att: director of software development
Established 1977

COMPANY PROFILE

Communications software, program generators written in machine language. Also buys recreation, personal productivity, business and professional management. **Micros; Operating Systems:** TRS-80 Color Computer. **Recent Titles:** *Source Generator, Microtext, Haywire, Colorpede.* **Distribution Channels:** catalogs, computer stores, consumer electronics stores, direct mail, software stores. Buys fewer than 10 programs annually; buying outlook the same.

SUBMISSION GUIDELINES

Preferred Media: floppy disk, cassette tape. Complete documentation required. **Average Company Response Time:** 2 to 3 weeks; rejected programs not returned. **Payment:** negotiable royalty or outright purchase. **Distribution Rights:** negotiable.

Microserve, Inc.
276 Fifth Ave.
New York, NY 10001
(212) 683-2811
Harold Bondy, president
Established 1978

COMPANY PROFILE

Extended support package for users of TURBO-DOS. **Micros; Operating Systems:** TURBO-DOS. **Recent Title:** *Turbo-Plus.* **Distribution Channel:** original equipment manufacturers. Buys 50 programs annually; buying outlook increasing.

SUBMISSION GUIDELINES

Preferred Medium: floppy disk. Initial documentation required. **Average Company Response Time:** 1 week; rejected programs returned. **Payment:** negotiable royalty or outright purchase. **Distribution Rights:** negotiable.

MicroSPARC, Inc.
10 Lewis St.
Lincoln, MA 01773
(617) 259-9710
David P. Szetela, technical editor
Established 1980

COMPANY PROFILE

Machine-level languages, communication programs, programming tools. Also buys recreation, personal productivity, business and professional management. **Micros; Operating Systems:** Apple II, II+, and IIe; Apple DOS. **Recent Titles:** *The Assembler and MacroSoft, Amperkit #1, GALE.* **Distribution Channels:** catalogs, computer stores, direct mail, software stores. Buys five programs annually; buying outlook increasing.

SUBMISSION GUIDELINES

Preferred Medium: floppy disk. Company provides complete documentation. **Average Company Response Time:** 3 to 4 weeks; rejected programs returned. **Payment:** 5 to 25 percent royalty paid quarterly. **Distribution Rights:** exclusive.

MicroStuf
1845 The Exchange, No. 140
Atlanta, GA 30339
(404) 952-0267
Does not actively solicit.

Mountain Computer, Inc.
300 El Pueblo
Scotts Valley, CA 95066
(408) 438-6650
Jim Sedin, president
Established 1977

COMPANY PROFILE

Music and speech synthesizers. **Micros; Operating Systems:** Apple, IBM PC, TRS-80. **Recent Titles:** *SpeechTalker, MusicSystem.* **Distribution Channels:** computer stores, software stores. Has not yet bought outside programs; company is now actively soliciting.

SUBMISSION GUIDELINES

Preferred Medium: floppy disk. Complete documentation required. **Average Company Response Time:** 2 to 4 weeks; rejected programs returned. **Payment:** 5 to 8 percent royalty paid quarterly or outright purchase. **Distribution Rights:** exclusive. **Plugging In:** Programs must interface with firm's peripherals.

Omega MicroWare Software Products
222 South Riverside Plaza
Chicago, IL 60606
(312) 648-4844
Ken Rose, president
Established 1979

COMPANY PROFILE

Antipiracy and other utilities. Also buys business and professional management. **Micros; Operating Systems:** Apple, IBM PC, TRS-80. **Recent Titles:** *Locksmith 5.0, The Savior, Chart Trader Plus, 1983 Tax Templates.* **Distribution Channels:** computer stores, direct mail, software stores. Buys three programs annually; buying outlook increasing.

SUBMISSION GUIDELINES

Preferred Medium: floppy disk. Complete documentation required. **Average Company Response Time:** 1 week; rejected programs returned. **Payment:** 15 to 30 percent royalty or outright purchase. **Distribution Rights:** exclusive.

Optimized Systems Software, Inc.
10379 Landsdale Ave.
Cupertino, CA 95014

(408) 446-3099
Bill Wilkinson, vice president of acquisitions
Established 1981

COMPANY PROFILE

Computer language interpreters, compilers. Also buys business and professional management. **Micros; Operating Systems:** Apple, Atari, Commodore 64; 68000-based systems. **Recent Titles:** *BASIC XL, ACTION!, SORT/65.* **Distribution Channels:** computer stores, consumer electronics stores, department stores, mass merchandisers, software stores. Buys six to 10 programs annually; buying outlook increasing.

SUBMISSION GUIDELINES

Preferred Medium: floppy disk. Complete documentation to be arranged between author and company. **Average Company Response Time:** 2 to 4 weeks; rejected programs returned. **Payment:** 6 to 12 percent royalty (based on retail sales) paid quarterly or outright purchase. **Distribution Rights:** exclusive "preferred." **Plugging In:** "Generally," Optimized claims, "our products are the best in their field in one or more aspects—speed, space, efficiency, ease of use, etc. Programs written in BASIC have, at best, a poor chance of acceptance. If *you* are *good*, we might be good for you."

Quadram Corporation
4357 Park Dr.
Norcross, GA 30093
(404) 923-6666
Does not actively solicit.

Racet Computes
1855 W. Katella, Suite 255
Orange, CA 92667
(714) 997-4950
Ron Johnston, chairperson
Established 1978

COMPANY PROFILE

Utilities, programming tools. **Micros; Operating Systems:** IBM PC, NEC Trek PC-6000, 8000 and 8800, TRS-80. **Recent Titles:** *Racet NEC-DOS, Electric Pencil, Fastload, Speed-up Kit.* **Distribution Channels:** computer stores, direct mail, software stores. Buys two programs annually; buying outlook increasing.

SUBMISSION GUIDELINES

Preferred Medium: floppy disk. Initial documentation required. **Average Company Response Time:** varies; rejected programs not returned. **Payment:** 15 to 25 percent royalty (based on gross receipts) paid quarterly. **Distribution Rights:** exclusive. **Plugging In:** "We are looking for proven programmers and prefer material written in assembly language."

Softech Microsystems, Inc.
9494 Black Mountain Rd.
San Diego, CA 92126
(619) 451-1230
Terry Rilling, director of software development
Established 1980

COMPANY PROFILE

Utilities, programmer's tools, and system support programs. **Micros; Operating Systems:** UCSD p-system. **Distribution Channels:** direct mail, original equipment manufacturers. Company "occasionally" purchases a program but more often functions as a distributor for finished application programs that run under the UCSD p-system. Includes successfully evaluated submissions in its catalog and direct mail promotions. Author remains the program's marketer and publisher.

SUBMISSION GUIDELINES

Preferred Medium: floppy disk. Complete documentation required. **Average Company Response Time:** varies; rejected programs returned. **Payment:** not applicable. **Distribution Rights:** nonexclusive.

The Software Toolworks
15233 Ventura Blvd., Suite 1118
Sherman Oaks, CA 91403

(213) 986-4885
Susan Hayes, director of software development
Established 1980

COMPANY PROFILE

Add-on programs for file management, graphics, and printing. Also buys recreation, personal productivity, classroom education, business and professional management. **Micros; Operating Systems:** DEC Rainbow, Kaypro, Heath/Zenith, Osborne; CP/M. **Recent Titles:** *C/80 Compiler Version 3.0, Autodiff, Word Wiggle.* **Distribution Channels:** catalogs, computer stores, software stores. Buys 10 programs annually; buying outlook increasing.

SUBMISSION GUIDELINES

Preferred medium: floppy disk. Complete documentation required; company edits. **Average Company Response Time:** 2 to 8 weeks; rejected programs returned on request. **Payment:** negotiable royalty paid monthly. **Distribution Rights:** exclusive. **Plugging In:** Software Toolworks concentrates heavily on systems software, but the company encourages authors to send home education and home hobbyist material. "We want programs that teach computer languages and programs that would help children with their schoolwork. Generally, we'll consider anything that can be learned via the computer."

Southeastern Software
7743 Briarwood Dr.
New Orleans, LA 70128
(504) 246-8438
George McClelland, director of software development
Established 1978

COMPANY PROFILE

Database management. Also buys recreation, personal productivity, business and professional management. **Micros; Operating Systems:** Apple, Columbia, Compaq, Corona, Franklin, IBM. **Recent Titles:** *Data Capture 4.0, BASIC/HELP.* **Distribution Channels:** bookstores, computer stores, consumer electronics stores, department stores, software stores, video stores. Buys two to three programs annually; buying outlook increasing.

SUBMISSION GUIDELINES

Preferred Medium: floppy disk. Complete documentation required. **Average Company Response Time:** 1 week; rejected programs returned. **Payment:** 15 to 25 percent royalty paid monthly. **Distribution Rights:** exclusive.

Southwestern Data Systems
10761 Woodside Ave., Suite E
Santee, CA 92071
(619) 562-3670
Tom Burns, director of software development
Established 1978

COMPANY PROFILE

Utilities, program tools. Also buys recreation, personal productivity. **Micros; Operating Systems:** Apple II, II+, and IIe, Commodore 64, IBM PC. **Recent Titles:** *The Routine Machine, Merline, Amper Array.* **Distribution Channels:** catalogs, computer stores, direct mail, software stores. Buys six programs annually; buying outlook increasing.

SUBMISSION GUIDELINES

Preferred Medium: floppy disk. Complete documentation required. **Average Company Response Time:** 6 weeks; rejected programs returned. **Payment:** 10 to 25 percent royalty paid monthly. **Distribution Rights:** exclusive. **Plugging In:** Author's guide available.

Stoneware, Inc.
50 Belvedere
San Rafael, CA 94901
(415) 454-6500
Frank Colin, director of software development
Established 1979

COMPANY PROFILE

Database management utilities. Also buys personal productivity. **Micros; Operating Systems:** Apple II and IIe, IBM PC and XT, IBM-compatible computers. **Recent Titles:** *DB Master Version Four, Advanced DB Master.* **Distribution Channels:** bookstores, catalogs, computer stores, consumer electronics stores, department stores, direct mail, discount stores, mass merchandisers, software stores, video stores. Buys 3 to 10 programs annually; buying outlook the same.

SUBMISSION GUIDELINES

Preferred Medium: floppy disk. Complete documentation required. **Average Company Response Time:** 6 weeks; rejected programs returned. **Payment:** negotiable royalty paid monthly. **Distribution Rights:** exclusive.

SuperSoft, Inc.
P.O. Box 1628
1713 S. Neil
Champaign, IL 61820
(217) 359-2112
Stephen Hagler, marketing director
Established 1977

COMPANY PROFILE

Language compilers, database management. Also buys personal productivity, business and professional management. **Micros; Operating Systems:** IBM; CP/M-80, CP/M-86, PC-DOS, MS-DOS. **Recent Titles:** *BASIC Tutor, FORTRAN, Personal Data Base.* **Distribution Channels:** catalogs, computer stores, direct mail, software stores. No annual buying limit.

SUBMISSION GUIDELINES

Preferred Medium: floppy disk. Complete documentation required. **Average Company Response Time:** 16 weeks; rejected programs returned on request. **Payment:** negotiable. **Distribution Rights:** negotiable.

CROSS-REFERENCES—SYSTEMS

The following companies also buy systems software. Their complete listings may be found under the major headings shown.

RECREATION

Adventure International, division of Scott Adams, Inc.
Atari, Inc.
Atari Program Exchange (APX)
Avant-Garde Creations, Inc.
Cload Publications, Inc.
ColorQuest, division of Softlaw Corporation
Comm*Data Computer House, Inc.
CompuServe, Inc.
Datasoft, Inc.
Dilithium Press
Don't Ask Computer Software, Inc.
Hayden Software Company
HESWARE (Human Engineered Software)
Insoft, Inc.
Instant Software, Inc., division of Wayne Green, Inc.
International Publishing & Software, Inc.
JMG Software International
Microcomputers Corporation
MicroLab, Inc.
Passport Designs, Inc.
Penguin Software, Inc.
Phoenix Software, Inc.
Prentice-Hall, Inc.
Quality Software
Rainbow Computing, Inc.
Ranco Software Games, Inc.
Rantom Software
Royal Software/COMPUTER PALACE
Softsel Computer Products, Inc.
Softside Magazine
The Software Guild
Source Telecomputing Corporation
Synapse Software
Tom Mix Software
Tronix Publishing, Inc.
United Microware Industries, Inc. (UMI)
Windcrest Software, Inc.

PERSONAL PRODUCTIVITY

Arlington Software + Systems
Continental Software

Digital Marketing Corporation
Dynacomp, Inc.
IJG, Inc.
Pacific TriMicro
PC Disk Magazine
Powersoft, Inc.
Sams Software, division of Howard W. Sams, Inc.
Silicon Valley Systems, Inc.

CLASSROOM EDUCATION

McGraw-Hill Book Company
Random House School Division
REMsoft, Inc.

BUSINESS AND PROFESSIONAL MANAGEMENT

AlphaBit Communications, Inc.
Aurora Systems, Inc.
The Business Division, division of Scott Adams, Inc.
CompuTech Group, Inc.
Designer Software
The Einstein Corporation
Epson America, Inc.
IBM External Submissions
Legend Industries
Lifeboat Associates
Mark of the Unicorn
MicroRIM, Inc.
Microsoft Corporation
MMG Micro Software
Omni Software Systems, Inc.
Phase One Systems, Inc.
Tristar Data Systems
Western Properties Investment Company, Software Division
Westico, Inc.

Magazines

Antic: The Atari Resource
524 Second St.
San Francisco, CA 94107
(415) 864-0886
Robert DeWitt, editor
Issued monthly

MAGAZINE PROFILE

Devoted to users of Atari home computers. **Wants:** recreation, personal productivity, classroom education, business and professional management, and systems written in BASIC or assembly language. **Recent Titles:** *Object Code to String (Using Assembly Language in BASIC), Pattern Maker, Fantasy Rolls, Hookey!* Buys 6 to 10 programs per issue, over 100 per year.

SUBMISSION GUIDELINES

Preferred Media: floppy disk or cassette tape and paper printout. Complete documentation required. **Average Company Response Time:** 8 weeks; rejected programs returned with SASE. **Payment:** $60 per published page. **Program Rights Purchased:** all rights for all media. **Plugging In:** Editor is particularly interested in business, utility, sound, and graphics programs. Magazine is also looking for articles on hardware and peripherals that require accompanying programs. Author's guide available.

Atari Connection: The Home Computer Magazine
Atari, Inc., Home Computer Division
P.O. Box 5047
San Jose, CA 95150
(408) 745-2000
Ted Richards, editor
Issued quarterly

MAGAZINE PROFILE

Devoted to users of Atari home computers. **Wants:** recreation, personal productivity, classroom education, business and professional management, and systems. **Recent Titles:** *Date, Dollar, Clock, Varnames, Disklook, Harmony.* Buys seven programs per issue.

SUBMISSION GUIDELINES

Preferred Media: floppy disk, cassette tape, or paper printout. Complete documentation required. **Average Company Response Time:** varies; rejected programs returned with SASE.

Payment: $20 gift certificate good for purchases from the Atari Program Exchange (APX). **Program Rights Purchased:** all print rights. **Plugging In:** "Even if you don't consider yourself an 'expert' or 'advanced programmer,' don't be discouraged. If you have created something neat or interesting, submit your program and explain its operation to the best of your ability."

Commander: The Monthly Journal for Commodore Computer Users
P.O. Box 98827
Tacoma, WA 98498
(206) 584-6757
Donald Elman, editor
Issued monthly

MAGAZINE PROFILE

Devoted to users of all Commodore computers (VIC-20, 64, and PET). **Wants:** recreation, personal productivity, classroom education, business and professional management, and systems. **Recent Titles:** *Telecommander, Data Base Files, Arithmetic at Nursery School.* Buys 5 to 10 programs per issue.

SUBMISSION GUIDELINES

Preferred Media: floppy disk or cassette tape and paper printout. Complete documentation required in duplicate. **Average Company Response Time:** 8 weeks; rejected programs returned with SASE. **Payment:** negotiable flat fee based on type and length of program. **Program Rights Purchased:** all rights to all media (company has recently added disk version). **Plugging In:** Magazine is particularly interested in high-quality game, education, home, and small-business management programs. Author's guide available.

Creative Computing
39 E. Hanover Ave.
Morris Plains, NY 07950
(201) 540-0445
Andrew Brill, editorial assistant
Issued monthly

MAGAZINE PROFILE

Devoted to Apple, Commodore, IBM PC, TRS-80 users and those with a general interest in computing. **Wants:** recreation, personal productivity, classroom education, business and professional management, systems. **Recent Titles:** *Computers against Crime* (antiprivacy program), *The Secret Code Machine* (code breaker), *The Apocalypse Equations, Medieval Combat.* No per issue buying limit.

SUBMISSION GUIDELINES

Preferred Media: floppy disk or cassette tape and paper printout. Complete documentation required. **Average Company Response Time:** 1 to 8 weeks; rejected programs returned with SASE. **Payment:** $50 to $75 per published page. **Program Rights Purchased:** one-time publishing rights, print only. **Plugging In:** Magazine has a heavy emphasis on games and prefers to tie programs into a specific theme issue (e.g., "games," "word processing," "education"). Also runs occasional programmers contests. Author's guide available.

Easy Home Computer
350 Fifth Ave.
New York, NY 10118
(212) 947-4322
Roger Sharpe, editor in chief
Issued monthly

MAGAZINE PROFILE

Devoted to new users of Apple, Atari, Commodore, IBM, TI, TRS-80, and other home computers. **Wants:** recreation, personal productivity, classroom education, systems. **Recent Titles:** in development. No per issue buying limit.

SUBMISSION GUIDELINES

Preferred Media: floppy disk or cassette tape, with paper printout. Complete documentation required. **Average Company Response Time:** 8 weeks; rejected programs returned with SASE. **Payment:** negotiable flat fee depending on length and type of program. **Program Rights Purchased:** one-time published rights, print only.

Plugging In: "Our magazine reaches beginners who want to know how they can get the most from their computer investment." Call to discuss current editorial needs.

80micro: The Magazine for TRS-80 Users
80 Pine St.
Peterborough, NH 03458
(603) 924-9471
Att.: submissions editor
Issued monthly

MAGAZINE PROFILE

Devoted to users of TRS-80. **Wants:** recreation, personal productivity, classroom education, business and professional management, systems. **Recent Titles:** *The Next Step* (keyboard programmer), *Rat Maze (game), Muddy Pig Simulator, My Foe Flicker, Model II Casino.* Buys 8 to 12 programs per issue.

SUBMISSION GUIDELINES

Preferred Media: floppy disk or cassette tape and paper printout. Complete documentation required. **Average Company Response Time:** 3 to 6 weeks; rejected programs returned with SASE. **Payment:** $50 to $75 per published page. **Program Rights Purchased:** all rights to all media. **Plugging In:** "Our audience is somewhat technically inclined, but all programs should be applicable to both the beginner and the intermediate computer user. We're particularly interested in utilities." Company sponsors annual Young Programmers Contest for ages 18 and younger every fall. Author's guide available.

Enter: The World of Computers and Electronic Games
1 Lincoln Pl.
New York, NY 10023
(212) 595-3456
Ira Wolfman, editor
Issued 10 times per year

MAGAZINE PROFILE

Devoted to first-time users of games and computers and those with a general interest in hardware and software. **Wants:** recreation, personal productivity for Apple, Atari, Commodore, TI 99/4A. **Recent Title:** *Make a Face.* No per issue buying limit.

SUBMISSION GUIDELINES

Preferred Medium: paper printout. Complete documentation required. **Average Company Response Time:** varies; rejected programs returned with SASE. **Payment:** "An *Enter* T-shirt." **Program Rights Purchased:** all rights for all media. **Plugging In:** Magazine wants original games or a variation on programs published by *Enter.*

Family Computing
730 Broadway
New York, NY 10003
(212) 505-3585
Claudia Cohn, editor in chief
Issued monthly

MAGAZINE PROFILE

"Family"-oriented publication devoted to first-time users of Apple, Atari, Commodore 64 and VIC-20, IBM PC and PCjr, TI 99/4A, Timex, TRS-80, and other "popular" home and personal computers. **Wants:** recreation, personal productivity, classroom education, business and professional management. **Recent Titles:** *Future Age Calculator, Rad Raymer, Learn Names Quicker!, Home Heat Loss Calculator.* Buys six programs per issue.

SUBMISSION GUIDELINES

Preferred Media: floppy disk or cassette tape and paper printout. Complete documentation required. **Average Company Response Time:** 8 weeks; rejected programs returned with SASE. **Payment:** $50 per program. **Program Rights Purchased:** all rights for all media. **Plugging In:** All programs must be written in BASIC and be sent in duplicate.

Home Computer Magazine (formerly *99'er Home Computer Magazine*)
1500 Valley River Dr., Suite 150

Eugene, OR 97401
(503) 485-8796
Robert Ackerman, editor
Issued monthly

MAGAZINE PROFILE

Devoted to users of Apple, Atari, Commodore 64, TI 99/4A, and TRS-80 Color Computer. **Wants:** recreation, personal productivity, business and professional management. **Recent Titles:** *Multiplan Medium* (spreadsheet), *Grisly Adventure* (game). Buys 4 to 6 programs per issue, 72 per year.

SUBMISSION GUIDELINES

Preferred Media: floppy disk or cassette tape and hard copy printout. Complete documentation required (in form of 200- to 1200-word article). **Average Company Response Time:** "minimum" 8 weeks; rejected programs returned with SASE. **Payment:** $50 to $300. **Program Rights Purchased:** all rights for all media. **Plugging In:** Author's fee depends on magazine's need, submission quality, and length. Author's guide available.

---

inCider: Green's Apple Magazine
80 Pine St.
Peterborough, NH 03458
(603) 924-9471
Hartley Lesser, technical and review editor
Issued monthly

MAGAZINE PROFILE

Devoted to users of Apple computers. **Wants:** recreation, personal productivity, classroom education, business and professional management, systems. **Recent Titles:** *Recipe for Random Access Salad, Blaising Bibliographies, Indy, EPROM Edification, Poking Perfection.* No per issue buying limit.

SUBMISSION GUIDELINES

Preferred Media: floppy disk or cassette tape and paper printout. Complete documentation required. **Average Company Response Time:** 3 to 6 weeks; rejected programs returned with SASE. **Payment:** $50 to $75 per published page. **Pro-**

gram Rights Purchased: all rights to all media. **Plugging In:** Particular interest in utilities and general interest software. Author's guide available.

The Rainbow: The Color Computer Monthly Magazine
9529 U.S. Highway 52
P.O. Box 200
Prospect, KY 40059
(503) 228-4492
Jetta Kapfhammer, submissions editor
Issued monthly

MAGAZINE PROFILE

Devoted to users of TRS-80 Color Computer. **Wants:** recreation, personal productivity, classroom education, business and professional management, and systems. **Recent Titles:** *A Glowing Tail of Battle, And the Winner Is, Long Distance Operator, Fast Talker.* Buys 20 to 30 programs per issue.

SUBMISSION GUIDELINES

Preferred Media: floppy disk or cassette tape and paper printout. Complete documentation required. **Average Company Response Time:** 8 weeks; rejected programs returned. **Payment:** $50 per published page. **Program Rights Purchased:** all rights for 3 months (from date of publication); rights revert to author after that time. **Plugging In:** Magazine seeks programs for theme issues and also runs occasional contests for specific applications. Author's guide available.

Softkey Publishing
3710 100th St. S.W.
Tacoma, WA 98499
(206) 581-6038
Julie Joringdal, managing editor
Issued quarterly

MAGAZINE PROFILES

Company publishes two magazines, *CORE* and *Hardcore*, devoted to users of Apple and compatible computers. **Wants:** recreation, personal productivity, business and professional management, and systems. **Recent Titles:** *String Plotter, 3-D Wall Draw* (both in *Hardcore*), *Quick Draw, Low Resolution Graphics* (in *CORE*). Buys 40 to 60 programs annually.

SUBMISSION GUIDELINES

Preferred Media: floppy disk and paper printout. Complete documentation required. **Average Company Response Time:** 6 to 8 weeks; rejected programs returned. **Payment:** $20 to $50 per published page. **Program Rights Purchased:** all rights for all media. **Plugging In:** *CORE* is aimed at the average Apple user, and *Hardcore* is designed for those interested in making backups of copy-protected software. All programs must be accompanied by article. For either magazine accepted programs always have the Apple user, not the programmer, in mind. So, accompanying articles should contain a step-by-step tutorial for the beginner. When programming "try to avoid long print statements and use TABS instead of spaces. In general, the more work our editors must do on the material they receive, the lower the amount paid to the author." Author's guide available.

Softside Magazine
10 Northern Blvd.
Northwood Executive Park
Amherst, NH 03031
(603) 882-2555
Carolyn Nolan, managing editor
Issued monthly

MAGAZINE PROFILE

Devoted to users of Apple, Atari, Commodore, IBM, TRS-80 home computers. **Wants:** recreation, personal productivity, classroom education, business and professional management, systems, written in BASIC. **Recent Titles:** *Graphic Writer, Shaped Wizard.* No per issue buying limit.

SUBMISSION GUIDELINES

Preferred Medium: floppy disk. Complete documentation required. **Average Company Response Time:** within 6 weeks; rejected programs returned with SASE. **Payment:** flat fee on acceptance; one-half the original amount is paid for reprint; 20 percent kill fee if program isn't

used. **Program Rights Purchased:** one-time publication rights. **Plugging In:** "The people whose work has appeared in *SoftSide* are thoughtful and intelligent authors and programmers. They include computer hobbyists, businessmen, scientists, and students . . . *SoftSide* authors are as bright and diverse as *SoftSide* readers."

Agents and Legal Resources

SOFTWARE AGENTS

John Brockman Associates, Inc.
2307 Broadway
New York, NY 10024
(212) 874-0500

Sterling Lord Agency, Inc.
660 Madison Avenue
New York, NY 10022
(212) 751-2533

Scott Meredith Agency, Inc.
845 Third Ave.
New York, NY 10022
(212) 245-5500

William Morris Agency, Inc.
1350 Avenue of the Americas
New York, NY 10019
(212) 586-5100

The Software Agency
825 Third Ave.
New York, NY 10022
(212) 675-5400

Synergistic Software
830 N. Riverside Dr., No. 201
Renton, WA 98055
(206) 226-3216

LEGAL RESOURCES

ADAPSO (Association of Data Processing
    Societies and Organizations)
1300 N. 17th St., Suite 300
Arlington, VA 22209
(703) 522-5055

Association for Computing Machinery
11 West 42d St.
New York, NY 10036
(212) 869-7440

Electronics Industries Association
2001 Eye St. N.W.
Washington, D.C. 20006
(202) 457-4919

Mark L. Levine, Attorney
58 East 83rd St.
New York, NY 10022
(212) 744-3901

Practising Law Institute, Computer Law Institute
810 Seventh Ave.
New York, NY 10019
(212) 765-5700

Remer, Remer and Dunaway
444 Castro St., Suite 400
Mountain View, CA 94041
(415) 964-7622

Software Author's Glossary

The software author's glossary is divided into two parts: the first covers key words and phrases relating to the marketing of computers and software; the second highlights words and phrases frequently used in the software publishing and legal worlds.

MARKETING

Audience: A group of potential or actual users or customers for a specific product or service.

Co-op Advertising Allowance: A financial arrangement between a hardware or software producer and its distributors and retailers in which stores are partially compensated for advertising certain manufacturers' products or brand names in newspapers and magazines, on radio and television, etc.

Customer Support: Any action that a manufacturer must undertake to satisfy product end users or retailers. End-user support includes specific product training, telephone hot lines, published product updates and revisions, written notices of product problems, etc. Retailer support includes co-op advertising allowances, fast product delivery, sales staff training, etc.

Demographics: The common characteristics that define a user or customer group for a particular product. Age, occupation, income, and education level are demographic segments which may define computer users.

Market Segmentation: The process of isolating a group of users or customers by one or more demographic criteria to sell them products or services. For example, Apple II users who live in California and earn more than $50,000 a year constitute a market segment. Also known as "target marketing."

Mass Merchant: A retailer carrying a broad selection of products and product lines appealing to a wide variety of customers.

Point of Purchase: The store cash register; figuratively, bringing the sale to a close.

Point-of-Purchase Materials: Anything supplied to retailers and distributors by the manufacturer that helps build store traffic and sell products. Window posters, banners, counter cards, and display racks are all point-of-purchase materials.

Specialty Retailer: A store carrying limited product lines (e.g., only computers or only software) and employing salespeople with expertise in those lines.

Target Marketing: See "Market Segmentation."

PUBLISHING AND LAW

Deliverables: In a licensing agreement, any item designated by a software publisher that is to be provided by the software author in order to create and market a finished product. Deliverables frequently include the program itself, program documentation, source code and source code documentation, and any supplementary user materials.

Documentation: A set of instructions.

Exclusive (Unlimited) Licensing Agreement: A contract in which a software author accords all mass production and marketing rights to a software publisher, regardless of machine or media format and geographic distribution or retail distribution channels, in exchange for monetary compensation.

Licensing Agreement: A binding contact in which software authors agree to make their program available to a software publisher for mass production and marketing in exchange for monetary compensation. The licensing agreement may be limited or unlimited.

Nonexclusive (Limited) Licensing Agreement: A contract in which a software author accords certain mass production and marketing rights to a software publisher in exchange for monetary compensation. Such rights may be limited to one or more machine or media formats, geographic areas, and/or retail distribution channels.

Program Documentation: A set of instructions that tells a user how to operate a software application.

Royalty: A frequently used method of compensation by software publishers in which software authors receive a percentage of their product's sales revenues on a periodic basis. Royalties may be based on a product's wholesale revenues or on a fixed dollar amount per copy sold.

Source Code Documentation: A set of instructions that helps the software publisher to evaluate a program.

User Documentation: Instruction booklet, manual, or other supplementary materials that help a user understand how to operate a software application.

Index of Directory Companies

Subject Index

ABOUT THE AUTHOR

Suzan D. Prince, a software reviewer and computer industry reporter, has written for *Creative Computing, Savvy,* and *Datamation.* She is a contributing editor and columnist for dozens of leading business and consumer publications, including *Consumer Electronics Monthly, Broadcast Week, Billboard, Video Review,* and *Home Entertainment,* and is also a consulting writer for Frank Barth, Inc., a New York public relations firm specializing in high technology. Ms. Prince began her free-lance career after receiving a journalism degree from New York University in 1978. She is married, lives on Long Island, and uses an Eagle PC.

1